Political Stratification and Democracy

Political Stratification and Democracy

IAN BUDGE, J. A. BRAND,
MICHAEL MARGOLIS and A. L. M. SMITH

Palgrave Macmillan

First published 1972 by
THE MACMILLAN PRESS LTD
London and Basingstoke
Associated companies in New York Toronto
Dublin Melbourne Johannesburg and Madras

SBN 333 12348 4

ISBN 978-1-349-01141-4   ISBN 978-1-349-01139-1 (eBook)
DOI 10.1007/978-1-349-01139-1

Contents

Contents

Acknowledgements

In the preparation of this book we have received essential help from many people. For the essential computer programmes on which analysis was based we owe a great debt to Eric Roughley, Brian O'Mahoney and A. J. S. Skinner. Much data-processing was performed by M. J. Fryatt and M. Marsh. M. J. Taylor suggested and largely performed the analysis of integrative behaviour carried through in Chapter 6. We received advice and criticism of the MS. itself from F. I. Greenstein, Anthony King, Brian Barry and Jean Blondel. The project was initiated with the help of A. M. Potter and the University of Strathclyde: analysis was subsequently supported by the Universities of Strathclyde, Essex and Pittsburgh.

The essential materials of the analysis were the responses of the Glasgow councillors, partyworkers and electors reported below. To all those who gave us time for interviews we extend our deepest appreciation. We hope they will find some recompense in the resulting insight obtained into the patterns of Glasgow politics.

Of course none of the individuals mentioned above has final responsibility for the reports and interpretations appearing in the book: that rests solely with us.

I.B.
J.A.B.
M.M.
A.L.M.S.

Introduction

Most of the immediately noticeable phenomena of democratic politics can be explained in terms of the obvious divisions which exist between different social classes, religious or ethnic groups, and political parties. These pervasive divisions influence electoral strategies, voting choices, issue-stands, governmental policies and pressure-group activities. Important though such decision-making processes are, it is apparent on deeper consideration that they form only one aspect of democratic politics. Of central relevance also are the toleration of one party for another, the submission of the Government to periodic elections, the existence of a broad cross-party consensus on some policies – phenomena which all relate to the maintenance and stability of democratic procedures. It is less easy to explain stability in terms of class or party cleavage than competition, although one ingenious argument based on the effects of cross-cutting cleavages emphasises the tendency to conciliation and compromise set up in an individual who finds himself grouped with different associates on one cleavage from those with whom he is grouped on another.[1] But cross-cutting theories do not explain why compromise rather than widespread withdrawal and alienation should result from individual cross-pressures, nor why at group level cross-cutting on cleavages of equal importance should not result in absolute intransigence and total inability to act (*immobilisme*). The failure of cross-cutting theories to discriminate satisfactorily between stable and *immobilistes* polities has led to speculation about influences on democratic stability which are less obvious than the familiar cleavages. One distinction common to these alternative speculations is drawn between persons of higher and lower political activity. The theory of differentiated consensus, for example, holds that democracies can operate in the face of considerable popular opposition and

[1] A useful summary of cross-cutting arguments is given in M. Taylor and D. Rae, 'Analysing Crosscutting Between Cleavages', *Comparative Politics*, Mar 1969.

confusion, provided that the politically active elements support their procedures.[2] Other theories stress the political apathy of potentially anti-democratic sections and the energy and effectiveness of the supporters of democracy.[3] Indeed it can be argued that cross-cutting cleavages likely to affect the behaviour of activists will differ from those which impinge on ordinary citizens,[4] so that cross-cutting theories too should take activity into account. It is precisely this differentiation of the democratic population by their varying levels of activity and involvement that we mean by political stratification.

Immediately political stratification is introduced as an explanation for democratic stability, its ability to account for other features of democratic politics becomes apparent. Some such features, such as the distribution of political information, and associated patterns of political communication, are linked very closely with the electoral and decision-making processes mentioned in the first paragraph. New questions are also raised. If persons at the same level of activity have many politically relevant characteristics in common, how do these interact with the party loyalties that otherwise divide them? And if communication between strata presents difficulties, do representatives – who by definition must belong to the upper strata – get enough information even to know what their constituents' views are?

The explanatory potential of political stratification in the areas of stability, representation, communication and party competition has never been systematically utilised.[5] The purpose of the present study is to devise and test a comprehensive framework which draws together the results of previous findings and theory, within which the effects of political stratification can be investigated. The remainder of this introduction gives a general description of the way we propose to conduct our investigation and of the data upon which it is based.

    [2] R. A. Dahl, *Who Governs?* (New Haven, 1963) pp. 311–25; V. O. Key, *Public Opinion and American Democracy* (New York, 1963) pp. 536–43; Ian Budge, *Agreement and The Stability of Democracy* (Chicago, 1970) chaps 1, 2, 12.

    [3] Budge, ibid., chap. 1; H. McClosky, 'Consensus and Ideology in American Politics', *APSR* LVIII (1964) 361–82.

    [4] R. A. Dahl, *Political Oppositions in Western Democracies* (New Haven, 1966) pp. 370–1.

    [5] In Chapter 1 we shall note the varied contexts within which the concept has been employed, but usually as an ad hoc interpretative device rather than in a systematic framework.

DATA

The data which resources and opportunity enabled us to collect consist of the responses of: 563 electors systematically selected from all persons on the electoral registers of the city of Glasgow; 64 ward chairmen and secretaries of the Glasgow City Labour Party; 52 of the most active Glasgow Progressive Party workers; 82 Glasgow City councillors; 6 municipal correspondents of Glasgow newspapers. All were interviewed between February and October 1966. The measure of political stratification obviously inheres in the basic survey design. Measures of the cleavages whose effects may cut across those of stratification were provided by reports of occupation, education, feelings about class and perceptions of the class structure, religious and party identifications. Dependent phenomena which might be affected by these political differences were ascertained through questions asked of all respondents on issues and problems facing Glasgow, reading and listening habits, ideas about councillors' tasks, and voting behaviour. Questions put only to partyworkers and councillors included queries as to how they first became politically involved. Questions put only to reporters included queries about their criteria for selecting and presenting news.

Appendix A gives a full account of the sampling design, questionnaire construction, interviewing and coding procedures employed in the survey, together with a comparison between various census statistics and comparable statistics resulting from the analysis of replies. In general we do not concern ourselves with developments in Glasgow after the interviewing period: that is to say, after 15 October 1966.

ORIENTATIONS

Whatever we do with these survey responses in the way of exploring the consequences of political stratification, they also have an inherent interest in describing aspects of the local political situation in Glasgow in 1966. This situation deserves investigation, for as a large and important city Glasgow has not only a unique political interest of its own but experiences which bear upon urban problems in general. Feeling both a deep fascination with Glasgow politics and a considerable interest in general urban problems, we have used our data to investigate Glasgow society and politics[6] as well as political stratification. Apart from the inherent interest of this other analysis it helps us in the present study to

6 Ian Budge, J. A. Brand, M. Margolis, A. L. M. Smith, *Class, Religion, Politics*: *Glasgow*, forthcoming.

distinguish general from Glasgow-specific phenomena, and to interpret some of the effects of parties in light of their historical development in Glasgow. At some points in the discussion we shall introduce
findings from this other research and assess their bearings on general
phenomena of cleavage and stratification.

One problem immediately posed by the concern of the present discussion with more abstract and general phenomena is the extent to
which we can extrapolate to other political systems from data collected
in Glasgow in 1966 – from one particular place at one particular time
to democracies in general.

It is of course obvious that our data are severely bounded by time and
place in a way in which experimental data of the physical sciences are
not. Political events cannot be re-run in the laboratory with the same
ease that physical scientists can re-run most experiments. We have
recognised this limitation to a particular time and place in speaking of
the opportunity it gives to illuminate unique features of Glasgow
politics – an opportunity which we welcome. But this does not prevent
the Glasgow data from offering one check on a general explanation:
especially when we face it with the intention of abstracting common
features from analogous events, wherever and whenever they occur.

In actual fact our analogies need not be forced, for it is easy to discern
important resemblances, not only between Glasgow and other large
Western cities, but between its political system and that of any modern
democracy. In common they have a party system, elections with virtually universal adult suffrage, representatives responsible to those who
elected them, citizens of varying degrees of political interest and activity,
mass media which devote a portion of their time and space to relaying
information about politics.

Unlike some democracies, which constitute independent nation-
states or autonomous provinces, the corporation elected locally in
Glasgow is formally subordinate to the central Parliament. However,
nation-states and provinces are not so autonomous as their formal
sovereignty would indicate, nor is the corporation of Glasgow strictly
confined to its legal powers. Many far-reaching decisions are debated
and made locally, and the central authorities are only the most important of the numerous bodies whose compliance the corporation has to
get on other matters. Nation-state, province and city are thus not
entities which are non-comparable because they are different in kind:
simply political bodies which lie at different points on a continuum
between complete autonomy and complete subordination in decision-

making. The differences in point of autonomy must qualify some conclusions[7] but the political resemblances between Glasgow and other democracies are sufficiently great to permit extensive generalisation from our findings to the functioning of democracy as such.[8]

Our concern with generalisation confronts us with a further difficulty. If we proceed by mere extrapolation from Glasgow findings we shall have no way of knowing which are general and which are specific to Glasgow. Certainly we have some criteria of generality in the substantial body of findings about politics elsewhere in Britain, and particularly in the United States, which have accumulated over the last thirty years. Should our findings replicate those made elsewhere, we can assume that they reflect general patterns of democratic political behaviour: if not, that they are Glasgow-specific.

This body of previous findings and interpretation which we apply as criteria to our own data is not wholly consistent within itself, however. Given the wide variation in the political, social and economic conditions which prevail in the different regions and cities of Britain and the United States – to go no further – different investigations have in many cases produced seemingly contradictory findings on the incidence and causes of the same political phenomenon. The necessarily probabilistic form of political generalisations aggravates this difficulty, since not enough parallel research has been done to determine which are the main statistical trends and which the statistical deviations.

In this situation we are forced, before we can separate the general from the particular in our Glasgow data, to select what we consider to be the most valid and reliable of previous findings, and the most plausible of previous interpretations, thus imposing a more systematic and consistent form on the conclusions derived from earlier research. How rigorous this formulation need be is a matter for individual decision. In the past it has commonly emerged (rather than been consciously shaped) in ad hoc interpretations applied to each new survey finding as it appeared. Our study accords with a growing tendency of political science in setting out from its inception to construct a more explicit frame of reference within which to view the Glasgow findings. This is

[7] For a similar viewpoint on the autonomy of much smaller communities than Glasgow, see J. Blondel and R. Hall, 'Consensus and Conflict in Community Decision-Making', *Political Studies*, Oct 1967.

[8] For an explicitly stated view of cities as democracies which can be directly compared with other democracies see R. A. Dahl, 'The City in the Future of Democracy', *APSR* LXI (Dec 1967) 953–70.

the model discussed in Chapter 1 and detailed in Appendix B. Like the usual conceptual framework it provides a vocabulary in which to discuss our research, and various predictions to direct analysis, but goes further in deriving its predictions from a set of explicitly related assumptions.

The statement of a set of specific predictions about the shape of the Glasgow data also had practical advantages in that it helped the physically separated authors to achieve a common focus in their chapters. Moreover it did not preclude supplementary investigation, and where its predictions fail (as they must often be expected to fail at this early stage of political research) we can proceed without hindrance to the equally interesting question of why they failed.

EXPOSITION

Chapter 1 justifies and summarises our model of political stratification in a mass democracy, and glosses its assumptions, definitions, derivations and data-predictions as these are laid out in Appendix B. Each following chapter then tests the success of the model as it attempts to predict patterns actually assumed by our data in different areas of substantive concern. Thus Chapter 2 is concerned with the interplay between model and data in so far as it relates to support of democratic procedures; Chapter 3 with its bearings on the coincidence or non-coincidence of ward activists' and electors' preferences – the question of representation. Chapter 4 attempts to explain the findings on representation by confirming theoretical expectations about types of political communication that prevail among, or between, political strata. Chapter 5 examines tendencies to internal agreement among electors and activist groups. Chapter 6 integrates these findings with our assumptions to form a coherent view of the nature and extent of politicians' autonomy, and of the effects on this of party competition; a view which is then confronted by actual data. Chapter 7 finally assesses the predictive success of the general model, and suggests modifications at some points to meet its failures.

1. A Predictive Model of Political Stratification in a Mass Democracy

If we are to use political stratification as the major explanatory concept in ensuing analyses of the Glasgow data, some theoretical rationale must be advanced to show why its effect on attitudes and behaviour should be anticipated, why it is important, and how it emerges. Systematic discussion of these points leads directly to an exposition of the assumptions we derive from previous research and of the predictions we deduce from them: thus to a full presentation of the *a priori* predictive model formulated before any of our analyses were undertaken.

DEFINITION AND MEASUREMENT OF POLITICAL STRATIFICATION

As we mentioned in the introduction, political stratification is a short-hand term for the differentiation of large democratic populations by their varying levels of political activity and involvement. We wish to distinguish those highly involved in politics from the mass of the population who are relatively inactive and generally uninterested in politics. Although the borders between different levels of activity are naturally fuzzy it is possible to make useful distinctions for any given governmental system. In Glasgow, for instance, we can reasonably argue that councillors are at the highest level because they are actively concerned with Glasgow politics almost every day. Forming the next most active stratum are the partyworkers whose political participation, while above that of the ordinary citizen, is less than that of councillors. Broadly speaking these two strata are composed of the relatively few citizens who engage in an 'above average' amount of political activity and whom we therefore term 'activists'. For Glasgow the third and final stratum is composed of ordinary electors who may be considered as engaged in an average, or even sub-average, amount of political activity. As is very often the case in political research we are here using a discrete variable – status – to represent an underlying continuous distribution from zero to complete activity, and our cutting points are inevitably arbitrary. We do in subsequent analyses try to approximate the underlying continuous distribution of activity by distinguishing inside the broad category of electors between those who perform slightly more than the minimal political act of voting (e.g. who attend meetings or hear of issues) and those who do less, the non-voters. These distinctions modify the discrete nature of the status groups but can only approximate the subtler gradations of the activity continuum.

Since our concern is with underlying activity rather than status we also equate the last of the Glasgow groups with which we are concerned – the municipal journalists – with councillors as the highest activist stratum. It is of course entirely possible that the different content of the political activity of journalists and councillors dominates their outlook more than their common high level of activity, thus making the assumed equivalence unrealistic. This however is an empirical question which will be tested by the success or failure of associated predictions.[9] A similar point can be made about the assumption of equivalence between all councillors, all partyworkers and all electors, regardless of their party identification. But even if these equivalences can only be ultimately justified by their predictive success, their integration into the model is not arbitrary, but based on theoretical considerations derived from previous research conclusions. These we now discuss.

IMPORTANCE OF POLITICAL STRATIFICATION

Our reasoning about the importance of political stratification starts from the general observation that persons of similar pursuits and inclinations tend to have more in common with each other than they do with persons of dissimilar inclinations: this is partly a cause and partly a consequence of their more extensive social interactions. Politics being a peculiarly absorbing pursuit for those committed to it, it appears likely that persons of equal degrees of involvement and activity will have more in common with each other – politically speaking – than with persons of different levels of involvement. This seems particularly true of activists when compared with electors, despite the other factors such as party, religion or class which divide them and despite the fact that they may be active and involved in quite disparate spheres of politics. For we assume that their common high involvement and political activity counteract in most spheres of behaviour the vertical differentiation which divergent loyalties might be expected to produce.

The validity of this assumption is crucial to the whole of our later

[9] For a justification of this procedure see James S. Coleman, *Introduction to Mathematical Sociology* (New York, 1964) pp. 71-3.

discussion, for if the differences between members of each stratum were more pronounced than the similarities, our model would have to take party or class or religion as its central explanatory variable rather than political stratification. A constant check on this possibility is maintained throughout subsequent analyses by the imposition of a party control on all tests of our hypotheses. At this point we are able to compare the unifying tendency of a common activism (or non-activism) with the divisive pull exerted by class and religion through evidence collected during our previous investigation of Glasgow politics.[10] There we took dichotomised political attitudes and perceptions stemming from forty-one different survey questions, and calculated the average change in the proportions having a particular attitude or perception between different class and stratification categories, and between different religious and stratification categories, under joint controls. If for example the average change in dependent proportions between stratification categories under the control for class were greater than the average change in the dependent proportions between class categories under the control for stratification, we took the influence of stratification on that particular attitude or perception as being stronger than that for class.[11] The measures of class and religion were those which related most closely to identification with one of the Glasgow parties.[12] Stratification was measured, where attitudinal questions had been put to all three groups, by the gradation from councillors through partyworkers to electors. Where the attitudinal questions had not been asked of councillors stratification was measured through the partyworker–elector dichotomy.

The actual results of the comparison were as follows: in the comparisons with class, stratification exerted a stronger effect over 23 attitudes, class a stronger effect over 14 attitudes, and equal effects were

[10] *Class, Religion*, chap. 7.

[11] The actual statistic used was Coleman's Effect Parameter, also employed in chap. 2 below.

[12] The measure of class was a combination of the occupational Manual–Non-manual distinction, and subjective class identification. This gave four class groups: Manual-(subjective) Working class, Manual–Non-working class, Non-manual Non-middle class, Non-manual Middle class. The measure of religion was a combination of self-identification with a particular denomination, and church-attendance. The actual classification was: Church of Scotland church-attenders, Church of Scotland non-church-attenders, Other Protestants, Non-believers, Catholics. A fuller description of these combinations, of their relationship to voting-choice, and of the questions on which they are based, is given in *Class, Religion*, chaps 6 and 7.

exerted over 4 attitudes. In the comparison with religion, stratification exerted a stronger effect over 20 attitudes, religion a stronger effect over 11 attitudes, and effects were equal over 2 attitudes. These scores are more illuminating when broken down between different areas. Class and religion more consistently influenced appraisals of voting behaviour and reactions to the parties. The preferences on current issues where class and religious effects outweighed those of activity were also closely related to party divisions. In view of the close relationship discovered in Glasgow between class, religion and party identification[13] this finding was not surprising. It does indicate, however, that class and religious effects are limited to those political attitudes affected by party competition. That these are not all or even the majority of political attitudes is suggested by the greater overall success of stratification compared with either class or religion. It might at first sight be thought that this predictive success of stratification was confined to the cognitive – that it primarily affected factual knowledge of issues, of the parties' position on the issue and so on. But in fact stratification had a greater effect on four out of five preferences on current issues, even on dislikes about the political parties and concern about the most important problem facing Glasgow. And in fact class and religion exerted their most consistent effects over one particular set of factual appraisals – of the voting behaviour of different groups. Thus the analysis points to stratification as the single strongest influence over attitudes taken as a whole. But this is a hollow generalisation. What really emerges is a distinction between stratification as the strongest direct predictor of attitudes unaffected by party competition, and class and religion as the strongest direct predictors of attitudes affected by party competition.

However other results from this analysis enable us to regard stratification of activity as a more pervasive influence over attitudes than its purely predictive success would indicate. In almost every comparison where the effects of class or religion appeared stronger than the direct effects of activity they gained their strength from the wider divergences between the class or religious grouping of activists rather than from divergences between electors. Thus the influence of activity was not really absent from those attitudes where class and religion exerted a stronger direct influence. What we really compared was the direct influence of activity, on the one hand, and the influence of class and religion in a multiplicitive relationship with activity, on the other – a relationship that is to say where higher activity extended and rendered

[13] Ibid., chap. 6.

more consistent the effects of class and religion. In other words, the greater political involvement associated with higher activity produces in common not only stronger attachments to procedures and a heightened political realism but also keener partisan feeling, carried over more consistently to certain types of political attitude.

This is only to be expected. Activists become involved through the parties rather than through a general orientation to politics as such. Naturally the ties of class and religion which bind together a party's adherents are felt more strongly by activists. A high level of partisan feeling thus becomes a general activist characteristic and at the same time activists seem to develop new orientations and new reactions which they share with their fellows of opposing parties – since all are exposed to similar problems and experiences.

The dual effects exerted by activism – as a promoter of a common outlook and at the same time stimulus of certain continuing divisions – make it possible to conceive of political stratification as the basis for a unified explanation of political reactions of the sort envisaged in the introduction, in spite of the greater direct predictive success of class and religion over certain reactions. An explanation of this kind certainly is obliged to account for the tendency of activism to promote similar attitudes in some areas, while stimulating partisan feelings on others, and in fact our later assumptions do allow for the divisive effects of party competition on members of the upper strata. But this is only within the context of their greater homogeneity when compared with members of lower strata over all their political reactions.

The empirical evidence for our emphasis on the overriding role of political stratification is not confined to the conclusions derived from this summary of Glasgow findings, which were at any rate not available when we formulated our model, for previous studies have already traced a close correlation between levels of political activity and political attitudes and opinions. Activists have been found better informed and better able to express a coherent set of political opinions on a wider number of public issues than members of less active strata.[14] They also feel themselves more capable of affecting government policies,[15] express greater agreement in their assessment of the content of political problems,[16] and support more consistently the fundamental procedural guarantees, rights and liberties of democratic

[14] Key, *Public Opinion*, pp. 150, 185–92.
[15] Ibid., pp. 192–3.
[16] Budge, *Agreement*, chap. 6.

government.[17] In addition there is some evidence of greater agreement on broad policy-preferences among activists compared with electors.[18]

Upon reflection the discovery of these communalities of attitude and opinion among political activists hardly seems surprising. The politically active generally emerge from similar socioeconomic backgrounds, characterised by prestigious religious affiliations and exceptional educational and occupational opportunities.[19] To a certain extent such similarities of background can be expected to promote the development of common perceptions and preferences in politics. This development is capable of being further enhanced by a tendency to extensive interactions. These may be face-to-face contacts or vicarious encounters brought on by reading the same newspapers and magazines or listening to the same radio and television programmes.

Of course there may be a tendency to read the media which favour one's own party and face-to-face contacts may also be confined to activists of the same party group. But at the highest level politicians are thrown into contact with their opposite numbers through the work of the legislature and its committees. And since persons active in party work are also likely to be active in other spheres of life they have a fair chance of meeting and exchanging views.

While party affiliations may promote disputes among activists on certain issues, party seems unlikely (in a stable democracy) to produce disagreement about the governmental system, nor even about most issues of the day. Evidence for this last point comes both from voting studies, which show that electors do not divide on consistent party lines for any type of issues except social and economic,[20] and for activists from a study of British Parliamentary politicians which demonstrated that disagreement on issue-preferences could not be explained by a party split.[21] Thus, given the relative disinterest and ignorance of

[17] Key, *Public Opinion*, p. 188; Budge, *Agreement*, chaps 8 and 9; S. Stouffer, *Communism, Conformity and Civil Liberties* (New York, 1955) chap. 3; McClosky, *APSR* LVIII (1964) 378.

[18] R. Rose, 'Political Ideas of English Party Activists', *APSR* LVI (1962) 360–71; Budge, *Agreement*, chap. 5.

[19] D. Matthews, *Social Background of Political Decision-makers* (New York, 1955) *passim*; *Class, Religion*, chaps 2, 4, 5.

[20] See for example Blondel's review of British voting studies which reports that even on socioeconomic issues electors' support for their own party line rarely exceeds 70 per cent: J. Blondel, *Voters, Parties and Leaders* (Harmondsworth, 1963) pp. 77–9.

[21] Budge, *Agreement*, chap. 5. H. McClosky and associates found that American activists tended to be more consistently divided on party lines than the American

the public on most political issues, it seems reasonable to expect that in most cases political activists will agree more with opposition members of their own political stratum than with ordinary supporters of their own party.

Our assumption about the concomitants of political stratification can be criticised not only in terms of the possible divisive effects exerted by party but also through our implicit postulate of a one-to-one relationship between activity levels and other political phenomena. Marvick and Nixon point to the differences which exist between American campaign workers on the one hand and either voters or political leaders in order to underline the problems of assuming that all political activities fall into one hierarchy: '. . . an active worker's behaviour and orientation to politics differ from a voter's, however active and partisan he is. The campaign worker has joined an organisation; the voter has not. . . . The campaign worker is engaged in activities that focus his attention upon influencing the electorate: the voter is intent largely upon the candidates and issues from which he must choose.[22] It can further be maintained that the politician, even more than the campaign worker, is removed from a general continuum of political participation through different orientations, motivations and expectations of reward.[23]

Ultimately these warnings against assuming a single hierarchy of political activity relate to the same problems of equivalence as those discussed above. The assumption of a single scale is a research judgement which must finally be justified against the usefulness of the predictions formulated on that basis. We do have indirect support for making the assumption, from an analysis of differences between councillors, partyworkers and electors undertaken in *Class, Religion and Politics*. There we discovered that some background characteristics distinguishing partyworkers from electors were also those which distinguished councillors from partyworkers, although some other differences existed between councillors and partyworkers which did not

---

electorate on current issues, but this may be explained as an artefact of the issues picked for study: 'Issue Conflict and Consensus among Party Leaders and Followers', *APSR* LIV (1960) 406–27. For an analysis of disagreements inside each of the major British Parliamentary parties see S. E. Finer, H. Berrington, D. J. Bartholomew, *Backbench Opinion in the House of Commons* (London, 1961).

[22] D. Marvick and C. Nixon, 'Recruitment Contrasts in Rival Campaign Groups', in D. Marvick (ed.), *Political Decision-Makers* (New York, 1961) p. 194.

[23] J. C. Davies, *Human Nature in Politics* (New York, 1962) p. 24.

appear when activists as a whole were contrasted with electors.[24] Thus we can infer that activity and its associated characteristics probably do have a monotonic relationship with some political phenomena and not with others. It happens that the phenomena with which our theory is mainly concerned – procedural and issue-agreements, conceptual ability, integrative behaviour – do probably show a monotonic relationship with activity and thus it is useful to make the assumption of monotonicity here.[25]

SUMMARY OF THE PREDICTIVE MODEL

The detailed assumptions, definitions, derivations and predictions of our Political Stratification model are spelt out precisely, exactly and at length in Appendix B. The present chapter is in a sense an exegesis of the model laid out there, our purpose being to justify the choice of assumptions in terms of previous research and speculation, to explain the reasoning which led from assumptions to predictions, and to expound the importance of both in a systematic account of the working of mass democracy, in Glasgow and elsewhere. Since the model is inevitably complex it is easy when reading Appendix B to lose sight of its overall structure in the course of detailed exposition. We shall therefore attempt at this point to summarise the model as a whole. Inevitably the clarification of terms and some very necessary qualifications are lost in such a drastic outline, but these can be filled in later. In this section we are simply concerned with the general view.

Basically our assumptions divide between two chains of reasoning.

[24] *Class, Religion*, chap. 5.

[25] The analysis summarised above was undertaken for a different purpose (to compare the independent effects of stratification, class and religion) but is capable of casting some light on the assumption of a one-to-one relationship between activity and other political characteristics. Under the separate controls for class and religion, effects of the elector–partyworker dichotomy fail to go in the same direction as the partyworker–councillor 20 times out of the 38 where these dichotomies were used jointly. In 13 of these cases discrepancies were quite substantial. This finding affords evidence that a one-to-one relation holds in some cases but not in others. However, discrepancies appeared under controls for class and religion not in a straight examination of the effects of increasing activity upon attitudes. Thus they are in many cases produced by the interactive effects of (class and religion-based) party differences on activity levels for which explicit allowance is made in our model and discussed later in this chapter. We therefore prefer to reserve final judgement on the usefulness of the assumption about a one-to-one relation until we have reported the detailed analyses carried out in the areas of our special interest (*Class, Religion*, chap. 7).

The first deals with manifestations and correlates of intra-strata cohesion compared with inter-strata variation. The second chain introduces the question of party competition and its effects on intra-strata cohesion. The processes summarised in these two chains are assumed to take place under constraints which render intra-strata communication easy and relatively accurate, and inter-strata communication difficult and relatively inaccurate. Taken together, all assumptions have important implications for the functioning of a democratic system, in particular for the shape taken by leader–follower and representative–constituent relations.

Both main chains of reasoning, with accompanying communication constraints, can be presented in the form of charts. We begin with the assumptions relating to intra-strata cohesion in a mass territorial democracy.

Although the systematic data at our disposal are limited to one point in time, we wish to link our speculations to the ongoing political processes of a mass democracy. The first assumption therefore relates previous socioeconomic conditions to the first fully observed datum we can get from our survey, the presence or absence of disagreement of a peculiarly intensive and pervasive sort. Such disagreement – because of its intensity and centrality – is then regarded as capable of severing the social and political contacts which activists are otherwise presumed to have with one another. In the absence of psychological barriers imposed by irreconcilable cleavage round an important issue, activists are assumed to behave more integratively than other groups in the population: to exchange information much more freely and even to act more supportively towards each other. Such behaviour is calculated to facilitate greater agreement on issue-preferences among activists as compared with electors.[26] It is also expected to produce agreement on political appraisals and perceptions. Agreements on topics which are currently being decided seem likely to promote further agreements – which may be quite implicit – on topics which have not yet come up for political decision, but which will come up in

[26] Mathematical formalisations of the effects of mutual influence attempts in an interacting group demonstrate a tendency towards ultimate agreement. See R. P. Abelson, 'Mathematical Models of the Distribution of Attitudes under Controversy' in Frederiksen and Gulliksen (eds), *Contributions to Mathematical Psychology* (New York, 1964); M. J. Taylor, 'Towards a Mathematical Theory of Influence and Attitude Change', *Human Relations*, Sep 1968, pp. 121–39. Connections between the present formulation of these processes and the mathematical treatments will be discussed in the note to this chapter.

the future – potential issues, in other words. And the more agreements there are on potential issues the less scope exists for the emergence of important or irreconcilable disagreements among activists. By this route we return to the beginning of the integrative behaviour – greater agreement cycle for the next time-period. The process described is therefore conceived as generating greater agreement in successive time-periods among activists at any rate. But it is not wholly self-contained, for adverse socioeconomic conditions can at any point halt or reverse the process in ways which are detailed later. For this reason the chart shows arrows to the future leading from 'Economic conditions' and 'Socioeconomic disparities' as well as from activists' greater agreement over potential issues.

A second chain of conditions facilitating agreement on political issue-preferences is shown on the left-hand side of Fig. 1.1. In line with findings previously cited activists are assumed – in a stable mass democracy – to support fundamental features of the democratic system more strongly than other groups. This reduces the scope for irreconcilable disagreements, since none would be likely to emerge on important procedural topics. The loyalty of activists to the existing constitutional arrangement is assumed to derive less from their integrative behaviour than simply from the realisation that they benefit most, by virtue of their activism, from the existing system, and would stand to lose if it were changed. This attitude would be altered if activists were split more or less equally by an important disagreement which could not be compromised, so that one set was bound to lose when a decision was taken. The activists who had lost on such a central issue would then feel that they had been penalised by the system under which they had suffered their defeat, and would lose any inclination to support its fundamental features. Through demand-satisfaction and procedural agreements as well as through integrative behaviour, therefore, the presence or absence of important irreconcilable disagreement exerts an effect on potential issue-agreements among activists.

The processes through which activists achieve greater solidarity are assumed to take place under restrictions on communication which are listed at the right-hand side of Fig. 1.1. It is difficult to conceive of any other ways in which activists and electors might exchange information and comment than through individual contacts (by letter, telephone or face-to-face encounters), meetings ranging from committees to public meetings, or mass media. The assumption that activists (in the absence of important irreconcilable disagreement) are more prone to exchange

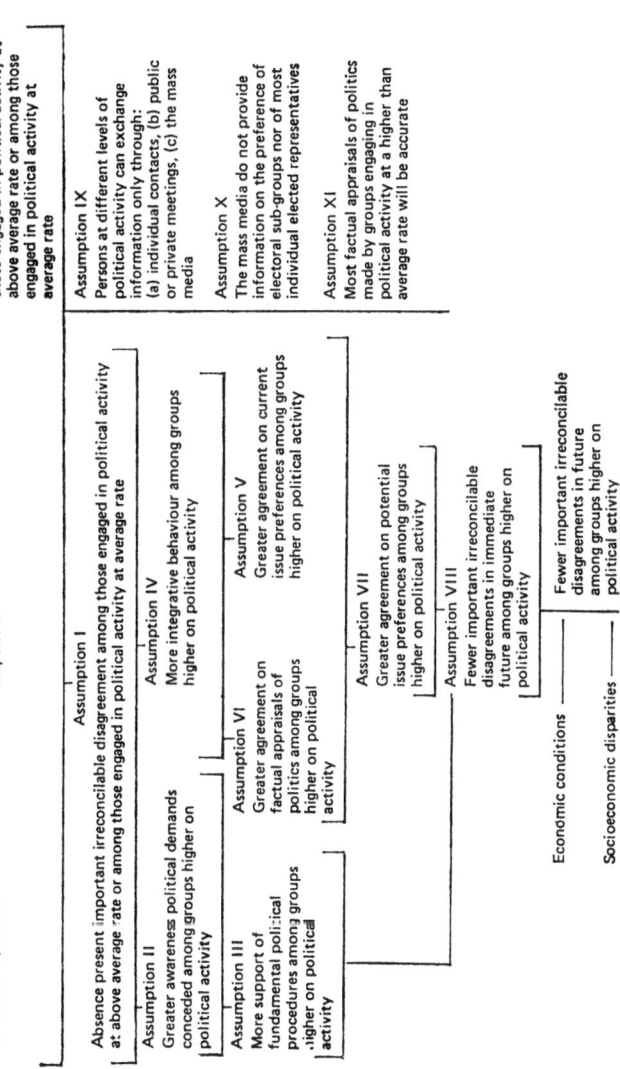

Fig 1.1

Assumptions of Predictive Model relating to intra-strata cohesion, with accompanying communication constraints, in a mass democracy

information and comment with other activists rather than non-activists does however immediately narrow the possibility that individual contacts form a central mode through which activists learn about popular preferences and opinions. Moreover one of the explicit points made in the previous discussion of political stratification was that persons who attend public meetings are themselves likely to be on a higher level of activity than the average member of the population and are thus not likely to represent his opinions very exactly. The point of Assumption XI is then that activists are likely to have an accurate perception of this state of affairs and to be aware of the inadequacy of their own knowledge about the opinions and preferences of the population. They are also likely, if our Assumptions approximate reality, to be aware of the inability of the mass media – the third possible channel of communication between population and activists – to purvey anything more than very general estimates of opinion on both sides.

The assumptions thus posit a state of affairs in which activists lack most information about the population, and the population is largely ignorant of the doings of activists. This situation has immediate consequences for representation, since activists are unlikely to make firm estimates about the preferences of constituents on most issues. It also implies that activists both individually and as a body are as a general rule freed from the danger of popular sanctions against their actions since not only are the population ignorant of what they do but activists are likely to be aware of this popular ignorance. These implications of our model are discussed in more detail later in this chapter.

The major fact of democratic politics so far omitted from theoretical consideration is party competition. This is capable of severely restricting the autonomy of politicians anticipated on the basis of the assumptions in Fig. 1.1, since popular ignorance is capable of being dispelled on certain matters by partisan controversy, which also appears capable of disrupting interactive processes and issue-agreements among activists themselves. We give explicit consideration to the impact of party competition in our second chain of assumptions, charted in Fig. 1.2.

A main assumption, XIII (b), is that activists have a keener appreciation than other groups that satisfaction of some of their personal political demands is bound up with the maintenance of their own party in power and hence (in a democracy) with its success in electoral competition.

This close association of some of their own causes and interests with those of their party is then capable of stimulating much keener partisan

Fig 1.2

Assumptions of Predictive Model relating to party competition with accompanying communication constraints, in a mass democracy

Higher rate of political activity than average

$\longleftarrow$ Assumption XII $\longrightarrow$

Political behaviour corresponds more closely to appraisals of how to gain some demands on current issues

Assumption XIII (b)
More widespread appraisal that some political demands can be gained by party vote maximisation

Assumption XIII (a)
More widespread appraisal that some political demands can be gained by increasing or maintaining political activity rate

Assumption XIV
More widespread appraisal that party vote-maximisation varies with extent to which party known to satisfy demands made by most of own party activists and by most electors, more than opposing parties.

Assumption XV
More widespread appraisal that most activists and most electors demand efficient running of government services and structure

Assumption IX
Persons at different levels of political activity can exchange information only through: (a) individual contacts, (b) public or private meetings, (c) the mass media

Assumption X
The mass media do not provide information on the preferences of electoral sub-groups nor of most individual elected representatives

Assumption XI
Most factual appraisals of politics made by groups engaging in political activity at a higher rate than average will be accurate

feeling and loyalty among activists compared with the general population. In order to predict specifically that such awareness of party will
affect their political reactions it is however also necessary to assume that
activists, more consistently than other groups, relate their political
behaviour to their political perceptions. Such a postulate is of course in
full accord with findings on the greater consistency of activists, which
we cited above. Note that party vote-maximisation is not regarded as
the only way through which activists feel that they can gain their
demands: they can be expected to have enough realism to perceive that
a continuing or increased investment in pressure- group activity or
individual lobbying might be more effective in some cases (Assumption
XIII (b)). This assumption is not further developed here, but encourages
expectations about politicians' own conscious reasons for continuing
their present rate of activity and attaining it in the first place. These
will be compared later in the chapter with findings from an analysis of
activists' recollections about their recruitment.[27]

Returning to the activists' awareness of their need for vote-maximisation, we state a further assumption which is almost a truism: activists
realise that vote-maximisation depends on pleasing a majority of
electors more than do the opposing parties.

Obviously the content of electors' political demands will vary from
one democracy to another. Seeking for a lowest common denominator,
it is likely that activists in all systems will see a majority of electors as
demanding at the minimum that governmental services be run efficiently and well. They may also demand much more, but this at least.
From Assumption XV which encapsulates this postulate we can deduce that most activists will see part of the job of representative as
showing concern about governmental services.

It will be noted that the whole trend of our assumptions is to limit
the areas in which activists' keener party feeling could undermine
tendencies towards agreement and joint action assumed in Fig. 1.1.
By Assumption XIV most activists should think that competition for
votes is relevant only where their own party is known to satisfy electoral demands to a greater extent than the other party. This implies that
their competition is confined to issues that are generally known: issues
that are not known to electors are not useful in gathering votes, and
other strategies such as the building of a cross-party consensus are open
to pursuit. In terms of constraints on between-strata communication,
the only way in which issues could become known to electors are

[27] *Class, Religion*, chap. 5.

through the mass media. However we have also assumed that what appears in the mass media is not independent of appraisals and agreements existing among activists, since media reports, written by political journalists, reflect – consciously or unconsciously – their extensive interaction with the highest activist strata. Thus electors will be familiarised, on the whole, with issues which activists think should be generally known, and not with those which activists are less keen to have publicised.

The end result of this chain of reasoning is then to reconcile the expectation that activists tend to greater agreement on political issues with the expectation that activists show keener partisan feeling. If such feeling is provoked only on a relatively narrow range of issues, it is in order to assume both that activists will agree more than electors over most issues and that they will display a sharper division on partisan issues. In terms of our assumptions these will turn to be a minority of current issues, if no irreconcilable and important disagreement exists.

Again we shall present these implications for various substantive areas of politics in more detail later in the chapter. At the moment however it is necessary to comment on various terms hitherto used in our assumptions without having had any very explicit meaning attached to them. Although exact statements are given in Appendix B our reasons for choosing these particular definitions need clarification at this point.

MASS TERRITORIAL DEMOCRACY

The whole structure of assumptions and predictions which we have put forward is only relevant in a mass territorial democracy. Some of the individual assumptions may be quite realistic in other contexts, but the particular patterns of activist interaction and party competition which we postulate are expressly tailored to this kind of political system. In the predictive model our conception of democracy derives from the ten conditions of Dahl's polyarchy – that is to say a political system in which the power to take policy decisions is allocated basically as the result of freely competitive elections in which every citizen's vote is weighted identically and all have access to information about the competing alternatives.[28]

A territorial democracy is any polity which meets these criteria but is composed only of the population in a given geographical area. A mass territorial democracy is one where the population is too large to permit

[28] R. A. Dahl, *Preface to Democratic Theory* (Chicago, 1956) p. 84.

decision-makers to be known personally by the majority of electors.

The fact that we limit our attention to only some out of the wide variety of democratic systems permits and indeed necessitates some additions to Dahl's more general definition, which is intended to apply to all democracies. It seems clear that where mass democracy has operated most effectively in the modern world it has done so in conjunction with a party system. We would argue that electors who have no personal acquaintance with candidates, and who lack a party label linking present candidates to past governmental and legislative records, are in fact suffering from inadequate information about competing alternatives. Where the population is large, parties are also necessary to narrow the main alternatives down to meaningful foci, to provide one line of communication between decision-makers and electorate, and – by supplying an enduring base for organised opposition – to ensure that prospects for the next election are one controlling influence on inter-election decisions.[29]

Since parties and their activities are so integrally necessary for implementing democratic procedures among a large population it is only realistic to take explicit account of their role in defining the fundamental political procedures of a mass territorial democracy. This raises another problem of definition – how to regard parties? They are taken here – again in the context of mass democracy – as autonomous organised groups that make nominations and contest elections in the hope of eventually gaining and exercising control of the personnel and policies of government. Used in this sense the term clearly refers to activists, not to party supporters among the electorate. It thus fits with the view, developed in Fig. 1.2, of party competition as a concern of activists rather than ordinary electors.[30]

Relationships other than parties have arisen in mass territorial democracies to ensure the responsiveness of decision-makers to electors. It would be too extreme to discern a norm that decision-makers did whatever a clear majority of electors obviously wished done – even though clarity is sufficiently rare in politics to leave decision-makers with considerable latitude still. It does seem realistic however to assume – with the same proviso – that elected representatives will not take

[29] F. I. Greenstein, *American Party System* (Englewood Heights, N.J., 1963) pp. 34–6, 40, 57–60, 73; R. A. Dahl, *Political Oppositions*, p. 333.

[30] A. Ranney and W. Kendall, *Democracy and the American Party System* (New York, 1956) p. 85; V. O. Key, *Politics, Parties and Pressure Groups* (New York, 1958) pp. 180–2.

positive action which they see as clearly opposed to the wishes of the majority of electors, since this does seem to be a prevalent norm among modern democratic politicians.

The final additional distinguishing mark of mass territorial democracies concerns the relationship of representative to constituency. Here we have a device – to some extent cross-cutting the party link – for focusing the otherwise tenuous voting rights of citizens on particular decision-makers. In this relationship not only is there a tighter degree of control by electors in view of the next election but there are also felt to be moral obligations on representatives to help all constituents who ask for help.

In light of this reasoning the definition of fundamental procedures in a mass democracy which appears in Appendix B (Definitions I.1 and I.2) adds to Dahl's general 'polyarchal' criteria a concern with party activity, constituency relationships and the norm that decision-makers will not take positive action contrary to clearly perceived majority preferences.

Since we propose to check our assumptions against Glasgow data it is obvious that we regard Glasgow as a mass territorial democracy. Its population, of approximately 1,000,000, and size, of 39,725 acres, qualify it on the first two counts. We are able to estimate its position on the third, democracy, through its score for the post-war period on Neubauer's Index of Democratic Practices. Neubauer's index, like our own definition of democracy, is based essentially on Dahl's conditions for polyarchy. But its additional concern with equality of representation and equality of party competition render it a good measure of our own concept of democracy in a mass territorial context.[31] The index

---

[31] The original index is described in D. E. Neubauer, 'Some Conditions of Democracy', in C. F. Cnudde and D. E. Neubauer (eds), *Empirical Democratic Theory* (Chicago, 1969) pp. 310–25. The component measures involve: (1) Percent of adults eligible to vote (the proportion of adults enfranchised); (2) Equality of Representation (the discrepancy between parties' share of votes and their share of legislative seats); (3) Equality of Information (number of separate newspaper owners $\times \dfrac{\text{average circulation}}{\text{size of population}}$); (4) Equality of Competition (percent of time-period the dominant party has not held office and average percent of votes not obtained by dominant party over time-period). These are the same here as in Neubauer's original measure but the method of scoring has been changed to yield a possible range of 0–1·00 on the combined index. Glasgow has thus a moderately high score. A fuller comparison between Glasgow and other cities and a more detailed description of the calculations involved is given in Ian Budge *et al.*, *The Political Development of Modern Glasgow* (unpublished MS), chap. 6.

score for Glasgow in the period 1946–66 is 0·692. This is somewhat, but not markedly, below the mean score of 0·746 for comparable British cities during the same period and well above the score of 0·404 for a comparable American city (Pittsburgh, Pennsylvania). We may conclude that the democratic nature of Glasgow politics is sufficiently marked to warrant a check of our model against responses drawn from that city.

ECONOMIC DEPRESSION AND SOCIOECONOMIC DISPARITIES

The initial assumption of our whole model links socioeconomic conditions to the emergence of important irreconcilable disagreement, which in turn is supposed to have immediate effects on procedural and issue-agreements and thus on the whole process maintaining democratic stability, as described in Fig. 1.1. We define socioeconomic stratification as the differentiation which exists between the members of a society in terms of their unequal prestige and resources, and this view is spelt out more exactly in Definition I.6 of Appendix B. Depression has been specified exactly enough in economic and other discussion to be left undefined by us. The indicator of depression which, because of its impact on the population, is most relevant to our purposes is the incidence of unemployment.

We made a speculative link between political processes and these factors because of the testimony of previous research that socioeconomic issues have a peculiarly strong influence over the emergence of important issue-disagreements. It is noteworthy for example that British cleavages over socioeconomic issues are the only ones which have any kind of consistent link to party divisions, at least among electors. Thus they are more likely to give rise to cumulative rather than cross-cutting divisions. They are also the issues which arouse the strongest feelings among the electorate. The same findings have been made for the United States.[32] On a world scale Lipset's investigation of relations between prosperity and socioeconomic stratification, on the one hand, and democracy and stability on the other, also supports the connection. We regard the conditions charted in Fig. 1.1 as being those under which the values of mass democracy will continue to be relatively highly implemented – that is to say, democratic stability maintained. Lipset demonstrated that for most countries of the world, considered inside broad culture areas, relative prosperity and low objective stratification

[32] Blondel, *Voters*, pp. 77–9; Budge, *Agreement*, chap. 3; A. Campbell, P. Converse, W. Miller, D. E. Stokes, *The American Voter* (New York, 1960) pp. 194–209.

did correlate with democratic stability.[33] Hence it is natural to consider such factors as encouraging or discouraging the emergence of central and important cleavages.

The way in which such cleavages might ensue is indicated by the findings cited above. It is unlikely that the impact of adverse circumstances would be felt by activists who, as we have seen, tend as a correlate of their status to belong to higher socioeconomic strata in any case. However, pressure from the lower strata of electors who would suffer the immediate effects of depression could either push their representatives into intransigent support of radical action or replace them bodily by intransigents. Representatives of the higher socioeconomic strata who suffered the effects of depression only very indirectly would be likely to oppose drastic action, which would endanger their own and their constituents' established position. Opposition would be even more bitter if a deflationary depression actually benefited the upper strata. The same bitter political cleavages can be seen as springing from an intensification of socioeconomic disparities, in which the lower strata would lose out either absolutely or relatively. In either case pressure would grow for redistributive measures likely to be strongly resisted by the upper strata and their representatives.

Obviously we are unable to test the connection between political processes and these socioeconomic factors with the same rigour as our other assumptions. Comparative data are lacking and our historical evidence is limited. On the basis of evidence presented earlier in *Class, Religion, Politics: Glasgow*, we are able to come to some conclusions about the relative values assumed by the independent variables in Glasgow in the 1960s. Unemployment at an average 3·4 per cent was heavier in Glasgow than in most other British cities. But the difference was not very great, looked at in general terms, a matter of 2–3 per cent. The really noticeable gap opens up between contemporary Glasgow and the Glasgow of the 1930s when unemployment averaged 25·2 per cent. By the standards of the inter-war period Glasgow could hardly be said to have an unemployment problem at the present time.[34]

Similarly with socioeconomic stratification, our evidence clearly shows that the trend is towards the elimination at least of wide occupational disparities. A comparison of survey respondents' descriptions

[33] S. M. Lipset, 'Some Social Requisites of Democracy', in Cnudde and Neubauer, *Empirical Democratic Theory*, pp. 151–92.

[34] *Class, Religion*, chap. 1.

B

of their own and fathers' occupations shows many more of the former to be non-manual and of higher status than the latter. Confirming the survey findings a division of the population between manual and non-manual occupations at various censuses between 1881 and 1961 shows an increase in the ratio of non-manual to manual from 1:16 to 1:2.[35]

Operationally therefore we have considerable justification for assuming that no lengthy or severe economic depression immediately antedated our survey nor that socioeconomic stratification increased. These are stated as Operational Assumptions B and C in Appendix B. As far as socioeconomic preconditions exert an influence therefore we should expect our survey data to reveal an absence of important irreconcilable disagreements in Glasgow in 1966.

Be it noted however that antecedent socioeconomic conditions are not regarded as the sole factors which might disrupt consensual political processes in a mass democracy. We concentrate upon them because their political effects alone have been systematically investigated to any extent. It is entirely probable that social factors such as certain distributions of religious preference or even political factors such as the growth of authoritarian movements might touch off irreconcilable disagreements. Since we have no hard evidence on these, we explicitly assume only the socioeconomic influence at this point. (It is in any case likely that social or political cleavages would be aggravated by adverse economic circumstances.) Room is left for the operation of other factors by our recognition that important cleavages which existed in the past can continue to affect the possibility of cleavage in the present.

IMPORTANT IRRECONCILABLE DISAGREEMENT

The situation through which adverse economic circumstances are regarded as capable of affecting the possibility of agreement among activists is one in which activists or population or both are divided between two relatively equal groups, each supporting completely incompatible policies on an issue they regard as important. (These positions obviously have to be ones they adopt spontaneously, not at the behest of an interviewer.) If the policies are truly incompatible it will

---

[35] Ibid., chap. 1; Budge, *The Political Development of Modern Glasgow* (MS), Table 2.9. The comparison is undoubtedly affected by differences in the census classification of occupations at various dates, but the broad trend is clear and undoubted.

be impossible to propose a compromise or composite policy which will give each group something of what it wants. An example of incompatible positions in Glasgow would be a disagreement on the question of council housing where one group wanted the housing programme expanded and another, pretty well equal in numbers, wanted the houses sold off. The only two outcomes which would satisfy even half the participants in this situation would be sale or expansion. Thus one side or the other would feel that their whole policy on this issue had been lost. Should they also happen to regard this issue as the most important on the political scene it is likely that their resentment at defeat would disrupt contacts with their opponents, thus diminishing the possibility of agreement even on issues which were not irreconcilable. It might also undermine their attachment to the procedures under which they had suffered defeat. Note that although the judgement of whether policies are irreconcilable is made by the analyst, the question of importance is settled entirely by activists and electors themselves: the issue must be one they nominate as centrally important. These points are more systematically stated in Definition I.3 of Appendix B.

The important irreconcilable disagreements capable of disrupting consensual processes may, in our view of the matter, arise either among the general population or among activists as a whole. Popular disagreements which were irreconcilable and regarded as important could exert enough of a strain upon activists to affect their internal cohesion. A further point to notice is our emphasis upon important and irreconcilable disagreement among population and activists as a whole. Disagreement among sub-groups of either population or activists might paradoxically increase the possiblity of cohesion among the group as a whole, by cross-cutting another line of cleavage which might otherwise have mustered the whole group into equal and opposing camps. This is precisely the situation which we feel might have prevailed in nineteenth-century Glasgow, where the religious divisions of the working class prevented a straight confrontation with the middle class, and permitted a highly consensual approach to local problems to develop among activists.[36]

Further terms involved in our assumptions are also specified in Appendix B, but none have the difficulties of the ones we have discussed and some (like agreement) are fully described in subsequent chapters. We turn at this point from classifying terms to summarising some of the consequences of the views we have put forward about the

[36] *The Political Development of Modern Glasgow*, chaps 2 and 3.

operation of mass democracy. These consequences are presented as they appear in various areas of substantive political concern, under appropriate headings.[37]

SPECIFIC IMPLICATIONS: COMMUNICATION

Communication refers to the interchange of appraisals about others' issue-preferences and appraisals. Such an interchange may take place between members of different political strata but in terms of our definitions and assumptions it is likely to be mainly confined to members of the same, and particularly activist, strata. The more politically active any group is, the greater the tendency for its members to communicate with fellow-members. Thus assuming the correctness of the operational assumptions, Glasgow councillors and correspondents will discuss current issues with more councillors and correspondents than partyworkers will with partyworkers: these in turn will discuss issues with more of their own group than will electors. It also follows from our assumptions that most councillors and correspondents will not discuss issues with partyworkers, and most partyworkers will not discuss them with electors.

These predictions militate against a classical model of information flow which is often assumed when discussing parties, namely that information is gathered at grass-roots level by the partyworkers and passed upwards to the party strategists, who in turn pass responses and directives down through the partyworkers. In contrast our assumptions point out the media as the main and practically the only channel through which members of one stratum can hear about the opinions and preferences formed by members in other strata. But appraisals given in the media are those formed by journalists' close interaction with other top activists. There may be tenuous exchanges between top- and middle-level activists but practically none with electors.

This revised model follows if we regard possible modes of inter-strata communication as being confined to individual exchanges, meetings and media (Assumption IX). The integrative behaviour of upper strata means that contacts will not normally be initiated by

[37] We do not discuss the implications of our model for support of democratic procedures, since these are immediately apparent from Assumptions II and III, given that we have already shown Glasgow to be characterised by a relatively high implementation of democratic practices in comparison with other cities and political systems. This topic is at any rate immediately taken up in the following chapter.

activists with ordinary electors, nor will meetings be spontaneously summoned by activists. On the other hand the generally low political activity of electors themselves will preclude much interchange with activists through letters or personal contacts, and those who attend meetings will by that very act be well on the way to activism themselves. Since activists can on the whole be expected to recognise the short-comings of personal contacts and meetings as methods of information-gathering, they are driven back on the media. They will probably also be sceptical of the estimates of opinion purveyed there. But it is the only source to which they can readily turn. Since most electors will have no contacts with activists and never attend political meetings they will be even more inclined to regard the media as their main source of political information. But in consequence of the impossibility (from considerations of time and space, if nothing else) of purveying estimates of representatives' and constituents' opinions there will be little opportunity for either group to know what the other is doing. Repre-sentatives must often take policy actions in ignorance of their constitu-ents' reactions, buttressed by the knowledge that the latter in most cases will have no idea of what they are doing.

As against this general block in communication between higher and lower strata one can expect to discover slight variations between one constituency and another. For it also follows from our assumptions that in constituencies where more electors are active (e.g. where more electors turn out to vote) there will be greater contact with party-workers and elected representatives than where less vote. Moreover those who attend meetings will in such constituencies have opinions which are more representative of electors than in constituencies where there is less general activity. Hence representatives' and partyworkers' appraisals of electors' issue-preferences will be more accurate and more definite in those constituencies where more electors vote than in others. This expectation has considerable implications for the question of representation.

SPECIFIC IMPLICATIONS: REPRESENTATION

By representation we mean the degree of correspondence between the opinions of groups higher in political activity and the opinions of groups lower in political activity, inside each constituency. We postu-late in Assumption V that integrative behaviour (including communi-cation) produces preferential agreement on current issues. Thus it follows from what has been said about communication that there will be greater agreement on current issue-preferences between representatives, partyworkers and electors in those wards where more electors vote. Integrative behaviour is also considered to bring about greater agreement on factual appraisals of politics (Assumption VI). Hence a concurrence of views in wards where more electors vote will similarly occur here. Greater agreement on preferences and appraisals of current issues is also assumed to foster greater agreement on potential issues (Assumption VII). Hence on most aspects of politics we predict greater agreement between activists and electors in the wards where more electors vote than in those wards where less electors vote.

However our postulates also lead to the expectation that these differences in agreement between activists and ward electors all occur within the larger situation where activists (by themselves) within each ward and party, or considered as a total group, agree more than electors, or any combination of activists and electors, over all aspects of politics.

PARTY COMPETITION AND AGREEMENT

Our reasoning about communications also has major implications for the shape assumed by party competition. We regard partisan feelings centring about the need to maximise votes as the main potential disrupter of consensual processes among activists, in the absence of important irreconcilable disagreements. The theoretical problem of reconciling the keener partisan feelings of activists with their superior cohesion has we hope been solved by the suggestion that party competition is confined to a relatively narrow sphere: to issues that are generally known to the public. From our remarks about communication it follows that issues can be made generally known only through the media, and thus not independently of the high-level activists.

SPECIFIC IMPLICATIONS: ROLE OF COUNCILLORS

What do councillors feel their duties ought to be? And are the expectations of partyworkers and electors the same as those of councillors or different? Our series of postulates enable us to make predictions on these points. We have anticipated in Assumptions II and III that the higher the rate of political activity the more support will be given to fundamental political procedures, one of which is assumed to be an obligation to help constituents who require help. Hence we expect that Glasgow councillors and partyworkers to a greater extent than electors will endorse a role for councillors of helping their constituents. We also anticipate that local voters will endorse this ward role to a greater extent than non-voters and hence that councillors, partyworkers and electors will agree more on a ward role in those wards where more electors vote than where less electors vote. Additionally, however, we have assumed that activists are more involved in party work and competition than others and hence will be more inclined to endorse a role for themselves related to work for a political party. From Assumptions XIV and XV we can also expect that activists will disproportionately see one of their main obligations as being to oversee services since they will feel they risk severe electoral sanctions if they fail to recognise this duty.

SPECIFIC IMPLICATIONS: RECRUITMENT OF ACTIVISTS

Our predictions about activist recruitment are almost a by-product of the model. We had to make it clear that activists had other ways of gaining their political demands than through party vote-maximisation and made this provision in Assumption XIII (a). It is true that activists could maintain or increase their rate of activity in party-related directions. Given our other assumptions, however, a profitable investment of their energy could also be made in lobbying within the activist group.

However this formulation has considerable bearings on recruitment – that is to say on the question of how some persons come to operate at an above-average level of political activity. The immediate answer provided by our assumption is that most present activists are past activists who have maintained or increased their activity to satisfy some of their political demands. This expectation is not exactly a truism either, for it leads to the concrete expectation that most councillors are former partyworkers, and that most activists as a whole have operated at an above-average rate of political activity from the start, either from having been born into a political family or through entering an occupation which involved political work, or through some other form of exposure. Moreover in terms of activists' own subjective orientations towards politics we should expect a majority to include the promotion of various political demands – either issue-policies or group interests – with which activists have become involved.

Whereas the success of our predictions in other substantive political areas will be assessed in subsequent chapters, we are immediately able to compare expectations about recruitment with findings already presented in *Class, Religion, Politics*.[38] These were made after the construction of our model, so they form just as good a test of its predictions as data not yet discussed.

On the first expectation that most councillors are former party-workers, it transpires that only 17 per cent of all councillors disclaimed previous political activity. This group was concentrated among Progressive councillors – in fact it formed a third of the total Progressive group. Even so a majority of Progressive councillors – a full 66 per cent – report previous political experience, and 98 per cent of Labour councillors.

The second expectation – that a substantial number of councillors and partyworkers have been exposed to politics from birth through their membership in an activist family – received some confirmation from the fact that 50 per cent of councillors and 40 per cent of party-workers mentioned a relative who engaged in politics. Inside the parties much the same proportions recur.

In regard to the occupational types of political exposure also mentioned above, 30 per cent of councillors and 21 per cent of partyworkers fell into the brokerage occupations which entail quasi-political activity. Thus a majority both of councillors and of partyworkers come either from a political family or from a brokerage occupation, and are consequently exposed to politics from the start of their whole life, or at least of their working life, in terms simply of these two specific characteristics, let alone through other modes of exposure. In a very real sense contemporary activists seem to have been active from the start.

The third prediction about recruitment relates to the motivations which prompt activists to continue their strenuous mode of existence: we expect them to have become involved in pushing political demands for themselves or others and to see the satisfaction of these demands as depending upon their continued activity.

From the answers of Glasgow councillors to a question about why they continued on the council it appeared that among both the whole group and each party group, over the whole array of answers, the promotion of causes and demands tied with general interest in council work as the main motivation behind continuing political activity. In their initial reply 22 of the 54 councillors who had served more than one term mentioned their support of policies or adherence to an ideology as their reason for standing for re-election to the council, compared to 28 who cited their general interest in politics. In their supporting

[38] Chap. 5.

replies 20 mentioned policies or ideology compared to only 7 who cited general interest.[39] About general interest as a motivating factor our assumptions say nothing, but the majority endorsement of causes (among those serving more than their first term) upholds our expectation that activists maintain their level of activity in order to promote their own political demands or those they have made their own.

THE PREDICTIVE MODEL AS RESEARCH STRATEGY

The relative success of those derived recruitment predictions serves to demonstrate an application of our hypotheses and the realism of our assumptions about one political phenomenon. However the actual testing of hypotheses is not the main concern of this chapter and we now consider the usefulness of our approach in political research since it is still uncommon among political scientists. Political inquiry is generally conducted within a less explicit conceptual framework, and concerns itself more with the interpretation than with the prediction of findings. This posture is probably adopted in most cases because investigators feel that the state of knowledge in their areas of interest is not sufficient to support extensively developed assumptions which have any chance of successful prediction.

It would be rash to claim that knowledge is exceptionally advanced in our areas of interest either. For that reason we suspect that many of our predictions may not enjoy the same degree of success as those relating to recruitment, and that as a result many assumptions will have to be re-cast at the end of the analysis.

Nevertheless it still seems worthwhile, as we mentioned in the introduction, to specify our initial expectations instead of leaving the analysis to be directed by a number of implicit hunches. Given that we had to evaluate the conclusions derived from previous research in order to assess the significance of our own findings, it seemed better to perform this assessment explicitly and systematically rather than in an ad hoc fashion at scattered points in the discussion. This procedure helps to emphasise the interconnectedness of our assumptions, if nothing else. Moreover it has in our case helped to point out novel areas for investigation. Starting from a concern with political stratification and a review of assumptions relating to activist agreement and support of democracy, we were led to extend our interest to representation and

---

[39] *Class, Religion*, chap. 5, Table 5.4. Partyworkers similarly put equal emphasis on causes and personal gratifications as motivations for continuing in politics (ibid., Table 5.7).

communication, and ultimately to the whole question of party competition and its effects on politicians' freedom of action. Systematisation thus prompts discovery of novel fields of interest and realisation of the bearings of analytic assumptions made in one area upon expectations in other areas. At the same time the mounting of certain predictions does not rigidify analysis into simple proof or disproof of our hypotheses. Especially where predictions are not upheld we can proceed to discover why the prediction failed, and to test alternative explanations of the phenomenon under consideration.[40]

It is as well to emphasise, that although the form taken by our initial assumptions may be new, their content is not. All are essentially based on previous research and speculation, as we have tried to demonstrate by references at various points in our exposition. This point will be made clear in the introductory discussion of each of the chapters concerned with testing predictions derived from the model.

One disadvantage in forming a comprehensive treatment prior to the actual analysis of data lies in the heavy investment of effort required to develop connections and eliminate inconsistencies, only to find that the model does not fit the data anyway. Because of this ever-present possibility we have made no attempt to develop the logical structure as far as we might have done. We have eliminated all inconsistencies which struck us at the verbal level, as well as those which appeared under elementary symbolic analysis. Doubtless however the model still harbours logical errors which would appear under more extensive examination. We have reasoned that the time to make a refined logical analysis is after it has stood up to an initial confrontation with data rather than before. Such a confrontation should tell us whether the further investment of time is worth while, yet still provide a valid test of the main assumptions.

A further caution should be given at this point in regard to our mode of evaluating the success of the model. In terms of classical hypothesis-testing our assumptions are upheld only if all derived predictions are

[40] Predictive theory (in a mathematical form) has been increasingly recognised as an ultimate goal of political science. The use of verbal theories of the kind set out above has been urged as an acceptable halfway house by such writers as Braybrooke, who has himself proposed a verbal 'Miniature Axiomatic Theory' based on Duverger's hypothesis about electoral systems and parties. See N. Polsby, R. A. Dentler, P. A. Smith (eds), *Politics and Social Life* (Boston, 1963). The *a priori* verbal propositions advanced by Anthony Downs in an attempt to explain democratic party competition have proved extremely fruitful. See A. Downs, *An Economic Theory of Democracy* (New York, 1957).

successful: failure of any one prediction means that some of our assumptions are wrong, though we may be uncertain as to which. Given the prior lack of hard knowledge in many of the areas we investigate, together with the unreliability of indicators in general, it would be unrealistic to embark on our investigation with these criteria. Instead we adopt an implicit Bayesian reasoning, whereby we shall try (in an approximate manner) to assess the posterior probability of our assumptions being right after their confrontation with data. A moderate assignment of probability after testing would indicate that they need to be supplemented or reorganised rather than completely abandoned.

One limitation on the assessment of predictive success is of course that some of our derivations would follow just as neatly from a different set of assumptions. The consequence that activists will recognise the value of political parties to a greater extent than others, which we derive from their support of party competition among other fundamental democratic procedures, could follow equally well from assumptions which elevated the activists' attachment to party above any tendency to integrative behaviour or support of democratic procedures. In looking at the model's overall predictive success we must ask ourselves how far it is due to such overlapping derivations – a question it is not easy to answer. We should point out however that deductive ambiguity of this type is paralleled by the inductive ambiguity of posterior interpretations – that is to say that many interpretations of data are susceptible to explanation by different sets of higher-level assumptions. So this kind of ambiguity is not peculiar to our approach.

Two other drawbacks are shared by our model with similar verbal formulations. In the first place the fact of being verbal means almost necessarily that they are verbose, when stated precisely. At a general level we are able to present our model in two figures and a short section of this chapter. However the exact statement of definitions, assumptions, derivations and data-predictions takes on the formidable bulk of Appendix B. Verbosity in turn leads to difficulty in keeping all consequences and relationships in mind at the same time, and lack of an exact summary means retention of inconsistencies and the potential to generate nonsensical consequences.

The second drawback is the absence of specified functions between variables. Relationships have inevitably to be stated in a 'more or less' form. In the present case this is not only a limitation of the model but also of the Glasgow data available to test the model. Moreover at each stage of the argument assumptions are stated in terms of one group compared with another – first activists compared with electors, then groups displaying more integrative behaviour with those displaying less and so on. As a result derivations are also worded in terms of group comparisons, and since our interest lies in the contrast between activists and electors the comparisons usually involve these groups.

TABLE I.I

Hypothetical distributions illustrating a possible fallacy in testing the Predictive Model

Straight group proportions on:

	Integrative behaviour		Factual agreement		Agreement on potential issues	
	High	*Low*	*High*	*Low*	*High*	*Low*
Group A	0·75	0·25	0·75	0·25	0·75	0·25

CASE I

Support at the individual level for result of group comparisons

	Group A			
	High integrative behaviour		*Low integrative behaviour*	
	High factual agreement	*Low factual agreement*	*High factual agreement*	*Low factual agreement*
High potential issue agreement	0·75	0·00	0·00	0·00
Low potential issue agreement	0·00	0·00	0·00	0·25 (1·00)

CASE II

Contrast at the individual level with result of group comparisons

	Group A			
	High integrative behaviour		*Low integrative behaviour*	
	High factual agreement	*Low factual agreement*	*High factual agreement*	*Low factual agreement*
High potential issue agreement	0·35	0·25	0·15	0·00
Low potential issue agreement	0·15	0·00	0·10	0·00 (1·00)

A possible fallacy in this approach is illustrated in Table 1.1 with hypothetical data. The straight group-based data of Group A seem to indicate that our assumptions are upheld. Group A, which displays a high degree of integrative behaviour, also agrees substantially on factual appraisals and on potential issues: 75 per cent of its members engage in highly integrative behaviour, and agree highly.

But it is by no means certain from these overall group results whether the individuals inside Group A who display integrative behaviour are the same individuals as those who display high agreement. It is possible that they are the same – this is Case I in Table 1.1 where the 75 per cent of the total membership of Group A who show high integrative behaviour also agree highly on factual appraisals and potential issues, and the 25 per cent who do not display integrative behaviour are not agreed in any respect. Even given the positive results from overall group comparisons it is possible however that only a minority of those who display high integrative behaviour in Group A agree highly on factual appraisals and potential issues, while a majority of those who display low integrative behaviour actually agree highly in both respects. This is the situation illustrated in Case II in Table 1.1.

Thus given the results shown from overall group comparisons on different variables it is possible to conclude that an anticipated better showing of Group A has been confirmed. An analysis of the behaviour of individuals inside the group would however reveal whether the interrelationships between variables inside each group actually confirmed the hypothesis, as in Case I, or failed to support it, as in Case II – *even in the event of group comparisons themselves upholding it*.[41]

In subsequent analyses we have often confined ourselves to group comparisons without examining relationships between variables at the individual level, as illustrated in Cases I and II in Table 1.1. The reason is that we conceive of most of our variables as group rather than individual phenomena. Agreement is by its very nature a group variable, since it is meaningless to talk about the agreement of a single individual, taken by himself. The same applies to integrative behaviour. If an ongoing group, e.g. political activists, is distinguished by a relatively high degree of integrative behaviour, the fact that some members are not at the moment of measurement taking part in its interactions is probably irrelevant, since their agreements with other members will

---

[41] This is one example of the general ecological fallacy originally pinpointed by W. S. Robinson, 'Ecological Correlations and the Behaviour of Individuals', *American Sociological Review* xv (June 1950).

still be shaped by their identification with a highly cohesive group. In this situation it would be misleading to cross-tabulate variables directly, since this procedure would ignore the vital part played by group processes. Where our hypotheses relate to purely individual reactions we have examined individual in addition to group-level data, as in Chapter 2 and parts of Chapters 3 and 4.

THE PREDICTIVE MODEL AND MATHEMATICAL TREATMENTS OF POLITICAL PHENOMENA

The criticism of our model's verbosity and lack of functional relationships between variables points to the superiority of mathematical treatments of the processes involved. This is not in question but their present feasibility is in view of the wide range of phenomena covered and limitations of data. In spite of their defects verbal models have at least the virtue of offering a reasonably systematic treatment of relationships which cannot as yet be mathematised. At the cost of precision they offer greater range and flexibility in examining relevant variables and specifying their relationships. Care should however be taken to relate verbal formulations to mathematical work being undertaken in similar areas, in order to avoid the ever-present dangers of vacuity and triviality which afflict them. To be any use such a comparison should as far as possible relate our model to specific mathematical treatments of parallel phenomena, in considerable detail. This is done in the note at the end of this chapter.

CONCLUSION: PREDICTIVE MODEL AND GLASGOW POLITICS

We have in this chapter put forward systematic research proposals which can be applied not only to the Glasgow data in our possession but to similar data elsewhere. The assumptions we make generate predictions which can be used to structure further data-analysis and to provide an overall framework for other investigations. Our Glasgow data can therefore be regarded as evidence required to test the model which could equally well have been collected in any other mass democracy. As mentioned in the introduction, however, Glasgow politics have an importance and general interest of their own, which we have recognised in a previous analysis. How do the interest in general explanation and the interest in Glasgow interlink?

The answer is of course that our general model is an attempt to explain certain aspects of politics in all mass territorial democracies. Since Glasgow constitutes such a polity, any general explanation will also cover the Glasgow case. To take one example, if our general expectations about the inability of representatives to form correct appraisals of constituents' opinions are correct, they will also explain the difficulty which Glasgow councillors have in ascertaining their ward electors' opinions. Thus the general model represents just as much of an attempt to explain why Glasgow politics fall into some of their present patterns and not others as any ad hoc interpretation of the data in a purely Glasgow context. It is in one respect a more satisfactory attempt at explanation of Glasgow politics, for it can be shown to be wrong. In subsequent chapters we expose its predictions to just such empirical checks.

Note: *The Predictive model and mathematical treatments of attitude change.* A mathematical model (or rather family of related models) has been developed to cover processes of influence, attitude change and agreement which are connected with some of the topics covered in Fig. 1.1.[42] Individuals are conceived as possessing attitudes which enable them to be located at particular points in a one-dimensional attitude continuum, which extends from -1 to $+1$. At the simplest level the rate of change in an individual's attitude is taken as a linear combination of his general persuadability, the attempts made by others to influence him, and the distance between his and their attitudes. On the additional assumption that individuals are at least in indirect contact through other individuals, analysis shows that the interaction process leads to universal agreement.

If the independent influence of constant communication sources is taken into account, the original linear combination can be extended (and in effect another model formed) by adding an analogous expression for the rate of contact between the individual and any given source, the distance between their positions, and the individual's persuadability. On the assumptions that all individuals are at least in indirect contact, through other individuals, and that all the constant sources take their position at 0 on the attitude continuum, it can be shown that the group tends to universal agreement. If the constant sources take different attitudes it is not impossible that universal agreement will ensue, but individuals can end up with divergent attitudes. The original models can be brought closer to reality by complicating these initial simple assumptions. In particular it can be assumed that the more extreme the attitude, the more resistant it will be to change: that the greater the difference

[42] M. J. Taylor, 'Towards a Mathematical Theory of Influence and Attitude Change', *Human Relations*, Winter 1968, pp. 121–39.

in attitude between individuals the less they will interact: that interaction is also shaped by fairly stable group structures independent of
given attitudes (these can be rendered in the equation by an associated
matrix of probabilities for interaction): that the 'attitude-distance'
which helps determine the rate of change under a given influence
attempt is less the real distance between attitudes than the distance perceived by the individual under persuasion, which is liable to be magni-
fied if the real distance is moderately large, minimised if it is small.
Such additional assumptions reduce the tendency to universal agreement, but it remains in attenuated fashion in a good many of the models
formed by the introduction of the new assumptions.

Relating the mathematical models to our verbal formulation, it is
obvious that the former concentrate entirely on the area covered by our
Assumption V. The mathematical models do not take the connection
between interaction and agreement as given. Instead they concentrate
on the tendency of interactions to produce agreement if persuadability
and some kind of attitude–distance are also considered to affect preferences. The fact that most of the models considered do point to the outcome of the influence process as universal agreement, lends some
plausibility to our more modest assumption on the relatively greater
agreement of the interactive groups.

These mathematical models are concerned with attitudes in the
psychological sense: that is, with an underlying predisposition to react
in the same way in a variety of social or political situations. Attitudes
have the additional advantage of being conceived as a continuous
distribution which eases mathematical formulation. Thus the models
considered above are not capable of being immediately applied to
discrete issue-preferences, unless all of them can be reduced by scaling
techniques to an underlying attitude dimension, and so rendered continuous. On the other hand our formulation is concerned with issue-
preferences which are not necessarily reducible to a generalised attitude
continuum. Thus one way to examine its usefulness in preparing the
way for future mathematical treatment is to see how far its reasoning
can suggest modifications which would equip mathematical attitude
models to deal with discrete issue-preferences in a mass territorial
democracy. Various suggestions are listed below:

(a) Our definition of integrative behaviour (Appendix B, Definition
IV. 1) points to the possibility that interaction may be supporting,
opposing, direction-giving or direction-seeking. Opposing interactions

– contradiction, abuse and the like – may not simply not contribute to bringing two positions closer together but may even push them further apart. And the probability of negative interaction may increase, the further apart two individuals originally are. On the other hand supportive interaction will tend to leave original positions as they were before. The mathematical models seem to have concentrated entirely on the direction-giving type of interaction, and this non-recognition of other types of interaction may have contributed to the unrealistic result of universal agreement. Our verbal theory thus suggests an alternative way of refining the original assumptions in order to reach consequences more consonant with general experience, and this applies as much to the original attitude models as to adaptations for discrete issues.

(b) Our reasoning postulates further that in the context of any ongoing political process an individual's susceptibility to persuasion by another individual is not independent of their relative position on other current issues, since these are being discussed concurrently. Discrete preferences should not be regarded as too discrete. The particular form in which this point comes out are in our assumptions linking the existence of important irreconcilable disagreement to the possibility of agreement on other issues.[43] Generally however it might be realistic to add to the attitude-distance on the issue under consideration an average (perhaps weighted) of attitude-distance on other current issues.

(c) The discussion here would also point to the possibility of two other types of 'distance' having an important effect on interaction rates, and hence on influence attempts. Most groups of any size will be politically stratified, with activists interacting a great deal among themselves but relatively little with ordinary group members, and the latter having a lower interaction rate among themselves. Influence attempts among activists are also likely to be two-sided, but activists are much more likely to persuade ordinary members than vice versa.

The activist–non-activist distinction is likely to be encountered on all issues. On some however an additional distance is likely to be that of party. On our assumption party divisions where they do occur are liable to be felt more keenly by activists than by electors. Such distinctions are perhaps common enough not to detract from the generality of a model in which they are incorporated, while at the same time

[43] Mathematically this could be expressed by a matrix linked to the other expressions, when an entry of 1 represents the fact that the two individuals are on the same side on such a central disagreement (if it exists) and 0 that they are on opposing sides so that no influence attempt would succeed.

providing more specific interaction values than could be obtained from a contentless assumption of mutual influence.

(*d*) A further differential effect of activism may be seen in the relationship with the mass media. For activist groups – particularly the top activists – relevant media should not be taken as purely external constant communication sources but should be regarded – through the journalists who formulate their messages – as themselves involved in the process of mutual influence attempts. The real difference between the media and individual activists would be in the range of their influence attempts: where the individual could reach only small numbers of his fellows the media could reach all. For ordinary members of the group the media could still be regarded as external communication sources, but so, on our assumptions, could the activists. The difference again would lie in the range of media influence attempts compared with any individual activist or even the entire activist group. The same points could be made with regard to pressure groups.

These suggestions imply that the lines of investigation involved in testing our verbal assumptions are not irrelevant to mathematical work in this area, and may indeed be capable of usefully supplementing it. Whether they should be adopted depends ultimately on two considerations: the difficulty of expressing them mathematically, and their success in anticipating the patterns of the Glasgow data.

2. Support for Established Procedures

The most compact and manageable part of our whole model is the left-hand chain of assumptions in Fig. 1.1, which lead from the absence of irreconcilable disagreements on the most important issues to a greater confidence among the politically active that their issue-demands will be satisfied, then from demand-satisfaction to the existence of positive attitudes towards established democratic procedures. The data-predictions arising from this little chain can readily be presented and tested within the bounds of one chapter, which will thus encapsulate the approach to the validation of hypotheses against data adopted in our handling of the other and more extended lines of reasoning in chapters 3/ to 6.

The two assumptions just summarised are typical of the rest in trying to provide a plausible explanation for an anomalous phenomenon while at the same time fitting this explanation into a wider account of ongoing political processes. This fit to a wider context has been attempted in the previous chapter: required here is a more detailed description of what the assumptions seek to explain and of how they relate to previous efforts to resolve the problem. For of course these starting assumptions are not plucked from the air. Normally they codify what seems to us the most relevant and plausible of previous speculations, and the most attested research findings.

In the present case our hypotheses seek to make some sense from the accumulation of recent evidence that democratic procedures – at least in the form in which they apply to specific situations – enjoy remarkably uneven approval among the populations of the United States and Britain. A series of American studies have tapped a widespread verbal reluctance to extend democratic freedoms to particular unpopular minorities or to acquiesce verbally in specific but disapproved majority decisions. This reluctance exists despite overwhelming endorsement of abstract democratic procedures and principles which logically imply these specific applications. Specific applications have attracted most widespread support among the better educated, the better off and the socially and politically active.[44] The same tendencies are evident in Britain although the differences in pro-democratic feeling between the more and less politically active are not so pronounced as in the United States.[45] Political distrust and cynicism about the actual application of democratic principles in decision-making are found to vary in the same way as these preferences through the different groups in the population.[46]

These puzzling and seemingly inconsistent findings have given rise to a number of widely divergent *a posteriori* interpretations. We shall summarise the main positions which arise from these and comment briefly upon each before we indicate how they stand in regard to our two assumptions.

1. *Internal inconsistency of democratic philosophy*

Because of the very muddled way in which the population appears to regard the procedures under which they live, some analysts have concluded that no unified concepts of 'democracy' exists, that there is no consistent set of democratic principles but only a changing bundle of ideas and values logically inconsistent with each other so that it is no wonder that they give rise to inconsistent derivations. For example, the idea that 'the majority should rule' is always in tension with the belief that elected representatives should be given wide discretion in

[44] The seminal research is that of Samuel Stouffer, *Communism, Conformity and Civil Liberties*, especially chap. 3; and J. W. Prothro and C. M. Grigg, 'Fundamental Principles of Democracy; Bases of Agreement and Disagreement', *Journal of Politics*, 22 (1960) 276–94. Also Herbert McClosky, *APSR* lviii, and A. M. Rose, 'Alienation and Participation', *American Sociological Review*, 27 (1962) 836–8. The way in which democratic support is measured in these studies is through dichotomised 'agree–disagree' statements: e.g. Prothro and Grigg's operationalisation of the abstract principle of majority rule is formed by two statements:
(i) Public officials should be chosen by majority vote. Agree/disagree.
(ii) Every citizen should have an equal chance to influence government policy. Agree/disagree. Support of abstract democracy is shown by agreement with these two statements. A specific application of this general principle is formed by agreement with the following agree/disagree statement: if an admitted Communist were legally elected Mayor of your city the people should not allow him to take office.
[45] Ian Budge, *Agreement*, chap. 8.
[46] Budge, *Agreement*, chap. 9; McClosky, *APSR* lviii, *passim*. G. A. Almond and S. Verba, *The Civic Culture* (Princeton, N.J., 1963) pp. 111–12, demonstrate that these conclusions hold true for a wider range of countries than simply Britain and the United States.

decision-making: minorities are supposed to have the right to criticise but at the same time representatives should be shielded from totally unfair and destructive criticism.[47]

This reaction is refreshingly iconoclastic and at the same time provides a plausible explanation for the inconsistencies in popular response. If no consistency inheres in the ideas themselves it is no wonder that popular responses appear muddled. But a weakness in the interpretation appears from the fact that not all replies are equally muddled. At the abstract level there is overwhelming endorsement of a number of generalised beliefs which by consequence show a high empirical correlation among all members of the population. Moreover, a high empirical correlation also exists for some groups between the abstract generalisations and their applications to certain specific situations. A general patterning, which goes against the interpretation of democratic doctrine as inherently inconsistent, is thus evident in the empirical findings, for if democratic doctrine were inconsistent, such inconsistencies should be apparent at the abstract as well as at the specific level and should be found equally among all groups. Nor have those who espouse this explanation by way of internal democratic inconsistencies yet produced a general philosophic critique of democracy which demonstrates the necessary inconsistency of its component ideas.[48] These criticisms do not completely dispose of the inconsistency interpretation but they do suggest that more positive and traditional explanations of the finding should be tested before the concepts of 'democracy' and 'support for democracy' are discounted for analytic purposes.

2. Apathy

A second interpretation similarly discounts the effects of any conscious or unconscious agreement about democratic norms on the operation of government. Hostility to these norms is still regarded as carrying

[47] R. R. Alford, *Bureaucracy and Participation* (Chicago, 1969) chap. 9. These points are made more strongly in the unpublished MS. on which chap. 9 is based, which was kindly lent to the authors by Professor Alford.

[48] Critics have demonstrated the inadequacy of one or two of Prothro and Grigg's operational statements about democratic norms. For example the statement that all public officials should be elected (quoted in footnote 44) is obviously far too sweeping even for the United States. All democracies in fact appoint many if not most public officials. However Prothro and Grigg's statements have been modified ('public officials' changed to 'representatives' for example) and also supplemented by other statements of the same type with much the same findings being obtained (Budge, *Agreement*, chap. 8).

potential dangers, but what keeps democracies stable on this view is the apathy of the elements in the population who might be most inclined to challenge them. This apathy derives from the fact that it is the less educated and less active who baulk at the practical consequences of democratic beliefs, and these are in fact the persons least inclined to take political action in Britain and the United States.[49]

3. Differentiated Consensus

Someone must take positive political action somewhere in the polity. The mere apathy of hostile elements seems a markedly incomplete explanation for stability. The empirical findings themselves indicate that the more active and the better educated offer the most consistent verbal endorsements of democratic action in specific situations. This fact has given rise to an argument that democratic agreement far from being irrelevant simply has its main locus among certain strategic groups in the population. It is the disproportionate support of these groups – in particular of the active politicians – which allows democratic procedures to be operated in concrete social and political situations as if there were no widespread disagreement upon their ability. On this view the apathy of the potentially anti-democratic is important but only because it is complemented by the activism of the potentially pro-democratic.[50]

The theory of differentiated consensus – which incorporates the views of the theorists of apathy – thus provides a plausible explanation for the pattern of findings described above and in particular for the discontinuities observed between the reactions of different groups. Moreover it fits commonsense ideas and recent findings more closely than does a mere dismissal of attitudes towards democracy as too shifting to be important in the maintenance of stability. They may be. But the alternative possibility demands prior attention.

The interpretation from which our present assumptions derive is

[49] H. McClosky, APSR LVIII, passim; W. H. Morris Jones, 'In Defence of Apathy', Political Studies II (1954) 25–34; Budge, Agreement, chap. 10, confirms for Britain that those least inclined to take political action are those least reliable in their democratic beliefs.

[50] R. A. Dahl, Who Governs?, chap. 28; V. O. Key, Public Opinion, pp. 536, 550. Budge, Agreement, states this position in detail in chaps. 1 and 2. Recent critiques of this position (which raise moral as well as empirical questions) are: Peter Bachrach, The Theory of Democratic Elitism (Boston, 1967); C. McCoy and J. Playford, Apolitical Politics (New York, 1967); W. Connolly, The Bias of Pluralism (New York, 1969).

then the notion that the greater agreement of certain groups – from whom the principal decision-makers derive – plays a major part in prompting them to a more extensive practice of democratic procedures in their actual behaviour. Chief credit for the maintenance of democratic operating procedures is thus attributed to activists – the councillors and partyworkers of our samples. They are aided of course by support from the richer and better-educated segments of the population and they are also able to invoke the respect for abstract democratic principles which almost everyone feels. Buttressing pro-democratic principles are the strong convictions of the active, richer and better-educated that democratic principles are actually being put into effect in their political system and that existent practices are therefore worth preserving.

A recent American discussion has amplified the earlier findings discussed above by showing that general and political tolerance is powerfully affected by education and almost unaffected by political activism.[51] This discovery might seem to raise some difficulties for the theory of differentiated consensus which emphasises the pro-democratic effects of activism rather than those of education (except in so far as the politically active tend to be better educated in any case). However the kind of outlook with which we are exclusively concerned is one needed to work the democratic rules and to see that others work them, in the relevant political system. Generalised tolerance might be one reason for abiding by them but by no means the only one, as we shall see. And in fact the investigators who found the stronger link between education and tolerance stress that activism probably exerts a stronger influence than education upon ideologies directly relevant to the political context in which respondents actually operate.

The question which now remains is just why the politically active should give this noteworthy support to democratic procedures? No doubt it stems in part from the greater regard for, and practice of, consistency between principles and action which comes from a concern with law-making and administration.[52] Such consistency would promote among activists a greater continuity between specific actions and abstract principles than appears to be present among other groups

[51] The discussion is contained in the unpublished MS. by R. R. Alford, 'Community Leadership, Social Status and Political Behaviour', which Professor Alford kindly showed us.

[52] This greater political consistency of activists is taken as a postulate of our discussion in Assumption XII. See Chapter 1 and Appendix B.

who endorse the same abstract principles but fail to follow them into practice.

But the mere habitual practice of consistency does not of itself explain why politicians show less scepticism about the extent to which democratic procedures are actually applied. Nor does it really explain the the intensity of their support for democratic procedures. Some warmer and more immediate influence seems to be at work and the most obvious explanation appears to lie in the self-interest of these pro-democratic groups. They – not only the politicians who exercise more influence on social and political affairs, but the better-off and the better-educated – are after all the main beneficiaries of the present system. They will tend to see democracy as a good thing because it is the system in which they flourish. Any change is liable to be adverse to these established figures. Their trust in the system can be seen as trust in themselves.

Our two assumptions summarise this simple rationalistic explanation of why the politically active in particular are likely to offer disproportionate support for fundamental present procedures. Activists are first assumed in the absence of any bitter internal division to feel to a greater extent than others that their system responds to their demands – that they are reasonably likely to get their way on issues when they exert themselves to do so. Then we assume secondly that those who feel likely to get their way are more likely to have pro-democratic preferences as expressed in positive attitudes to the fundamental present political procedures we describe in Appendix B. Since on the first assumption the political activists will include more people who feel likely to get their way they will also include more who express pro-democratic appraisals.

Our theory thus seizes on the most obvious initial explanation for activists',[53] stronger attachment to democratic norms, ignoring possible complicating factors that might be at work. It could easily be argued, for example, that quite apart from self-interest both active and educated persons had been exposed to longer and more intensive processes of democratic socialisation than others[54] and that such socialisation

[53] But also all other established groups which benefit from the system – the better educated, better off, dominant ethnic group and so on. It is a commonplace sociological proposition that those who benefit most from a situation are most inclined to maintain the status quo.

[54] For example R. A. Dahl, *Who Governs?*, pp. 319–20 stresses the effects of these socialisation processes well as the strength of self-interest.

exerted an independent pressure towards pro-democratic attitudes. Moreover education may give a value to consistency between speech and action which is much more than instrumental, and it may also (as noted above) promote attitudes of general social tolerance which foster support of democratic procedures. Our theory is a simplification which deliberately ignores these possibilities. Where so few tests have been applied to any explanation of politicians' stronger attachment to democracy the best strategy lies in postulating and checking the most economical. Only if the latter is disproved need more complex aspects of activists' experience be drafted to serve as explanations. These are at any rate put to indirect test in the comparisons of councillors' partyworkers' and electors' attitudes required to test the simple model. For unless the (more highly educated and more intensively socialised) activists do appear as more pro-democratic than electors, the role of these other factors will also appear to be negligible. But our more rigorous tests are geared to the self-interest theory.

Two further points must be made before we proceed to these tests. In the first place we anticipate at the outset of the discussion an empirical finding which is presented in Chapter 5 – that there are no important and irreconcilable disagreements in Glasgow among electors or activists. This being given we are concerned here solely with the link between political activity and demand-satisfaction on issues, and the further link between these two factors and pro-democratic attitudes.

A second caveat must be entered with regard to the measurement of these pro-democratic attitudes. Whether or not the concept of democracy is internally inconsistent it is certainly complex and value-laden. We have tried to encompass the relevant meanings of the concept for a mass society in our definition of fundamental present political procedures which by consequence has in itself become a complex and many faceted concept. It would be unrealistic to claim that the survey-responses we examine for signs of pro-democratic attitudes are capable of reflecting all aspects of the definition. Most in fact relate only to single constituent items such as the stipulation that representatives normally follow clear majority wishes on current issues. And some of these items may be queried as being less relevant than others to the essential functioning of democracy. In these circumstances the best we can do is to indicate clearly what indicators we are using at each point in the discussion[55] and how they relate to our concept of fundamental present political procedures, then distinguish the actual results

[55] These points will be made principally in the notes to each table.

obtained with such indicators from the interpretation we place upon the results. In this way the reader will be free to accept our conclusions or to reinterpret them in the context of previous research as he thinks fit.

POLITICAL ACTIVITY AND DEMAND-SATISFACTION

The first step in judging whether our simple self-interest model does satisfactorily account for the variation observed in our Glasgow data is to discover whether more councillors than partyworkers and more partyworkers than electors actually do feel likely to get their way on issues. We can also compare voters' and non-voters' feelings of efficacy on this point since we do after all associate increased demand-satisfaction with any increment in political activity. The four current issues over which demand-satisfaction is assessed are: (1) the placing of pubs in corporation housing estates; (2) the elimination of corporation-sponsored fee-paying schools; (3) the extension of parking-meters in the city centre; (4) the raising of rates.[56]

First impressions of the distribution of replies gratifyingly support our assumptions. Councillors as a body are more confident of being successful and confidence declines as we go through the groups at lower and lower levels of activity, all the way down to non-voters.[57] Even in the case of councillors who refuse to give a general estimate of their likely success on issues, 7 per cent out of 11 per cent think they will be very or quite likely to succeed on pubs although they doubt their ability on rates. Only 3 per cent out of the 7 per cent of party-workers who similarly qualify their estimate judge that they will be successful on a specific issue, so that this subsidiary comparison also reveals a decline in confidence from councillors to partyworkers.

Since our assumptions regard political stratification as the sole influence upon demand-satisfaction, the derived predictions about the degree of confidence which councillors and the other groups feel in their success extend to all the possible subdivisions into which they

[56] The background to these issues is fully described in chapter one of *Class, Religion*. The questions from which preferences were ascertained are reported in notes to Table 2.1.

[57] The 7 per cent of Glasgow electors who feel very likely to succeed compares with the 12 per cent of all English and Welsh local electors who felt likely to take action and to succeed on local government affairs: 54 per cent of these electors thought they would not succeed or not take action, compared to the 69 per cent of Glasgow electors who felt unlikely to succeed. *Maud Committee Report* (London, H.M.S.O., 1968) vol. 3, p. 75.

might be split. Obviously not all such subdivisions can be compared. Indeed the labour involved in analysis of most of the ensuing data restricts us to the imposition of only one control. Of all the criteria on which sub-groups of the various strata might be chosen, party, class and religion are the most immediately obvious alternative explanations of phenomena to stratification. The effects of class and religion on general political attitudes have already been examined in some detail.[58] Moreover we also know that party identification correlates strongly with (objective and subjective) class and with religious affiliations,[59] so that conclusions reached about the success of the model under a control for party will generally apply to the success it would have had if class and religion were held constant. Party therefore appears to be the strategic split we should make in each political stratum to provide a more severe test of the success of the model.

But inside each party too the anticipated ordering of councillors–partyworkers–electors is encountered on most comparisons. The marginally greater confidence of Progressive partyworkers compared with Progressive councillors disappears when it is noted that most of the 16 per cent of councillors who qualify their answer actually feel quite confident of satisfaction on pubs although not on rates.

When we proceed less formalistically however, comparing the various groups between parties as well as internally, it emerges that demand-satisfaction is related to party-membership as well as to political activity. Labour partyworkers display greater confidence that their demands will be satisfied than do Progressive councillors, and Labour electors almost as much. The superior showing of councillors in the overall comparison is due solely to the overwhelming confidence of the Labour group. Party thus emerges as an independent influence on demand satisfaction. However estimates of relative influence in the shape of effect parameters show that its effect is only about half that exerted by activism. Our model is thus inadequate in entirely dis-counting the influence of party dominance on demand-satisfaction, but upheld to the extent that political stratification is a more important influence. It is interesting to see that party effects consistently decline from councillors to partyworkers to electors, since other assumptions in our model (XII and XIII (b)) link the strength of party feeling to levels of activity.

This conclusion still leaves untouched the possibility that demand-

[58] *Class, Religion*, chap. 7: summarised in Chapter 1 above.
[59] *Ibid.*, chap. 6.

TABLE 2.1

Confidence in likelihood of successful action on four current issues (percentage of councillors, partyworkers, electors and non-voters)

	Successful action:			Discriminates between likelihood on different issues	DK	Effect Parameters
	Very likely	Quite likely	Not likely			
All councillors	21	26	28	11	10	
All partyworkers	13	25	45	7	11	
All electors	7	10	69	1	9	
All non-voters	6	8	70	—	12	
Prog. councillors	8	18	50	16	8	
Prog. partyworkers	9	20	57	2	11	$a_1 = 0\cdot19$
Prog. electors	5	9	73	1	10	$a_2 = 0\cdot18$
Lab. councillors	30	33	9	7	12	$A = 0\cdot37$
Lab. partyworkers	16	28	34	11	11	$P = 0\cdot20$
Lab. electors	10	12	68	1	9	

The questions which prompted respondents' estimates of their likely success were: 'If you felt strongly about any of these problems, pubs in housing estates, eliminating fee-paying schools, extending parking-meters or raising rates, what do you think you could do?'; 'If you did do anything about them, how likely is it that you would succeed? Very likely, quite likely or not likely?' Percentages in this and following tables do not add precisely to 100 per cent, partly because of rounding and partly because varying (but usually small) numbers of respondents did not give relevant answers to the questions. To reduce complexity in this and subsequent tables percentages for party sub-groups are reported only for councillors, partyworkers and electors: not for narrower strata like non-voters except where these percentages are especially relevant or interesting. For the same reason no percentages for voters are presented, since they can be inferred from the comparison of non-voters and all electors. Party identification in this and subsequent tables is estimated through the known affiliations of councillors and partyworkers and for electors from replies to the following question: Generally speaking do you usually think of yourself as Unionist, Labour or Liberal? [Unionists (Scottish Conservatives) are practically identical with Progressive supporters.]

P stands for the effect exerted by party; a_1 stands for the effect of the difference between electors and partyworkers and a_2 for the effect of the difference between partyworkers and councillors. A stands for the total effect of activism ($A = a_1 + a_2$). Effects are calculated on the dichotomy between those who feel 'very' and 'quite likely' to succeed plus those who discriminate between different issues, and others. Those who discriminate are included with those who feel likely to succeed because many of these persons feel reasonably likely to succeed on at least one issue. In line with our textual discussion we assume that demand satisfaction increases from Progressive to Labour and with increases in activity.

Given the dependent dichotomy described above between those confident of demand-satisfaction and those not confident, and the assumptions about the increase in demand satisfaction between categories of the independent variables, the part of Table 2.1 relating to the calculation of effect parameters can be represented as follows, in the expected order of demand-satisfaction.

Electors		Partyworkers		Councillors	
Prog.	Prog.	Prog.	Lab.	Prog.	Lab.
0·15	0·23	0·31	0·55	0·42	0·70

The proportions represent the percentage of all those in each category who are confident of demand-satisfaction (e.g. 0·15 of all Progressive electors are confident of demand-satisfaction: the 0·85 of all Progressives not confident of demand-satisfaction are not explicitly reported but left to be inferred). The effect on demand-satisfaction exerted by party independently of activity can then be obtained by averaging the proportional difference between party groups inside each activity level, i.e.

$$\frac{(0·23 - 0·15) + (0·55 - 0·31) + (0·70 - 0·42)}{3} = 0·20 = P.$$

P is the effect of party reported in Table 2.1.

The effect on demand-satisfaction of the elector–partyworker dichotomy can be obtained by averaging the proportional difference between activity-levels inside each party group, i.e.

$$\frac{(0·31 - 0·15) + (0·55 - 0·23)}{2} = 0·24 = a_1.$$

By a similar procedure the effect of the councillor–partyworker dichotomy can be ascertained, i.e.

$$\frac{(0·42 - 0·31) + (0·70 - 0·55)}{2} = 0·13 = a_2.$$

Because we have assumed that the elector–partyworker–councillor distinctions constitute a gradated rank-order scale of political activity we can add the effects on demand-satisfaction of the two component gradations to obtain an estimate for the overall effect of activity. The mathematical derivation of these effect parameters and a general formalisation of the procedures involved are given in James Coleman, *Introduction to Mathematical Sociology*, chap. 6, pp. 116–19. The fact that a_1 and a_2 are added does of course strongly reflect our theoretical emphasis on the total effect of activism, and in many cases a higher final effect parameter is obtained by treating activism as a trichotomised gradation than if it were treated as a simple dichotomy-like party. On the other hand our treatment of the measure does make the rather severe requirement that both gradations of the activity measure produce changes in the dependent variable which move in the same direction: otherwise the algebraic summing of a_1 and a_2 will substantially reduce the final measure of effect (A).

satisfaction itself is closely related to pro-democratic attitudes. The proposition now implies not only that councillors offer more support than others but also that Labour councillors offer somewhat more support than Progressives, since they include more persons who feel their demands are likely to be satisfied. This modification of the original assumptions has indeed its own plausibility. On exactly the same self-interest argument one can maintain that the potential decision-makers of the majority party are those who have most reason to be satisfied with the system which has placed them on top. They are therefore the persons with more strongly self-interested motives than others in its operation: stronger than supporters of their own party because of their greater influence on decisions, stronger than their defeated opponents at the same level of activity for precisely the same reason. Therefore their attitudes towards the existent democratic system should be warmer.

These modified assumptions still rest solely on a presumed connection between demand-satisfaction and approval of established democratic practices. The comparison of proportions showing such approval between different strata and now between Labour and Progressives offers one set of tests of this connection. Another and severer test can be applied by combining all councillors, partyworkers and electors of whatever party who feel very likely to succeed in the action they undertake on issues, and examining their pro-democratic attitudes. On the assumption that confidence of success promotes pro-democratic feeling this group should appear as more pro-democratic than any other, for its members are literally 100 per cent confident while doubters of their own efficacy appear even among Labour councillors.

MAJORITY VERSUS MINORITY RULE ON CURRENT ISSUES

As first indicators of pro-democratic feeling we use responses evoked in response to a hypothetical situation on the four current issues mentioned above where the views of a particular and directly affected minority were clearly contrasted with those of the majority in Glasgow and we asked which ought to decide the issue. We are thus using the term 'majority rule' in a different sense from that employed by Prothro and Grigg, who related it almost exclusively to electoral majorities. Replies to these questions will be likely to bear on acceptance of majority electoral decisions, in so far as those who accept majority decisions here will be almost bound to accept them in elections. However those who oppose the majority in these situations cannot be taken as necessarily opposed to majority electoral decisions. The questions are the data-equivalents of the stipulation in our definition of fundamental present political procedures that in a functioning mass democracy representatives will normally follow clearly-expressed majority wishes on current issues. The stipulation is very restrictive and these questions are capable of testing it severely, for they are posed in regard to live and particularised issues on which respondents had previously stated their own preferences and their appraisals of the party positions. In such a context concern with general democratic principle is liable to be smothered in the strong feelings aroused by the issue itself.

The first striking conclusion which emerges from the overall distribution of responses is that the combination of councillors, partyworkers and electors who feel very likely to succeed on issues does not show the most undeviating support for majority as against minority rule over all issues[60] – only on pubs do they offer more unanimous support than other groups. The groups offering most support to majority rule on other issues are councillors on parking and partyworkers on fees and rates. Councillors are less majoritarian than electors on pubs and fees. The group which gives most consistent support to majority rule over the whole array seems to be partyworkers.

We can summarise the bearings of these data as a whole on our hypotheses by noting the numbers of group comparisons which do and do not fall into the expected order over all four issues. In one sense our initial assumptions constitute a prediction about the order into which groups will fall on the extent of their pro-democratic attitudes – in this case support of majority decision-making: the predicted order is that in which groups appear in Table 2.2. Thus those who feel likely to succeed should show more support for the majority and less for the minority than councillors, partyworkers, electors and non-voters, and so on. Each comparison of one group with another constitutes a test of our model. Sometimes the model passes and sometimes it fails this test. Where a variety of data are being used as indicators of the same underlying phenomenon – support of democratic procedures – this can cause confusion. However the theory's predictive success – the surplus of times we could trust to it over the times we would be let down – can be usefully summarised by subtracting the number of failures from the number of successes and dividing by the total number

[60] Nor do the councillors, partyworkers and electors who feel very likely to succeed offer more pronounced support for majority rule when they are separately compared with other councillors, partyworkers and electors. A minor difficulty in evaluating the results of Table 2.2 arises from the fact that in some cases a group offers more support for *both* minority and majority than does another: for example, partyworkers compared with councillors, since more councillors than partyworkers qualify their answers. Ignoring this group and any 'don't knows' – of whom we cannot say either that they support or oppose the majority – we can reach a decision as to which group offers more unanimous support for majority *v*. minority by subtracting the proportion supporting the minority from the proportion supporting the majority and comparing the difference for all groups. This procedure is the one followed in the text.

TABLE 2.2

Support for majority or minority decision of four current issues (percentages of the 73 councillors, partyworkers and electors who felt very likely to succeed in action undertaken on the four current issues, all councillors, all partyworkers, all electors and all non-voters)

	Issue should be decided by:				Per cent majority support – per cent minority support
	Affected minority	*Glasgow majority*	*Qualified answer*	*DK*	
Pubs					
Those who feel likely to succeed	68	23	4	4	—45
All councillors	73	16	10	1	—57
All party workers	75	23	—	2	—52
All electors	71	25	—	4	—46
All non-voters	73	23	—	4	—50
Fees					
Those who feel likely to succeed	40	53	3	4	+13
All councillors	48	44	5	4	—4
All partyworkers	42	58	—	—	+16
All electors	48	44	—	7	—4
All non-voters	45	46	—	9	+1
Parking					
Those who feel likely to succeed	23	64	7	5	+41
All councillors	11	68	12	6	+57
All partyworkers	25	68	3	4	+43
All electors	44	49	1	7	+5
All non-voters	49	44	—	7	—5
Rates					
Those who feel likely to succeed	38	49	7	5	+11
All councillors	15	52	23	9	+37
All partyworkers	26	64	1	8	+38
All electors	50	39	2	9	—11
All non-voters	46	42	3	10	—4

The four questions which prompted respondents' endorsements of majority or minority decision are: 'If the majority of people in the corporation housing estates wanted pubs there, but the majority of all people in Glasgow were against such a proposal, which side do you think ought to win?' (pubs); 'If the majority of parents whose children go to these schools wanted the schools to be fee-paying, but the majority of all people in Glasgow wanted to stop fee-paying in corporation schools, which side do you think ought to win?' (fees); 'If the majority of motorists in Glasgow didn't want more parking-meters but the majority of all people in Glasgow did want them, which side do you think ought to win?' (parking); 'If the majority of people living in private houses were against raising the rates but the majority of all the people in Glasgow were for it, which side do you think ought to win?' (rates).

of comparisons. We can term the resultant fraction a 'success ratio'. If all predictions are upheld the success ratio will be 1·00. If only half are upheld (and correspondingly half fail) the success ratio will be zero – as it should be for our predictions are then producing no more than chance success. The overall success ratio for Table 2.2 is in fact zero. Thus the model does not adequately account for our data.[61] With the relative failure of the explanation by demand-satisfaction (at any rate for this set of data), the partyworkers' more consistent support of the majority might be seen as deriving from their relatively more intense socialisation into democratic norms, uncontaminated by the councillors' brushes with determined minorities in practical decision-making.

Support for majority/minority does however vary in roughly the same way for all groups over the four issues. About three-quarters of each group favour the people living in corporation estates on the introduction there of pubs.[62] On parking, however, the position of most councillors and partyworkers is reversed: overwhelming numbers in each of these groups support majority decision, although electors are evenly divided. Now pubs and parking happen to be the issues on which councillors and partyworkers agree most in their preferences;[63] the largest numbers favour a forward policy on both. It is interesting therefore that most councillors and partyworkers endorse council tenants' desire for the introduction of pubs and then switch to support of the Glasgow majority on the extension of parking meters, for it

[61] Success ratios for each issue are: pubs 0·00; fees 0·00; parking 0·60; rates 0·20.
[62] Support for the minority on this issue could be strengthened by regard for the rights given to affected minorities by Scottish licensing law – the objections of even a substantial minority of residents in any area can prevent the sale of liquor. On the other hand this right is one of veto while the minority envisaged in the question was one which wanted pubs to be introduced.
[63] See Fig. 5.1 below.

c

appears that they approve whatever group happens to support their own preference. This interpretation gains additional reinforcement from the close split between majority and minority support on fees, which seems likely to reflect the clash of preferences which exists on that issue between relatively equal groups of councillors and party-workers.[64] Only in the case of rates does relatively extensive endorse-ment of the hypothetical majority position (for an increase) not seem an exact reflection of personal preferences. Even electors, who in fact overwhelmingly oppose an increase, divide fairly evenly between approval of minority opposition and majority advocacy. And the majority is upheld by most partyworkers and councillors,[65] in spite of the fact that here too a clash of preference exists.

The link between personal preferences and support for minority views can be examined directly in terms of the correlation which exists between them. From Table 2.3 there appears to be a very high

TABLE 2.3

Correlations between personal preferences and support of affected minority on four current issues (Tau$_a$ values for councillors, partyworkers and electors)

	Electors	Partyworkers	Councillors
Pubs	0·90	0·24	0·33
Fees	0·90	0·80	1·00
Parking	0·90	0·73	0·60
Rates	0·60	1·00	0·43

Given rank-order on the independent variable (here issue-preferences) T$_a$ indicates the degree to which pairs of ranks in corresponding order on the dependent variable (here support for affected minority) exceed pairs of ranks in non-corresponding order. Tau$_a$ values for this table were calculated on the expectation that the per cent supporting the minority would increase steadily from the group expressing strong disagreement to the group expressing strong agreement, where the minority were depicted as agreeing with the proposal, and vice versa where the minority were depicted as disagreeing with the proposal. See H. M. Blalock, Social Statistics (New York, 1960) pp. 319–20.

correlation between electors' own feelings and their support or non-support of the affected minority on three of the issues, and a moderately high correlation on rates. There is a very high correlation for party-workers on all issues except pubs, where it is very low. For councillors

[64] See Fig. 5.1 below.
[65] Most of the 23 per cent of councillors who give qualified answers on the rates question deny – quite correctly – that the majority do in fact support a rates increase.

the correlation is moderately high on parking and relatively low on pubs and rates (on rates the order of magnitude resembles that obtained for electors rather than the one obtained for partyworkers).

The array of correlations, taken as a whole over all issues, shows that the connection between personal feelings and minority support is strongest for electors, next strongest for partyworkers and least strong for councillors. This finding offers limited support for the interpretation that activists' procedural attitudes are influenced more by the long-term benefits they derive from the political system than by their immediate interest in each issue. Such an interpretation is consonant with the assumption contained in our model. But it should not be over-stressed in view of the fact that the main difference seems to lie between councillors and partyworkers rather than between partyworkers and electors.

TABLE 2.4

Support for majority or minority decision of four current issues by party (percentage supporting majority minus percentage supporting minority, among Progressive and Labour councillors, partyworkers and electors)

Pubs	Per cent majority support − per cent minority support		Per cent majority support − per cent minority support
Prog. councillors	−58	Lab. councillors	−55
Prog. partyworkers	−34	Lab. partyworkers	−69
Prog. electors	−42	Lab. electors	−45
Fees			
Prog. councillors	−58	Lab. councillors	+46
Prog. partyworkers	−56	Lab. partyworkers	+78
Prog. electors	−33	Lab. electors	+9
Parking			
Prog. councillors	+45	Lab. councillors	+67
Prog. partyworkers	+23	Lab. partyworkers	+61
Prog. electors	−12	Lab. electors	+12
Rates			
Prog. councillors	+10	Lab. councillors	+61
Prog. partyworkers	−13	Lab. partyworkers	+80
Prog. electors	−37	Lab. electors	−1

The association between personal preferences and support of majority or minority points of view emerges much more clearly from the imposition of a control for party. The party groups of councillors and workers spread themselves in much the same way between support of the minority on pubs and majority on parking, with Labour showing more support of the majority on parking. The relative similarity of attributes here is explained by the fact that these are not party issues. But on fees – which is a party issue – most Progressive councillors and partyworkers support the parents who would wish to retain fees (their own position). The corresponding Labour groups side with a Glasgow majority which (as the statement was put) shares their own preference for abolition.

Rates display a less clear-cut pattern. Labour – councillors and partyworkers – strongly endorse the hypothetical majority position of support for an increase. In view of the general tendency to majority or minority support on the basis of personal preferences this finding causes no surprise. But the Progressives do not line up with the minority in straightforwardly opposing the increase. Fifty per cent of Progressive partyworkers support the minority but the substantial proportion of 37 per cent line up with the majority. And the largest single cluster of Progressive councillors, 40 per cent, endorse the majority preference opposed to their own. This explains the relatively low correlation between personal preferences and minority support on this issue which we found among councillors (Table 2.3). Here for the first and only time among activists we find large groups supporting the majority even though its views are opposed to their own. Any interpretation of this anomaly must be speculative. In view of later findings on the longer-term considerations applied in making political decisions by activists compared with electors,[66] it does seem possible that many Progressive councillors may recognise rates increases as necessary and inevitable in order to meet rising costs and increasing demands for city services. For the opposition party however antagonism to rates increases forms a valuable electoral posture. Those Progressive councillors who recognise both facts find themselves in a typical politicians' dilemma: they wish the city government to fulfil its obligations, but they have no mind to lose votes. The hypothetical statement that the majority in fact supports a rate increase offers a notional escape route: they can at least verbally support a rates increase without losing votes.

Labour electors on fees, parking and rates tend to split almost evenly

[66] See Chap. 6 below.

between majority and minority endorsement. A similar split appears on parking among Progressive electors – the greater number supporting the motoring minority in spite of their councillors' and partyworkers' endorsement of the majority position. On fees all Progressive strata unite in support of affected parents. And on rates Progressive electors show more internal solidarity in favouring minority hostility to an increase than do partyworkers or councillors. The 44 per cent of Labour electors (almost all personally opposed to a rates increase) who endorse majority support of the measure thus share with Progressive councillors and partyworkers the distinction of being the only groups to offer considerable support to a (hypothetical) popular majority with opposing preferences. This elucidates the finding presented in Table 2.3 where the correlation between electors' preferences and minority support appeared lowest on rates preferences. But the most probable explanation for Labour electors' altruism on this point is party loyalty.[67]

Looking more systematically at the influence of party and activism on majority support, it appears from resulting effect parameters that the Labour–Progressive split exerts a more consistent and generally stronger effect than gradations in activity. On pubs both party, with an effect of –0·04, and activism, with an effect of −0·10, detract from support of the majority, rather than enhancing it. On parking majoritarianism is promoted slightly more by activism (0·20) than by party (0·15). However on rates the effect of party at 0·30 is twice, and on fees at 0·45 forty-five times, as great as that exerted by activism. The weaker influence of activism on fees and rates is explained by the contrary effects exerted by the elector–partyworker difference – which promotes majoritarianism – and the partyworker–councillor difference – which detracts from majoritarianism. This discovery adds support to the trend noted in Table 2.2, for partyworkers to offer more consistent support than other groups for majority rule.

The increase in majority support from Progressives to Labour was in a sense anticipated by the self-interest argument as soon as we discovered that Labour was more confident of demand-satisfaction. But demand-satisfaction was more strongly influenced by activism than by party, hence on the pure self-interest argument majoritarianism ought to be more strongly influenced by activism. Since the reverse is the case, there

[67] The strongest Labour identifiers fall somewhat disproportionately into this group: 48 per cent of strong identifiers siding with majority support for the increase compared to 39 per cent of weak identifiers.

must be more behind the strong effects of party than feelings of demand-satisfaction, although these may play a part.

The general conclusion must be that long term pro-democratic attitudes are simply not discernable in these endorsements of majority as against minority decision. Support for majority rule does not appear as strongly linked to demand-satisfaction nor indeed does it seem to vary to any great extent with degree of political activity.[68] There is of course always the possibility that endorsement of the majority over the minority on current issues has nothing to do with support for democracy, and that the negative result casts more doubt on the relevance of some of our more severe requirements for a functioning democracy than on the assumptions which link demand-satisfaction and political activity to pro-democratic attitudes. This possibility can be checked by examining responses to another question whose scope relates it to our definition of democracy as a whole rather than to one specific item in that definition.

CHANGES IN GLASGOW GOVERNMENT

If those confident of demand-satisfaction and higher on political activity do feel more concern for democracy we should expect them to a greater extent than other groups when confronted by the possibility of changes to suggest ones which strengthened or preserved the representative character of the régime. At the minimum they should be less inclined to mention changes which transferred power from electors and elected representatives to officials or which vitiated electoral competition.

On the initial question of change or no change, more electors than partyworkers and more partyworkers than councillors or those who feel confident of demand-satisfaction oppose any innovation whatsoever. This finding is probably to be attributed more to the hidebound conservatism of electors than to their desire to defend democratic principles. It is linked to the fact that they mention fewer changes of any kind in reply to the question. Both characteristics probably stem from a lack of articulateness and of ability to envisage changes which is probably bound up with their lower degree of political activity. Regardless of its origins the electors' conservatism lends support to the existent system, and since this is democratic the end-result is to

[68] The success ratio for all comparisons on the question of majority rule including those under party control is 0·22, a low figure which reveals the inadequacy of the model, although not its complete rejection.

safe-guard democratic principles whatever the motive for the action.

It is probably more illuminating for our purposes to consider opposition to any change at all along with attempts to strengthen the representative principle. For all are in a broad way responses which support the democratic functioning of the system. It is true that the most popular of pro-representative responses – make councillors more efficient – may have its origins in a desire for technocracy rather than democracy, but again we are concerned with the end-tendency rather than the initial impulse. If we proceed on this basis it emerges that the order of the various groups is that predicted by our model apart from the support given by partyworkers, which is stronger than that given by either councillors or those confident of success. However substantially more partyworkers than electors and somewhat more councillors and persons confident of success also back changes such as increasing officials' power and weakening the political parties which seem potentially capable of weakening the representative principle. We encountered this seeming contradiction on the last set of responses, and as before it is partly due to the fact that more electors and non-voters made a neutral and irrelevant reply such as 'don't know' and hence fewer than in other groups endorsed both pro- and anti-representative positions. One way of getting round the confusion is again to estimate the degree to which each group agrees on strengthening representation by the disparity between the percentages who are pro- and anti-representation. This difference varies with the proportion who support representation, the proportion who oppose it and the proportion who are neutral and indifferent: hence it summarises in one statistic all the possible reactions in the table.[69] The difference is greatest for partyworkers (39 per cent), next greatest for those confident of success (33 per cent), then for councillors (31 per cent), electors (28 per cent) and non-voters (25 per cent). The relative support given by councillors and those confident of success increases on the second and third replies to the question.

The final ordering for democratic support is thus reasonably consistent with our predictions.[70] One point to note is the wide support given by all groups, which is perhaps as important a phenomenon as the variation which exists between them.[71]

[69] This measure has already been used in the discussion of majority rule. For a fuller discussion of the measures of agreement which can be applied to data deriving from various types of survey questions see Budge, *Agreement*, chap. 3.

[70] The success ratio is 0·60.

[71] For the strong general support given to democratic norms by British electors see Budge, *Agreement*, chap. 8.

TABLE 2.5   Changes preferred in Glasgow local government

(Percentages of the 73 councillors, partyworkers and electors who felt very likely to succeed in action undertaken on the four current issues; all councillors, all partyworkers, all electors and all non-voters)

	Changes which would preserve/strengthen present modes of representation				Changes which would weaken present modes of representation				Changes which do not affect present modes of representation					Per cent support for representation—per cent for weakening representation
	Desire no change of any kind	Broaden council representation	Make councillors more efficient	Total endorsing changes preserving/strengthening representation	Make appointed officials more powerful	Weaken the party system	Reduce influence of various groups	Total endorsing changes weakening representation	Reform corporation finances	Transfer some services to central government	Regionalise local government	Have smaller local government areas	Get Labour out	
First-mentioned changes														
Those feel likely to succeed	23	3	22	48	10	5	—	15	4	1	8	3	4	+33
All councillors	13	1	30	44	5	7	1	13	5	7	18	5	1	+31
All partyworkers	24	8	28	60	13	8	—	21	4	1	5	1	1	+39
All electors	34	1	5	40	7	4	1	12	2	1	1	1	3	+28
All non-voters	31	—	3	34	4	3	1	9	2	1	1	1	2	+25
Second-mentioned changes														
Those feel likely to succeed	—	1	13	14	3	2	—	5	3	2	2	—	—	+9
All councillors	—	1	18	19	2	2	—	4	5	6	6	4	1	+15
All partyworkers	—	3	19	22	7	—	1	8	—	3	1	—	—	+14
All electors	—	—	2	2	1	1	—	2	1	—	—	—	—	—
All non-voters	—	—	1	1	—	1	—	1	—	—	—	—	—	—
Third-mentioned changes														
Those feel likely to succeed	—	—	7	7	—	—	—	—	1	—	—	—	—	+7
All councillors	—	—	11	11	—	—	—	—	2	4	—	—	—	+11
All partyworkers	—	—	3	3	—	2	—	2	1	—	1	—	—	+1
All electors	—	—	—	—	—	—	—	—	—	—	—	—	—	—
All non-voters	—	—	—	—	—	—	—	—	—	—	—	—	—	—

NOTES TO TABLE 2.5
The questions which prompted respondents' preferences were: 'Do you think that any changes should be made in the arrangements for running local government in Glasgow?' [*If Yes*] 'What changes are these?' Respondents' answers were taken verbatim and subsequently coded into forty categories of a much more detailed character than was required for our research but which facilitate recombinations in secondary analysis by other investigators. For our own purposes these detailed categories have been formed into the ten broader groupings which appear in the table. The eleventh, *desire no change*, simply reports negative replies to the introductory question and therefore appears only among the first-mentioned changes. Up to three separate changes as distinguished by our forty detailed coding categories could be recorded for each respondent in order of mention. Hence distributions are presented in Table 2.5 for first-mentioned, second-mentioned and third-mentioned changes. The distributions are separated because of the danger of double counting if they were combined in a multiple-response distribution. Respondents could in that case be possibly counted twice as mentioning one of the broader changes presented in the table if they had originally been coded into two of the more detailed categories which now form part of the same broader grouping. This cannot happen on any single mention, however, since respondents could be coded into one and only one of the detailed categories at a time. Conclusions are drawn largely from the first-mentioned changes – these being the most salient for respondents. But percentages from the other two distributions are used to check that conclusions fit with later replies as well. Normally in this and following tables of the same type the most popular initial preferences are also those which attract heavier subsequent endorsement.

The eleven broad preferences for changes are linked according to whether they seem to maintain or improve the direction of Glasgow government by representatives elected on a universal adult franchise; on the other hand tend to change that system by increasing the powers of appointed officials, reducing the representation of various groups, or weakening the party competition through which elections become more meaningful choices for the bulk of the population; or are technical proposals which do not affect the modes of representation.

When party is controlled, pro-representative feeling turns out to be concentrated among Labour councillors rather than spread throughout the whole stratum. The ordering of overall support for representation is partyworkers, electors and councillors among Progressives – a result which decidedly reverses our expectations. The Labour figures are closer to those we predicted but, as with the Progressives, partyworkers emerge as the group most strongly committed to representation. Even Labour electors are more strongly committed than Progressive party-workers. The striking connection between party and pro-representation feeling might seem to support the argument that adherents of the party in power will more strongly support the existent system. But on the same argument we would expect inside the Labour party to find councillors more strongly for the representative principle than partyworkers, since it is the operation of this principle which has given them their closer proximity to the seats of power. It is true that on their second and third replies Labour councillors emerge more strongly in support of

TABLE 2.6

Changes preferred in Glasgow local government, by party (percentage support for representative practices minus percentage for weakening representative practices, among Progressive and Labour councillors, partyworkers and electors)

Per cent representation support – *Per cent weakening representation*		*Per cent representation support –* *per cent weakening representation*	
First-mentioned changes			
Prog. councillors	+15	Lab. councillors	+46
Prog. partyworkers	+25	Lab. partyworkers	+57
Prog. electors	+21	Lab. electors	+39
Second-mentioned changes			
Prog. councillors	−2	Lab. councillors	+30
Prog. partyworkers	+8	Lab. partyworkers	+20
Prog. electors	—	Lab. electors	—
Third-mentioned changes			
Prog. councillors	8	Lab. councillors	+14
Prog. partyworkers	4	Lab. partyworkers	—
Prog. electors	1	Lab. electors	—

representation. But on the initial question of change or no change, where the securely established might be expected to resist, fewer Labour than Progressive councillors plump for stability (12 per cent compared to 16 per cent).

The failure of our predicted ordering of pro-representative feeling by activism among Progressives greatly impairs its ability to explain all variations in the data.[72] Party emerges as a more useful indicator than level of activity.[73] And confidence of demand-satisfaction appears to have less effect on this manifestation of pro-democratic feeling than does status as a partyworker.

Again we must face the question of the validity of these replies as measures of pro-democratic feeling. After all, the changes which are suggested by respondents are all incremental. They may reveal tendencies to extend or limit the operation of representation but nobody

[72] The model's overall success ratio is lowered to 0·37 when the results for each party are taken into account.

[73] If the influence of party in promoting support for representation (as opposed to all other replies) is compared with that exerted by activism, effect parameters are: party, 0·10; partyworker–elector difference, 0·25; partyworker–councillor difference, −0·175; activism, 0·075.

proposes to abolish it altogether. Like Holmes' dog which barked in the night the significant fact about our respondents may lie in what they did not say: they did not advocate revolution or dictatorship. But this argument from what was left unsaid simply reinforces the conclusions reached from the analysis of spoken preferences. For silence on these points is common to all groups: if the silence is significant we can at least conclude that activism and demand-satisfaction – and party – have nothing to do with it. For the rest here was a question directly related to procedural changes. The responses elicited by it seem to have implications for all definitions of democracy, whether broader or narrower than that adopted here. And they confirm the impression left by replies on majority/minority decision on issues: that they are governed more by party than by either activity or demand-satisfaction.

POLITICAL PARTIES IN GLASGOW GOVERNMENT

We regard political parties as a necessary means of representation in mass democracies, through which majority opinion can be translated into action and minority opinions expressed. We are bound to point out however that this view does not command universal acceptance and hence that the findings we reach through the use of derived measures may not be acceptable to some as evidence of the democratic feeling of our samples.

Whether the parties engaging in electoral competition are purely local or affiliated to a wider national organisation is of course irrelevant from our point of view. Hence we can examine attitudes to the parties directly through the various likes and dislikes expressed by workers and electors about the two major parties in Glasgow and also in a more long-term perspective through reactions to the possibility of parties disappearing from the corporation.

In terms of our original arguments on the necessity of party competition for a mass democracy and on the positive attitudes engendered by demand-satisfaction and activity towards all the procedures of democracy, we should expect more persons who feel likely to succeed on issues, and more partyworkers than electors, to express positive attitudes to parties, i.e. to express definite likes not only about their own parties but also about the parties opposed to them. Moreover we anticipate in the two first-mentioned groups a superior ability to avoid simplistic black-and-white views of party politics, to be able to see things that are wrong with their own party as well as with the opposing party. Otherwise we can hardly say their members are reacting to parties as parties but to parties as 'mine' and 'theirs'. These expectations can be compared with the proportions in each of the three groups saying that they liked or disliked 'nothing' about a party and the proportion making some definite reply. We are able to make an additional distinction between those who replied to the party questions 'nothing' – a mild disclaimer which may simply reflect lack of interest in the other party – and those who more vigorously indicated that there was 'nothing at all' they liked or disliked, a reply with stronger positive or negative affect as the case may be.

Since responses to such directly party-related questions are bound to be affected by partisan loyalty the overall distribution is inevitably less illuminating than the breakdown by party. Suffice it to note that those confident of demand-satisfaction consistently incline less to definite appraisals and more to negative replies than partyworkers, although such tendencies are less apparent in this group than among electors. This is just what would be expected however from a group drawn from both partyworkers and voters: what we are getting is more of a statistical average rather than a unique and powerful influence of demand-satisfaction upon positive reactions to the parties. However the success ratio for our model on these data is 0·66, which indicates a reasonable fit.

For each of the separate party groups of workers and electors there is a tendency for negative affect to increase in remarks about the opposing party.[74] What really concerns us however is the question of whether reluctance to praise the opposing party and criticise one's own is less pronounced among partyworkers compared with electors. As it turns out they are less inclined than electors to reply that there is simply 'nothing' they like about the other party and more inclined to say there is 'nothing at all' they like. This pattern would unambiguously indicate that partyworkers harboured more intensely negative feelings than electors towards the other party were it not for the fact that both Progressive and Labour partyworkers are also more inclined than corresponding electors to mention definite likes about the opposing party. In the case of Progressives however the tendency of partyworkers to find something they like about Labour is markedly weaker than the opposing tendency to find nothing at all they like. But the proportion of Labour workers making definite appraisals of Progressives is actually slightly greater than the proportion harbouring strongly negative

[74] An exception here occurs with Labour partyworkers and electors who both prove as willing to criticise Labour as the Progressive Party. This finding is discussed in more detail below.

TABLE 2.7

Incidence of negative and definite appraisals of Labour and Progressives by party (percentage of partyworkers and electors)

	Prog. party-workers	Prog. electors	Labour party-workers	Labour electors	Effect parameters
Like about Progressives					
Some definite aspect	94	42	25	8	P = 0·515; A = 0·345
DK what	4	24	8	23	
Nothing	2	32	44	56	
Nothing at all	—	2	23	12	
Like about Labour					
Some definite aspect	19	12	76	46	P = 0·455; A = 0·185
DK what	4	11	15	23	
Nothing	39	51	8	29	
Nothing at all	39	27	2	3	
Dislike about Progressives					
Some definite aspect	54	15	75	18	P = 0·120; A = 0·480
DK what	6	14	15	32	
Nothing	33	65	9	46	
Nothing at all	7	7	2	4	
Dislike about Labour					
Some definite aspect	85	48	75	16	P = 0·210; A = 0·480
DK what	11	28	12	27	
Nothing	4	21	13	50	
Nothing at all	—	2	—	6	

Summary distributions of responses to questions: 'Is there anything in particular you like about the Progressive Party in Glasgow?' 'Is there anything in particular you like about the Labour Party in Glasgow?' 'Is there anything in particular you don't like about the Labour Party in Glasgow?' 'Is there anything in particular you don't like about the Progressive Party in Glasgow?'

Effect parameters are calculated for the dichotomy between some definite response v. all other responses. The assumptions about the direction of effects are: that party loyalty promotes a tendency to like some definite aspect of one's own party and dislike some definite aspect of the opposing party; that activism tends to promote a definite response whatever the party loyalty.

feeling, while for the corresponding electors there is a marked decrease in both the proportions making definite and those making strongly negative appraisals. Both sets of partyworkers are less likely than their electors to refrain from criticising their own party but Labour party-workers are still less likely to refrain than Progressive. The greater

TABLE 2.8

Appraisals of changes if there were no parties on Glasgow corporation

(Percentages of the 73 councillors, partyworkers and electors who felt very likely to succeed in action undertaken on the four current issues; all councillors, all partyworkers, all electors and all non-voters)

	Appraisals of parties as necessary or beneficial					Appraisals of parties as harmful					Appraisals of parties as neutral	
	Parties promote public service	Parties necessary to democracy	Parties promote efficiency	Parties are inevitable	Total seeing parties as necessary or beneficial	Without parties politics would be more disinterested	Without parties politics would be more businesslike	Without parties there would be less control by national government	Parties favour special groups	Total seeing parties as harmful	Politics are the same with parties or without	Per cent seeing parties as necessary or beneficial – per cent seeing parties as harmful
First-mentioned appraisals												
Those feel likely to succeed	3	5	12	23	43	26	3	3	1	33	11	+10
All councillors	—	2	33	28	63	24	4	—	—	28	5	+35
All partyworkers	2	16	13	10	41	30	12	3	—	45	5	-4
All electors	1	7	6	11	25	34	5	1	1	41	3	-16
All non-voters	2	8	4	13	27	29	3	—	—	32	4	-5
Second-mentioned appraisals												
Those feel likely to succeed	1	7	3	3	14	10	—	1	—	11	—	+3
All councillors	1	7	7	10	25	11	1	—	—	12	—	+13
All partyworkers	1	3	3	3	10	14	4	1	—	19	1	-9
All electors	1	1	1	—	3	9	1	—	—	10	—	-7
All non-voters	—	—	1	—	1	6	—	—	—	6	—	-5

NOTES TO TABLE 2.8

The questions which produced appraisals in the table were: 'If there were no parties on Glasgow corporation do you think it would make a difference in the way the corporation is run?' 'Why is that?' Responses were coded into thirty detailed substantive categories which have been collapsed into the nine broader categories shown in the table. These in turn can be grouped in terms of whether the view taken of parties is positive, negative or neutral. As in previous tables, the difference between the percentage taking a positive view of parties and the percentage taking a negative view can be used as a summary index of the support given to the idea of local parties by each group of respondents.

warmth towards all parties displayed by Labour activists is perhaps natural in the strong adherents of the party which introduced organised competition into local politics and stressed its own affiliation to a national machine. Labour stalwarts may feel the more benevolence towards local parties inasmuch as Labour has dominated the more intense party competition. Progressives on the other hand have resisted the encroachment even of sympathetic national parties into the local arena and had (up to 1966) proved unable to break the Labour grip on the corporation. The systematic comparison of influences on definite versus negative appraisals, reported through the effect parameters of Table 2.7, shows that party consistently promotes negative appraisals and that activism in this case consistently works against them. Party exerts a more powerful influence than activism on likes about the parties: activism a somewhat greater effect than party on dislikes. However the finding that activism consistently damps down negative appraisals is exactly in line with the expectations we derive from our model. Its success ratio over all appraisals of parties (with and without the party control) is 0·75. The model's fit with data on appraisals of parties is thus very adequate and much greater than has appeared with the indicators of pro–democratic attitudes examined hitherto.

Further reactions to the party system can be examined in the shape of effects anticipated from the disappearance of local parties. These effects can be grouped according to whether they indicate a view of the party system as good, bad or indifferent and again we expect those confident of demand-satisfaction and activists to see most good and least bad about the operations of parties. The actual ordering of groups on their overall replies corresponds closely to that anticipated. Although those who feel very likely to get their way on issues are less inclined than councillors to take a favourable view of parties and to avoid a negative view, they do prove more inclined to such attitudes than partyworkers, electors and non-voters. The success ratio for the predictive model is thus 0·60, for the data in Table 2.8.

Our expectations are reasonably confirmed on these aggregate figures. However the previous effects of party affiliation have been sufficiently great that it is not unexpected to find that pro-party sentiment is strongly concentrated among Labour adherents. Inside both parties it is still true that councillors make the most favourable and least unfavourable allusions (although Progressive partyworkers are much more hostile than Progressive electors). But Labour electors emerge as more favourable and less hostile than Progressive councillors, a finding rather contrary to our expectations. Effect parameters calculated for the dichotomy between pro-party and all other answers do however show the overall influence of party and activism to be almost comparable – 0·35 for party and 0·36 for activism. Activism consistently promotes an appraisal of parties as necessary or beneficial, except in the case of Progressive partyworkers and electors where the difference involved is not great.

TABLE 2.9

Appraisals of changes if there were no parties on Glasgow corporation, by party (percentage seeing parties as necessary or beneficial minus percentage seeing parties as harmful, among Progressive and Labour councillors, partyworkers and electors)

	Per cent consider parties beneficial – per cent consider parties harmful		Per cent consider parties beneficial – per cent consider parties harmful
First-mentioned appraisals			
Prog. councillors	−11	Lab. councillors	+78
Prog. partyworkers	−74	Lab. partyworkers	+55
Prog. electors	−33	Lab. electors	−1
Second-mentioned appraisals			
Prog. councillors	−7	Lab. councillors	+39
Prog. partyworkers	−39	Lab. partyworkers	+16
Prog. electors	−18	Lab. electors	−1

The success ratio for the model over all comparisons with and without party controls is 0·62. Again this is a good formal fit. But when Labour adherence inclines respondents so powerfully to a favourable view of party over both likes and dislikes for parties and appraisals of change if parties disappeared, there are inadequacies in an explanation solely by level of political activity. Nor can we interpret the benevolence of Labour councillors and partyworkers towards party purely in terms of demand-satisfaction, for the group unanimously confident of its ability to achieve such satisfaction proved less favourable to parties than these two Labour groups.

THE IMPARTIALITY OF GLASGOW GOVERNMENT

A group undistinguished from other groups by greater warmth towards democratic procedures may yet prove more inclined to defend
such procedures in a concrete situation because its appraisals of that
situation are different. If for example more members of a group regard
the existing situation as democratic than do members of other groups,
the equal pro-democratic feeling of the first group will be more effective in prompting it to defend the existing order. For the choice of
action depends on the factual appraisals one makes as well as on the
values one holds.[75]

An examination of the extent to which our different groups see
Glasgow government as fair and impartial is therefore capable of further testing our original assertion that pro-democratic orientations are
associated with demand-satisfaction and political activity, as well as
seeing whether party continues to exert its powerful effect on these
relationships. We first analyse the role of the Lord Provost, the civic
head and chairman of the council, as perceived by each of our groups.
The provost should stand, if anyone does, for the unity of the city and
its government over and above partisan strife. If his activities are
regarded as purely factional the implication is that the whole government proceeds on partisan lines without regard to the general good.

What we discover is that even aggregate replies offer inconsistent
support for the connection between activity, demand-satisfaction and
belief in the Provost's impartiality. Partyworkers are as sure of his
representation of the whole city as those confident of demand-satisfaction, and electors have more faith than councillors. (This conclusion
emerges if the comparison is based on the differences between proportions saying the Provost stands for the whole city and proportions
saying he stands for his own party.) Again the distributions show a
radical contrast between Progressive and Labour responses. Among the
Progressives it produces a perfect negative correlation between levels of
activity and positive appraisals of the Provosts' freedom from party considerations: councillors, the group most directly in contact with the
Provost are most inclined to view him as a partisan figure (owing in

[75] See Budge, *Agreement*, chaps 8 and 9 for an extended argument on these
lines: and also for the finding that British Parliamentary politicians are distinguished from British electors by only somewhat more intense and consistent pro-
democratic preference but quite strongly by their belief that British government is
fair and democratic.

TABLE 2.10

Appraisals of the behaviour of Lord Provosts (percentages of the 73 councillors, partyworkers and electors who felt very likely to succeed in action taken on the four current
issues, councillors, partyworkers, electors and non-voters)

	Provost stands for all Glasgow	Provost stands for own party	Qualified reply	DK	Per cent saying Provost stands for all Glasgow – per cent saying Provost stands for own party
Those feel likely to succeed	68	21	—	11	+47
All councillors	65	29	2	4	+36
All partyworkers	69	22	7	3	+47
All electors	64	21	—	15	+43
All non-voters	59	21	—	19	+38
Progressive councillors	39	53	3	5	−14
Progressive partyworkers	50	41	7	2	+9
Progressive electors	58	26	—	16	+32
Labour councillors	88	7	2	2	+81
Labour partyworkers	84	6	6	3	+78
Labour electors	71	17	1	11	+54

The question which produced these replies is: 'Do you feel the Lord Provost stands for
the interests of everyone in Glasgow or just those of his own party group?'

part, as appears from *obiter dicta* on this question, to his continuing to
vote regularly with the Labour Party in the Council Chamber).
Progressive partyworkers are more inclined to share their councillors'
views on this point than ordinary electors. Most Labour councillors
on the other hand view the Provost as standing for Glasgow, and more
partyworkers take this view than electors. What emerges in fact is a
strong interaction between party and activity in which the two in
combination produce a different result than either would separately.
Any attempt at prediction of these appraisals which does not take party
explicitly into account is bound to prove inadequate.[76]

The investigation can be pursued further through answers to another
question, on who runs Glasgow. Again our concern is to discover which
groups display the most pro-democratic orientation, in the shape this
time of appraisals that the only groups running Glasgow are those duly

[76] In view of these considerations it is not surprising that our overall success
ratio on these appraisals is only 0·12, and that effect parameters for the dichotomy
between appraisals of the Provost as standing for all Glasgow and all other answers
are 0·35 for party and —0·01 for activism.

elected to the office – that there is no hidden conspiracy behind a façade of sham representation.

Actually it appears that electors are more inclined to view elected groups as ruling, by a majority of 71 per cent to 17 per cent. A majority of 71 per cent of partyworkers share this appraisal, but proportionately more than electors (27 per cent) attribute final power to non-elected groups, chiefly to corporation officials and businessmen. The combined group of electors and partyworkers who feel very likely to get their demands on issues take no more favourable a view of the power of elected representatives than do non-voters (71 per cent to 16 per cent).

It is true that electors' rejection of conspiracy ideas may owe more to their limited political insight than to their pro-democratic fervour. A majority (52 per cent) nominate the two most visible political bodies: the corporation (undifferentiated between councillors and officials) and councillors as a body. Most ignore the key roles of the ruling Labour Party and of appointed officials, which are named by a majority of partyworkers. However the aspect of immediate concern is simply this more widespread perception by partyworkers that non-elective groups really run Glasgow. Whether prompted by cynicism or realism this appraisal is not calculated to prompt a warmer defence of established procedures on grounds of their democratic character.

As it turns out the Labour partyworkers are primarily responsible for this effect. In contrast to 65 per cent of Progressive partyworkers only 15 per cent are inclined to attribute power to the Labour Party as a whole. The largest single cluster (29 per cent) places control with the appointed officials. The contrast between the two party groups seems again to spring from reasons quite remote from democratic sentiment. From comments at the time of interviewing it seems unlikely that either group of partyworkers feel they have much control over corporation affairs. For Progressives there is an obvious explanation: the Labour Party is in power. Labour partyworkers have to explain their lack of control by reference to factors outside the electoral battle: hence the more widespread attribution of controlling influence to officials and business interests. The balance of replies naming elected representatives as running the city over replies naming non-elected groups is 73 per cent for Progressive partyworkers, 69 per cent for Progressive electors, 19 per cent for Labour partyworkers and 75 per cent for Labour electors. Thus pro-democratic and pro-representative appraisals are not uniformly associated with levels of political activity. While a majority of every group sees control as held by elected

TABLE 2.11

Appraisals of groups with undue influence in Glasgow

(Percentages of the 73 councillors, partyworkers, electors and non-voters who felt very likely to succeed in action undertaken on the four current issues, councillors, partyworkers, electors and non-voters)

| | No groups have undue influence | Appraisals implying that Glasgow government is representative | | | | Total implying Glasgow government is representative | Appraisals implying that Glasgow government is unrepresentative | | | | | | | | Total implying Glasgow government is unrepresentative | per cent implying Glasgow government is representative – per cent implying Glasgow government is unrepresentative |
		Councillors	Labour group	Labour party as a whole	Convenors		Corporation officials	Progressives	Scottish Nationalists	Economic interests	Religious groups	Friends, relatives of councillors	Various special groups	Unspecified groups		
Those felt likely to succeed	33	3	1	8	1	46	3	3		7	5		3	12	33	+13
All councillors	48		10	17		75	2		1	6	5		2	9	25	+50
All partyworkers	31	1	8	14	2	56		1		11	10	1	4	3	30	+26
All electors	19	3	2	2		26	1	1		10	3	4	2	15	36	−10
All non-voters	15	2	2			19		1	1	11	3	5		15	36	−17
Progressive councillors	26		21	29		76				8	5		3	8	24	+52
Progressive partyworkers	15		13	30	4	62				13	2	2	2	4	23	+39
Progressive electors	19	4	5	2		30	1			11	4	2		15	33	−3
Labour councillors	65			7		72	5		2	5	5		2	9	28	+44
Labour partyworkers	44	2	5			51		2		9	17		6	5	39	+12
Labour electors	19	3	1	1		24	1	1		10	3	5	1	16	37	−13

NOTES TO TABLE 2.11

The questions which produced the answers were: 'You sometimes hear that people or groups have so much influence on corporation affairs that the interests of the majority are ignored. Do you agree or disagree that there are such groups?' 'What groups are these?' The question was adapted from G. A. Almond and S. Verba, *The Civic Culture* (Princeton, N.J., 1962). Respondents' replies were recorded verbatim and subsequently coded into thirty-five detailed categories which are further grouped into thirteen broad categories used here. These are divided between appraisals which see Glasgow government as representative at least to the extent that groups chosen by popular vote exercise undue influence and those which attribute such influence to non-elected groups and minority parties. Up to two replies as distinguished by our detailed categories were recorded for each respondent: since the overwhelming majority ventured only one appraisal second-mentioned appraisals have been omitted in the interests of clear presentation. They are so few that they do not affect conclusions drawn from the first distributions presented here.

representatives, partyworkers are not more strongly inclined to this view. Hence – other things being equal – they will not be prompted to a stronger attachment to established democratic institutions through more sanguine estimates of the power of elected representatives.[77]

Further appraisals of Glasgow democracy can be examined in con- nection with a question on whether any groups exert undue influence in Glasgow. Such a query fairly invites the exposition of a conspiracy theory, and in fact a much clearer distinction emerges here between the readiness of the different groups to trust in the representative nature of the political system. The differences between the overall proportions showing trust in the system and those showing mistrust are greatest for councillors, next greatest for partyworkers, next for those confident of demand-satisfaction, next for electors and least for non-voters. Only those confident of demand-satisfaction deviate from the pre- dicted order. This anticipated order holds too for political strata inside each of the parties. Party effects are most evident in the initial disposi- tion of activists to deny that any group exerts undue influence (only a quarter of Progressive councillors compared to two-thirds of Labour councillors, 15 per cent of Progressive partyworkers compared to 44 per cent of Labour partyworkers). But the Progressives have a compen- sating tendency to attribute the excessive influence which they feel to exist either to Labour councillors or to the Labour group as a whole. Thus party exerts little influence on replies attributing a representative character to Glasgow government (as opposed to any other reply): the effect parameter is only 0·07. Activity exerts a strong effect of 0·47, to which both gradations contribute substantially. The influence of

[77] Party exerts its effect on these appraisals really only within the group of partyworkers (the total effect parameter is 0·165), while level of activity has no consistent effect at all (the total effect parameter is −0·065). Our success ratio over these appraisals is zero.

activism in producing the ordering of trust predicted by our model is reflected in a good success ratio of 0·75.

The evidence of these replies is reinforced by answers to a subsidiary question on patronage in corporation jobs. Fifty-five per cent of all partyworkers denied that certain groups were favoured compared to 31 per cent of electors (and 31 per cent of non-voters). Forty-one per cent of Progressive partyworkers made this denial compared to 26 per cent of Progressive electors and 52 per cent of Labour partyworkers compared to 32 per cent of Labour electors. Effect parameters are 0·085 for Party and 0·175 for activism. Party allegiance does affect these appraisals but not to the extent of political activity.

CONCLUSIONS

It is comforting to end the analysis with evidence which upholds our initial ideas. Their success ratio over all our data on pro-democratic feeling is however only 0·38. This figure indicates that our stratification model has some predictive success, but not enough to be considered the sole explanation of the patterns we have discovered. The clearest result from the analysis is the purely negative finding that self-interest, as measured by confidence of demand-satisfaction, does not explain pro-democratic attitudes. The feelings of superior efficacy which were supposed to motivate the politically active have proved almost irrelevant. The responses of the combination of those who felt very likely to succeed on issues can be accounted for more plausibly on the grounds that they constitute averages of councillors', partyworkers' and electors' responses than by any unique experience of demand-satisfaction.

The second major finding is that party exerts a somewhat stronger influence than activism over all the indicators of democratic feeling we have observed. Since the explanation of differences in such feeling through self-interest has been rejected, the most plausible explanation for differences in party reactions comes from the historical experiences and traditions of the Glasgow parties – which are paralleled in many Western mass democracies. In Glasgow as elsewhere Labour is the party which within living memory has broken through to power on the impetus of a popular mass movement. It is therefore natural for its adherents to stress the desire of their representatives to serve the general good and to favour change in the direction of wider representation in government. Having won the party competition it is only human nature to approve of it. Progressives on the other hand have sought to counter Labour stress on the clash of interests involved in policymaking by emphasising the purely administrative and routine nature of local government work, best carried on by experienced persons applying agreed criteria, with only very general responsibility to the electorate. These different traditions developed over time, and they still exercise powerful effects at the present day.[78]

However understandable the different party reactions in terms of tradition and outlook, they still pose problems in terms of democratic stability. If only activists of the majority party are strongly concerned with upholding representative modes of government, what holds the democratic system together in the long run? One possibility inherent in our initial assumptions and examined in Chapter 5 is that the procedural differences discovered to exist between party groupings of activists are offset by considerable agreement over policies currently being discussed and settled. We still need to know more about the practice of democracy in Glasgow before we come to any definite conclusions, however, and having examined general attitudes in this chapter we proceed in the next to evidence bearing directly upon the actual workings of representation in the city.

[78] A summary of these developments is given in *Class, Religion*, chap. 4. A full account is given in *The Political Development of Modern Glasgow*, chap. 6.

3. Representation

The fundamental political procedures of mass democracy are linked, in our conception, by a common focus upon the responsiveness of politicians to electors. All the provisions relating to voting rights, to equality of information, to the predominance of the electoral decision over intervening decisions, are designed to ensure that elected representatives do carry out popular desires, so far as these can be ascertained. In discussing fundamental procedures we gave explicit recognition to the role of parties and of relationships between representatives and their constituents, since we regard both as essential means by which mass democracies ensure some responsiveness of politicians to electors. We have already examined attitudes to parties – in Chapter 2 specifically with regard to their involvement in democratic processes. This chapter analyses the second means of electoral control which has developed particularly in mass democracies – the constituency relationship between elector and representative.

MODES OF REPRESENTATION

Although there may be dissent from any particular definition, all conceptions of democratic government hinge upon some form of control of leaders by non-leaders. In the end, it is expected that the acts of the citizen's representative somehow reflect the best ideas and interests of the citizen himself. The means by which the citizen controls his representative may vary from a periodic authorisation, during which the representative may exercise his own judgement over all pertinent decisions, to a delegation of specifically enumerated powers over a limited number of decisions.[79] While the alleged merits and demerits of these various forms of control over the representative have been discussed at length, surprisingly few studies have dealt directly with

[79] Cf. Robert A. Dahl, *A Preface to Democratic Theory* (Chicago, 1956) chap. 1; Hanna Pitkin, *The Concept of Representation* (Berkeley, 1969); John W. Chapman and J. Roland Pennock (eds), *Representation* (New York, 1968); Heinz Eulau *et al.*, 'The Role of the Representative', *APSR*, LIII (1958) 742–56.

the actual correspondence of the representative's decisions with the opinions of his constituents.[80]

But the work that has been done has suggested that in modern democracies, whatever may be the ideal model, the citizen authorises his representative to act in his stead on most issues. Given the complexity and multiplicity of political decisions to be made in a modern democracy, the citizen would have to invest an enormous amount of time in studying the issues at hand in order to delegate specific powers for each political decision. Yet investing such a great amount of time would hardly be rational, for it would defeat the main purpose of having a representative – saving the citizen most of the time and trouble required to run the government.[81] In point of fact, most citizens are rational enough not to worry about the day-to-day issues of politics, but many have adopted an attitude of indifference that extends even to the most pressing political issues.[82] Coupled with this, representatives generally admit that even on important issues they have little systematic information about what interested constituents think.[83] Furthermore, many representatives feel that they need not follow their constituents' preferences anyway, if such preferences run against the representatives' expert judgements of the merits of the issue or the best interests of their constituents.[84] Clearly, representatives have a great deal of autonomy.

Still the authorisation given to a representative need not be a universal one. Citizens may reserve control over those issues they consider most vital to their interests in a number of ways. To begin with, they may scrutinise their representatives' behaviour over certain issues, and

[80] Among these few are: Warren E. Miller and Donald E. Stokes, 'Constituency Influence on Congress', APSR LVII (1963) 45–56; Roberta Sigel and H. Paul Friesema, 'Urban Community Leaders' Knowledge of Public Opinion', Western Political Quarterly, XVIII (1965) 881–95; Frank Cantwell, 'Public Opinion and the Legislative Process', APSR XL (1946) 924–35.

[81] See Anthony Downs, An Economic Theory of Democracy (New York, 1958) chaps 11–13, for a discussion of information costs.

[82] Robert Lane and David Sears, Public Opinion (Englewood Heights, N.J., 1963) chap. 6; Richard Rose, Politics in England (Boston, 1964) chap. 8.

[83] Cf. Miller and Stokes, loc. cit.; Sigel and Friesema, loc. cit.; also Lewis A. Dexter, 'The Representative and his District', Human Organization, XVI (1957) 1–13.

[84] Eulau et al. loc. cit.; John Wahlke, Heinz Eulau et al., The Legislative System (New York, 1962) chap. 12; see also the discussion of the role of the representative below.

quickly punish those who violate their preferences.[85] This seems to be the case with regard to civil rights in the United States: congressmen's perceptions of constituents' opinions and congressmen's votes correspond closely to constituents' actual opinions on civil rights; where such correspondence is lacking, the congressman is less likely to be re-elected.[86] Second, citizens may exert some control by voting for a particular party, thereby authorising a particular party programme or outlook while rejecting other programmes and outlooks.[87] This is what informed British citizens do when they cast their votes in a general election. Finally, a modicum of control may be exerted indirectly through the socialisation process. A representative sharing the same values as his constituents will find it more difficult to vote for alternatives violating these values than will a representative with an independent set of values.[88] Because of similarities in the background of Scotsmen, for instance, on matters relating to Scotland, it is generally expected that a Scottish MPs judgement of the opinion of a Scottish constituency will be more accurate than an English MPs assessment of that opinion. Citizens may exert control, therefore, by electing representatives who share their values.

The question of how far the actual relationship between the representative and constituent in Glasgow corresponds to these general modes can be approached on our data from two points of view. In the first place we can look at the general responsibilities attributed to councillors by electors, partyworkers and councillors themselves. In the second place we can formulate more specific models of what the representative–constituent relationship might be, and see how these correspond to actual coincidences and divergences of opinion on current Glasgow issues. Role conceptions will obviously yield more general and less precise evidence about forms of representation than the application of specific models to issue relationships, but at the same time they are likely to set long-term constraints on the types of issue-relationship which will emerge. Consequently we examine role conceptions be-

[85] Cf. Peter G. J. Pulzer, *Political Representation and Elections* (New York, 1967) chap. 3; also Nigel Nicolson, *People and Parliament* (London, 1958) *passim.*

[86] Miller and Stokes, loc. cit.

[87] Cf. Downs, chap. 3; E. E. Schattschneider, *Party Government* (New York, 1942) chaps 8–9; R. T. McKenzie, *British Political Parties* (London, 1955) chap. 11.

[88] Dahl, chaps 4 and 5; Rose, chap. 3; Christopher Martin, 'In Praise of Political Apathy', *The Listener*, LXIII (1960) 1079–80; W. H. Morris Jones, 'In Defense of Apathy; Some doubts on the Duty to Vote', *Political Studies* II (1954) 25–34; V. O. Key, *Public Opinion*, chap. 21.

fore formulating exact models for the analysis of our data on current issues.

It is immediately apparent that a very wide range of ideas exists among our groups on the question of what councillors should do. Equally however it appears that all concur in stressing certain responsibilities more than others. Two are endorsed particularly heavily: these are ward representation and working for the good of the city as a whole. Ward representation is mentioned by 64 per cent of councillors at some stage in their reply, by 61 per cent of partyworkers and by 34 per cent of electors: working for the whole city by 50 per cent of councillors at some point, by 47 per cent of partyworkers and by 26 per cent of electors. Representation of Glaswegians as a whole, which seems to fall between representation of constituents only and working for the whole city attracts 14 per cent of councillors, 15 per cent of partyworkers and 18 per cent of electors. The other 'governing' function which attracts mention from councillors is attending to city finances. This is stressed less by partyworkers and electors.

Looking at the broad groupings of councillors' responsibilities which have been made in Table 3.1, it appears that no group mentions individual moral qualities to any great extent, that electors pay more immediate attention to the provision of services than activists, that councillors themselves stress administration more than the other two groups, and that party loyalties receive more attention from partyworkers than councillors, and from councillors than electors, but are in no case particularly underlined.

From our theoretical assumption of the increasing support produced by activism for fundamental democratic procedures – which include ward representation – we correctly anticipate the greater stress laid on that responsibility by councillors and the placing of partyworkers between councillors and electors. Our second role prediction – that because the provision of efficient government is a minimal requirement for electoral success, concern about city government will increase with activism – is also borne out. It further follows from our assumptions about activists' greater involvement in party competition that they will be more conscious than electors of their party attachments. The data in fact show activists as a whole to be more conscious of party than electors, but in the order partyworkers – councillors – electors rather than in strict order of increasing activism.

TABLE 3.1

Perceived responsibilities of Glasgow councillors (percentage of electors, partyworkers and councillors)

	First mention			Second mention			Third mention		
	Cllrs.	Pwk.	Ele.	Cllrs.	Pwk.	Ele.	Cllrs.	Pwk.	Ele.
Representation									
Represent his ward	45	50	29	17	8	4	2	3	1
Personal contact with constituents and surgeries	1	3	2	2	5	2	1	3	1
Ward and local party committees	—	1	1	1	4	1	1	—	—
Represent populace	6	3	11	6	11	6	2	1	1
Party Loyalty									
Carry out party policy	—	3	1	5	4	1	1	1	—
Carry out election promises	—	3	2	—	1	1	1	—	—
Be true to political ideology	1	1	—	1	1	—	—	—	—
Individual Moral Qualities									
Sincerity, honesty	2	1	1	2	1	—	2	1	—
Consider others	1	—	1	—	—	1	—	—	—
Do very well	—	—	1	—	—	—	—	—	—
Provide Services									
Services in general	1	—	1	5	—	2	4	1	1
Provide housing	—	3	7	4	2	4	7	3	1
Provide schools	—	—	1	—	—	2	1	1	1
Look after old-age pensioners	—	—	1	—	—	1	1	—	1
Help handicapped	1	—	—	4	—	—	1	1	—
Provide other services	—	—	1	—	2	2	—	—	2
Administration									
Control officials	1	1	—	1	1	—	2	—	—
Work on committees	6	3	1	1	—	1	5	2	—
Finance									
Keep down rents	—	—	—	—	—	1	—	—	—
Keep down rates	—	1	1	1	—	2	—	—	—
Attend to city finances	6	4	4	5	2	3	1	1	—
Govern City									
Keep business in city	—	—	—	—	3	1	—	—	—
Plan and develop city	—	—	—	2	2	1	—	—	—
Work for city as a whole	26	26	21	15	19	5	9	2	—
No (further) comments	3	—	13	27	34	59	59	80	91

The question to which the replies shown in Table 3.1 were given was: 'What would you say should be the main job of a councillor?' Coding categories were devised on the basis of clusters in a sample of replies. Percentages may not be exactly 100 per cent because of rounding.

The broad roles defined for Glasgow councillors by these replies centre around ward representation, on the one hand, and city government on the other, especially if the latter is conceived as extending to finance, administration and the provision of city services. The former corresponds generally to a mode of representation whereby constituency influences are the main consideration – whether or not the councillor is a strictly mandated delegate, decides for himself where his constituents' interests lie, or is seen more simply as dispensing aid and advice to the individual constituents who seek his help. The city-wide role is more likely to accord a degree of autonomy and independence to the representative once elected – he has to decide where the general interest lies, to balance the interests of opposing factions (which may be ward-based), and to provide the expertise necessary in administration.

The party form of representation mentioned earlier is largely ignored in these replies. This is anomalous because party divisions obviously have a strong effect on procedural attitudes, and we anticipate that they will also affect some issue preferences. Furthermore there can be no doubt that the corporation itself gives substantial recognition in its procedures to the importance of party, and that most decisions taken in full council committees are previously discussed in the party group. Electors and even partyworkers might be unaware of the effects of such arrangements but councillors could hardly fail to be.

The failure of 88 per cent of partyworkers (at least) to stress councillors' party duties contrasts strongly with the opinion of 46 per cent that electoral organisation and activity is one of their own main tasks, this percentage rising to 59 per cent among Progressives although only 34 per cent among Labour.[89]

The substantial absence of party from the responsibilities attributed to councillors cannot therefore be regarded as indicating the unimportance

[89] The difference in this case probably arises from the fact that Progressive workers are mobilised only for elections, while the permanent Labour Party organisation serves other than electoral functions for many Labour activists. The contrast between conceptions of the partyworkers' and councillors' role supports Marvick and Nixon's point cited previously (Chapter 1, n. 22) that there are role differences between different types of activists additional to sheer increases in the extent of participation.

of parties. Probably rather it stems from a widespread belief that councillors in their public personae ought not to represent only one segment of the community (i.e. adherents of a single party), but all constituents or all citizens, as the case may be. It is quite apparent in Glasgow politics that councillors often do act in partisan fashion. Nevertheless the political argument usually consists in demonstrating that each party in taking its stand is acting for the general good, while the other is selfishly serving some particular interest. And on many matters, as we argued in Chapter 1, policymaking is by consent in any case. Both partisan and consensual processes demonstrate the power of the belief that councillors will act for the public and not simply for the party good.

The opposing pulls of public duty and party loyalty form only one example of the clash of expectations with which councillors are beset. There is also a potential for conflict in the main responsibilities overtly mentioned, to the ward and to the city. A councillors' constituents may well have certain demands which they expect him to represent to the corporation. His committee and council colleagues on the other hand may expect him to forget his parochial concerns and to concentrate upon the good of the city as a whole. The different demands made by groups with whom he is in relationship are likely to be simultaneously internalised by the representative and to combine in varying proportions at different times to affect his decisions. Because councillors are more exposed to the conflicting demands of various groups we should expect a greater number than among partyworkers or electors to mention both ward and city responsibilities.

From a regrouping of the answers listed in Table 3.1 into broad mutually exclusive categories, we can see whether councillors do more often see themselves as combining a ward and city role. In order to obtain a regrouping to investigate the overlapping of these roles we can take advantage of the fact that most answers in Table 3.1 other than those specifically mentioning the ward can be regarded as pertaining to a city role. The parties are city-wide organisations and the services mentioned are all run by the corporation for Glaswegians as a whole. Without serious distortion therefore we can trichotomise all answers between city, ward and mixed. Furthermore, we can try to distinguish between mixed answers themselves.

Respondents' answers often reveal the priority they give to ward as opposed to city responsibilities, in a way which is not directly reflected by coding. However, in the case of mixed answers we can take the responsibility mentioned first by respondents, reasoning that this is likely to be most salient to them. When answers have been re-analysed so that persons who mention a ward responsibility before mentioning a city responsibility are classed as 'mixed ward', and persons mentioning a city responsibility before a ward responsibility are classed as 'mixed city' we get the distribution shown in Table 3.2. A majority

TABLE 3.2

Perceived responsibilities of Glasgow councillors as they divide between ward roles, city roles and two types of mixed roles (percentage of electors, party-workers and councillors)

	Pure ward role	Mixed ward role	Mixed city role	Pure city role
Councillors	8	38	21	33
		46		54
Partyworkers	31	25	10	34
		56		44
Electors	20	13	5	62
		33		67

Table 3.2 is the result of a computer recoding of the responses given in Table 3.1. 'Pure ward role' groups all respondents who at some point answered 'represent ward', 'personal contact with constituents', 'ward and local party committees' in Table 3.1 and gave no other reply. All responses other than those designated above as 'ward' responses are taken as 'city' responses. Respondents who gave 'city' responses without mentioning 'ward' responses are grouped under 'Pure city role'. 'Mixed roles' (grouping respondents who mentioned both ward and city roles as now defined) are distinguished as 'mixed ward role' if the respondent mentioned a ward responsibility before mentioning a city responsibility and as 'mixed city role' if the respondent mentioned a city responsibility (as now defined) before mentioning a ward responsibility.

of councillors appear from this to adopt a mixed role (with mixed ward roles predominating): recognition of mixed roles declines from councillors to partyworkers to electors. On this grouping of roles, partyworkers are much more concerned than councillors to plump for a pure ward role, which is understandable in terms of the fact that their whole activity is framed by the ward and they are less exposed to the diverse demands which inspire councillors' adoption of mixed roles.

Party makes no real difference to the distribution reported in Table 3.2. Progressives in all groups tend very slightly to endorse the pure city role more than Labour, and Labour the mixed ward role more than Progressives. But all the conclusions reached on the basis of overall comparisons still stand under the party control.

With a view to casting light on the genesis of these role conceptions, further comparisons were made between age cohorts, socioeconomic groups, subjective classes and those born inside and outside Glasgow. None revealed substantial differences however, nor did comparisons between respondents from high- and low-turnout wards.

Among councillors themselves a general tendency emerged for those serving their first term to endorse ward commitments more heavily than other councillors. This difference might be due to council influences on longer-serving councillors, which orient them more towards the city as a whole. Alternatively however it can be argued that councillors serving their first term were in 1966 heavily Progressive (owing to recent electoral successes of that party), and are in any case likely to come from marginal wards where party competition is more intense, and where representatives feel they have to pay more attention to the ward in order to retain the seat. The first interpretation (in terms of council influences) receives support however from the fact that past or present tenure of a council office (usually convenorship of committees) predisposes Labour councillors to adopt somewhat more of a pure city role and Progressives not to endorse a pure ward role. Among Progressive councillors only, the holding of party office increases endorsement of the mixed role from 5 to 33 per cent with a corresponding reduction in other ward orientations. Previous party activity before becoming a Progressive councillor leads to more emphasis on ward reponsibilities: 47 per cent of those councillors who had not participated in (ward) political activity before entry to the council adopt a pure city role, compared to 29 per cent of those who had.

Generally, although interesting differences emerge among councillors, it is clear that variation in these role conceptions inside Glasgow is limited. The comparison which might well produce substantial differences would contrast Glasgow with another community.

The presumed effect of role conceptions in which we are primarily interested from the point of view of representation is their influence on agreement between representatives and constituents. We shall look at this effect along with the effects of other factors in the next section.

Regardless of the immediate influence of role conceptions upon issue-reactions it is probable that their main effects are long-term and less direct. In considering stands upon issues, most representatives are at least expected – and expect themselves – to take ward views into account, although they may not automatically endorse them. The widespread acceptance of city roles on the other hand possibly secures recognition of the councillors' special expertise and independent responsibility, and this promotes respect for his autonomy of judgement among the majority of electors who endorse city roles.

SPECIFIC MODELS OF REPRESENTATIVE–CONSTITUENT RELATIONSHIPS

What kinds of day-to-day control do citizens have over their representatives in Glasgow? Our study provides an excellent opportunity to explore at length representation of constituent opinion with regard to the four specific issues previously discussed. These are: (1) the placing of pubs in corporation housing estates; (2) the elimination of corporation-sponsored fee-paying schools; (3) the extension of parking-meters in the city centre; (4) the raising of rates. We also asked about a fifth issue which was only just coming under consideration at the time of our survey. This was the possibility of integration between Catholic and Protestant schools.[90]

To answer our question, let us proceed by investigating how well the representation of opinion on these issues fits each of five alternative models. The first is the Burkean model of representation. This model assumes that the representative uses his best judgement to serve the the interests, though not necessarily the opinions, of his constituents. According to this model, there need be no positive correlation between the opinions held by representatives and those held by their constituents, nor need the representatives let their impressions of their constituents' opinions affect their own attitudes or votes.[91]

The second model, which we call the 'microcosm' model, incorporates elements of proportional representation, guild socialism, and the Fabian socialism of Beatrice and Sidney Webb. Basically, this model asserts that the legislature should be a microcosm of the society as a whole. The distribution of opinions, interests and social backgrounds of the representatives should as nearly as possible reflect the

[90] The first four of the issues listed below were the subject of a whole battery of questions relating to factual appraisals of the issue, support of minority, methods of gaining information, etc., as well as to preferences. The integration issue was the subject of only a single question about preferences. The actual questions relating to preferences were: Do you agree or disagree with this proposal? (to introduce pubs into corporation housing estates, to abolish the fee-paying in the corporation schools where fees are still paid, to extend parking meters all over the city centre, to raise rates, to mix Catholic and Protestant schoolchildren together in the same schools).

[91] Cf. Pitkin, chap. 8; Eulau *et al.*, *Legislative System*, chap. 12.

D

distribution of these respective elements in the society as a whole. A legislature is not truly democratic until labourers represent labour, capitalists represent capital, and in general members of group X represent group X roughly in proportion to the membership of each significant group in the population. Although it is not a logically necessary condition of this model, it is usually expected that representatives should, in contrast to the Burkean model, reflect as nearly as possible the opinions of the constituent groups they represent. With the geographical or party models discussed immediately below, the microcosm model does not assume that representatives need consciously bring their opinions into congruence with those of their constituents. Simply by being a social reflection of their constituents, their preferences will automatically mirror theirs.[92]

The third model is a geographic or areal model. The pattern of interests and interaction is expected to vary regionally, and as a consequence representatives are required from each area. Other than residence, no assumptions are necessarily made about the representative's socioeconomic background, but it is fully expected that his opinions and votes will reflect those of the majority of his constituents, owing to the interaction stimulated between them by their common areal ties.[93] Although there are a large variety of criteria of normative and practical importance which one can use to determine the composition of constituencies to be represented, for the present study the choices have been predetermined – Glasgow councillors represent geographically defined units or wards. There are three representatives from each ward, elected for staggered three-year terms.

The fourth model stresses party representation and responsibility. Instead of the representative's opinions and votes reflecting those of his district or some particular interest, the representative is expected to conform to his party's programme. Competing parties present the voters with the broad-based party programmes at each election, and on the basis of past and expected party performance, the voters decide

[92] In *Class, Religion*, chaps 2, 3, 4, 5 have already addressed the question of how far the social composition of the councillor and partyworker groups constitutes a microcosm of the Glasgow electorate. In this chapter we concentrate on the extent to which the behaviour of councillors and partyworkers reflects the opinion of their constituents. Cf. Pitkin, chap. 4; J. S. Mill, *Considerations on Representative Government* (Chicago, 1962) chaps 7, 12.

[93] Cf. Arthur Maas (ed.), *Area and Power*, (Glencoe, 1959) *passim*; William H. Riker, *Federalism* (Boston, 1964) *passim*; K. C. Wheare, *Federal Government* (New York, 1968) chap. 1.

which party programme to adopt by electing representatives pledged to those programmes.[94]

Finally, we deal with a stratification model of representation which arises from our theoretical framework. This model suggests that while in some cases there may be a fair degree of correspondence between the opinions of leaders and followers, the leaders and followers generally will not have very accurate pictures of one another's opinions. The main reason for these inaccuracies is a postulated absence of communication between the political strata. There is no such lack of communication within the leadership strata, however, so the stratification model also expects that groups of leaders will agree among themselves more than with their constituents: in other words representatives will inevitably represent themselves more than they will their constituents.[95] Finally, since election votes are a form of communication between constituents and their representatives, and since high turnout is expected to be accompanied by other types of communication, the model predicts that appraisals of the opinions held by other strata will be more accurate (or less inaccurate) in wards where turnout for local elections is high.

These five models are by no means mutually exclusive. Indeed, it is easy to conceive of combinations of them such as a party-microcosm model or a party-geographic model. Nor are they intended to represent an exhaustive list of possible models of representation. We do not consider, for instance, models of representation in the divine right vein, which postulate a supreme leader who interprets and embodies the will and traditions of his people. None the less, our five models do contain the major elements of most modes of representation which have been given serious consideration by political theorists in recent years, and for this reason are of considerable heuristic value for our discussion.

[94] Schattschneider, *Party Government* (New York, 1942) *passim*; Committee on Political Parties of the American Political Science Association, *Toward a More Responsible Two Party System*, *passim*; Pulzer, *Representation*, chap. 5.

[95] Some difference between the first four models listed, and the stratification model, may seem to emerge in that the first four address the question of what the activist represents (or ought to represent) while the stratification model is concerned with the nature of communication between representative and represented. The quality and extent of communication in the stratification model is however posited as an explanation as to *why* the representative must represent himself and other activists, so that it does address the same question as the other models. The real difference is that the stratification model gives a detailed explanation as to why the representative acts as he is predicted to do.

GENERAL PATTERNS OF REPRESENTATION IN GLASGOW

Table 3.3 presents the preferences of our three political strata on the five issues, and in addition the preferences of the 'attentive public', the local voters and those who had heard of the issues before they were interviewed.

TABLE 3.3

Preferences on five current issues (percentage of councillors, partyworkers, electors, local voters and those electors who had heard of issues)

	(1) All		(2) Progs.		(3) Labour	
	For	Against	For	Against	For	Against
Pubs						
Councillors	85	12	76	21	93	5
Partyworkers	77	17	65	26	88	9
Electors	56	36	52	40	58	35
Voters	58	36	56	38	60	30
Heard	57	36	54	40	58	34
Fees						
Councillors	42	56	13	84	68	30
Partyworkers	49	46	6	89	86	9
Electors	44	45	32	60	51	37
Voters	41	50	29	67	47	39
Heard	37	49	28	66	47	36
Parking						
Councillors	72	23	58	34	84	14
Partyworkers	59	28	63	30	55	19
Electors	48	32	48	36	49	30
Voters	50	32	51	36	51	28
Heard	49	33	47	38	52	30
Rates						
Councillors	45	43	5	84	81	5
Partyworkers	31	58	9	89	48	33
Electors	7	87	2	93	10	82
Voters	8	87	5	86	11	83
Heard	7	87	2	93	9	83
Integration						
Councillors	84	13	92	5	77	21
Partyworkers	76	23	69	30	83	17
Electors	64	33	68	31	60	36
Voters	61	35	67	31	55	39
Heard	—	—	—	—	—	—

As can be seen from the table, opinions among all three strata run in the same direction only on three of the five issues covered. The majority of councillors oppose the elimination of fee-paying schools, while the partyworkers and electors are divided about evenly on this issue; the councillors, on the other hand, are split evenly over the rates issue, but majorities in the other strata clearly oppose increases. When the data are controlled for party, however, the extent of agreement among the strata increases. With the exception of the rates issue among Labour supporters, all three strata share the same modal position on all given issues. Two of the issues, fees and rates, are clearly party-related, in both cases the Labour party favouring the proposals, the Progressives opposing. Interestingly, the distribution of opinion among the attentive public closely resembles that of the electorate in general for all breakdowns of the data. This finding has some general relevance in view of the considerable speculation that has emerged about ways in which the opinions of the more informed and more active members of the population might differ from those of the more apathetic.[96] If we can generalise from the Glasgow case, it may be that under relatively open conditions the politically active are simply more prominent carriers of generally accepted views. As far as our own analysis goes the absence of policy-differences between 'attentive' and 'inattentive' publics means that it will not be necessary to consider voters and informed electors separately from the general electorate in most of the subsequent analysis in this chapter.

Using the data in Table 3.3, we can inquire into how well the distributions of opinion on these issues fit four of the models of representation we have discussed. For instance, if the city council formed a microcosm of Glasgow as a whole, then the distribution of opinions among councillors would correlate strongly with the distribution of opinions among the electorate. If the Burkean model held, then there would be less likelihood of high correlation, for representatives would not be concerned whether or not their opinions matched those of their constituents. If the party model held, then correlations between

[96] The term 'attentive public' was first given currency by Gabriel Almond, *The American People and Foreign Policy* (New York, 1950). V. O. Key, *Public Opinion*, pp. 9–10, 265, 282–5, 413–14, 544–8, makes extensive use of the term in his theoretical discussion but does not compare the actual opinions of the attentive and non-attentive. An analysis of other Glasgow survey evidence reveals no significant distinction between voters and non-voters over a series of questions touching on rate-related expenditure; Ian Budge and D. W. Urwin, *Scottish Political Behaviour* (London, 1966) Table 6.12.

distributions of opinion between the strata would be higher within the parties than for all members of our samples. If the situation were best described by the stratification model, then the correlation of the distribution of opinion should be greater within the activist strata than between these strata and the electorate, and furthermore, the correlation of the distributions of opinion within any strata, even among members of opposite parties, should be greater than the correlation of distributions of opinion between strata; i.e., councillors and partyworkers should agree with each other more than with electors; and councillors, partyworkers, and electors should agree more with members of the opposite party in their own strata than they agree with members of their own party in other strata.

Table 3.4 contains four correlational matrices. The first consists of product-moment correlations between the distribution of agreement and disagreement over all five issues for all political strata using the data in column 1 of Table 3.3. The next two matrices consist of the correlations between strata, using columns 2 and 3 of Table 3.3 in which controls for party are introduced. The final matrix contains the correlations within strata between members of different parties.

The pattern of correlations in the first matrix indicates a mix of at least two models of representation. The occurrence of fairly substantial positive correlations among all three strata indicates that the data are more compatible with the microcosm model of representation than with the Burkean model. That the largest correlation ($r = 0.92$) is between councillors and partyworkers, however, provides evidence for the stratification model as well.

When party factors are introduced (matrices 2 and 3), the picture changes somewhat. The Progressives are shown to hold closely related distributions of opinion across all three strata, but the opinion distributions of Labour councillors and electors are found to be virtually unrelated ($r = 0.02$). The distributions of Labour councillor and partyworker opinions remain similar ($r = 0.84$), but the partyworkers and electors are found further apart ($r = 0.38$) than was the case in matrix 1 ($r = 0.69$). This disparity between electors and other strata is due of course primarily to the difference of opinion over the rates issue. When rates are dropped from the calculations the correspondence between councillors and electors changes to 0.93 and between partyworkers and electors to 0.94.

For the Progressives, therefore, a party-microcosm model of representation describes the relationships among all three strata across the

TABLE 3.4

Product-moment correlation matrices of agreement among and between Glasgow councillors, partyworkers and electors

All	Councillors	Party-workers	Electors	Voters	Heard
Councillors	—	0·92	0·44	0·32	0·29
Partyworkers	0·92	—	0·69	0·66	0·63
Electors	0·44	0·69	—	—	—
Voters	0·32	0·66	—	—	—
Heard	0·29	0·63	—	—	—
Progressives					
Councillors	—	0·93	0·86	0·92	0·89
Partyworkers	0·93	—	0·87	0·92	0·89
Electors	0·86	0·87	—	—	—
Voters	0·92	0·92	—	—	—
Heard	0·89	0·89	—	—	—
Labour					
Councillors	—	0·84	—0·02	—0·08	—0·14
Partyworkers	0·84	—	0·38	0·29	0·25
Electors	—0·01	0·38	—	—	—
Voters	—0·08	0·29	—	—	—
Heard	—0·14	0·25	—	—	—
Cross-Party					
Councillors	0·12	—	—	—	—
Partyworkers	—	—0·05	—	—	—
Electors	—	—	0·88	—	—
Voters	—	—	—	0·84	—
Heard	—	—	—	—	0·84

The statistic used in Table 3.4 is the product-moment correlation coefficient (r), which measures the extent to which variation in one variable is associated with variation in another variable. See H. M. Blalock, *Social Statistics*, chap. 17. Each entry in the table is a correlation coefficient summarising the extent to which the percentages in each group agreeing and disagreeing with the five issue-proposals vary together.

five issues surveyed. For Labour, however, the description is not so simple. While the party-microcosm model fits four of the issues rather well, the distributions of opinions over all five issues do not appear to be accurately described by this model. Instead, for the Labour party either a Burkean or perhaps geographic model might provide a better description.

A glance at matrix 4 indicates that across parties the stratification model of representation implied by our theory holds well for electors, but does not describe the distribution of opinions among councillors or activists. Among the more active strata, party differences appear to produce important divergences of opinion which evidently are not easily overcome by the postulated high levels of communication within strata. Although activists may be found willing to compromise in the long run, their initial distributions of opinion on the five issues studied are further apart across parties than is the distribution of opinion among electors.

TABLE 3.5

Product-moment correlation matrices of agreement among and between Glasgow councillors, partyworkers and electors; fees and rates issues only

	Councillors	Party-workers	Electors	Voters	Heard
All					
Councillors	—	−0·15	−0·13	−0·03	−0·02
Partyworkers	−0·15	—	0·97	0·95	0·94
Electors	−0·13	0·97	—	—	—
Voters	−0·04	0·95	—	—	—
Heard	−0·02	0·94	—	—	—
Progressives					
Councillors	—	0·99	0·90	0·95	0·94
Partyworkers	0·99	—	0·87	0·93	0·91
Electors	0·90	0·87	—	—	—
Voters	0·95	0·93	—	—	—
Heard	0·94	0·91	—	—	—
Labour					
Councillors	—	0·22	−0·79	−0·84	−0·82
Partyworkers	0·22	—	−0·01	−0·09	−0·05
Electors	−0·79	−0·01	—	—	—
Voters	−0·84	−0·09	—	—	—
Heard	−0·82	−0·05	—	—	—
Cross-Party					
Councillors	−0·95	—	—	—	—
Partyworkers	—	−0·83	—	—	—
Electors	—	—	0·88	—	—
Voters	—	—	—	0·84	—
Heard	—	—	—	—	0·85

Since two of the issues, elimination of school-fees and raising of the rates, produce clear party-related differences of opinion among the activist strata, it is necessary in view of the distinction drawn between partisan and other issues, in our original model (Figs 1.1 and 1.2) to compare the correlations among our three strata for these party-related issues with the correlations for the remaining three issues, pubs in housing estates, extension of parking-meters, and integration of Catholic and Protestant schools, to see if the results are similar to those of Table 3.4. The resulting correlation matrices are presented in Tables 3.5 and 3.6.

TABLE 3.6

Product-moment correlation matrices of agreement among and between Glasgow councillors, partyworkers and electors; pubs, meters and integration issues only

	Councillors	Party-workers	Electors	Voters	Heard
All					
Councillors	—	0·99	0·93	0·96	0·96
Partyworkers	0·99	—	0·95	0·97	0·96
Electors	0·93	0·95	—	—	—
Voters	0·96	0·97	—	—	—
Heard	0·96	0·96	—	—	—
Progressives					
Councillors	—	0·93	0·94	0·98	0·94
Partyworkers	0·93	—	0·87	0·93	0·92
Electors	0·94	0·87	—	—	—
Voters	0·98	0·93	—	—	—
Heard	0·94	0·92	—	—	—
Labour					
Councillors	—	0·95	0·93	0·96	0·97
Partyworkers	0·95	—	0·97	0·95	0·95
Electors	0·93	0·97	—	—	—
Voters	0·96	0·95	—	—	—
Heard	0·97	0·95	—	—	—
Cross-Party					
Councillors	0·86	—	—	—	—
Partyworkers	—	0·96	—	—	—
Electors	—	—	0·90	—	—
Voters	—	—	—	0·83	—
Heard	—	—	—	—	0·98

Only for Progressives are there no marked contrasts between the data in the two tables. Progressive activists continue to show the same high correlations among themselves and with less active strata that were evident in Table 3.4. It makes virtually no difference whether or not the issues are party-related: Progressive activists and their constituents hold substantially similar opinions. For all the other matrices the differences between Tables 3.5 and 3.6 are considerable.

To begin with, for the fees and pubs issues councillors show a set of weak negative correlations with other strata (matrix 1, Table 3.5) in contrast to the strong positive correlations in Table 3.6. These latter correlations are considerably stronger than the moderately positive correlations found between councillors and non-activist strata in Table 3.4, and even the previously strong correlation of 0·92 between councillors and partyworkers is surpassed by a nearly perfect correlation of 0·99. In somewhat surprising contrast, the correlations between partyworkers and non-activist strata are high and positive in both Tables 3.5 and 3.6 and the magnitude of these correlations is larger than the positive correlations in matrix 1 of Table 3.4. This means that whether or not the issues were party-related, partyworkers and electors tended to have similar distributions of opinions.

Turning our attention to the third correlation matrix, it is clear that on fees and pubs, the party-related issues, Labour councillors' opinions differed greatly from those of their constituents, the correlations varying from —0·79 to —0·84. Labour partyworkers, on the other hand, seem to lie midway between councillors and electors, having opinions but weakly related to those of either group. For the pubs, meters and integration issues, however, the Labour councillors and partyworkers agree with one another and with their constituents to the same high degree that was found for Progressives (matrix 3, Table 3.6). The results in these two tables help to explain the weak relationship between the Labour councillors and non-activist strata found in Table 3.4.

The final matrix in Table 3.5 indicates that for party-related issues the stratification theory does not describe activist opinions, but still holds for non-activists. On the remaining three issues, correlations across party within both activist and non-activist strata are consistently high (Table 3.6, final matrix). None the less, even on non-party issues, the correlations within strata are no higher than those between strata, thus detracting somewhat from the credibility of the stratification model.

The overall results seem to suggest that when the effects of party strife are reduced (Table 3.6), the microcosm model of representation holds rather well, although the stratification model cannot be rejected. When party-related issues are surveyed, however, the stratification model fails to explain the behaviour of party activists and a party-microcosm model is the best description.[97] But additionally, it must be noted that Labour, the party in power, tends to be more Burkean than the Progressives.

CONSTITUENCY REPRESENTATION BY GLASGOW COUNCILLORS

So far we have looked only at the total distributions of opinion for each stratum or at the total distribution broken down by party alone. In the course of our analysis we have seen how well the Burkean, microcosm, party and stratification models fit the data. In order to examine the fit of the geographic model to the data, we must break down the data by wards.

Table 3.7 contains our data on the extent of agreement between councillors and constituents in their wards across all five issues investigated. Although the percentage of councillors agreeing with the modal opinion of their constituents is impressively high only on the issue of integration of corporation schools, the general trend indicates more agreement than disagreement between the opinions of councillors and those of their constituents. Only on the rates issue is the percentage of disagreements greater than that of agreements. On a geographic basis, ward by ward, therefore, the opinions of councillors may be said to represent the opinions of their constituents with a fair degree of accuracy. The data fit the geographic representation model in four out of five cases.

When comparisons are made between the opinions of councillors and the modal opinions of their party supporters on a ward by ward basis, the picture changes somewhat. In comparison with agreements in Table 3.7, agreement between Progressive councillors and their constituents is extremely high (84 per cent) on the rates issue and is about the same or slightly higher on the fees, meters and integration

[97] It should be noted that the full statement of our predictive theory allows for the effects of party competition in promoting greater differences among activists than among electors (Fig. 1.2), only stipulating that issues affected by party competition are a minority of current issues (as they are here). It further predicts that party competition is confined to issues which receive wide coverage from the mass media. For a test of this prediction see Chapter 6.

TABLE 3.7

Correspondence of councillors' and ward electors' preferences on five current issues (percentages of councillors whose preference is the same as or different from the preference held by the majority of their ward constituents on each issue)

	Pubs (per cent)	Fees (per cent)	Parking (per cent)	Rates (per cent)	Integration (per cent)
Same	54	51	45	43	80
Different	25	43	25	46	15
Indeterminate	21	5	30	11	5
(N = 80)					

Ward constituent opinion is counted as 'for' or 'against' an issue if the modal opinion is 'for' or 'against' and is more than 10 per cent greater than endorsements of any other choice. Other cases are regarded as neutral. Illustrative examples of this procedure are tabulated below:

For (per cent)	Against (per cent)	Neutral (per cent)	Ward placement
55	45	—	For
54	46	—	Neutral
40	30	30	For
30	30	40	Neutral
30	20	50	Neutral
40	20	40	Neutral

Councillors' and constituents' preferences are termed the same if the councillors' preference coincides with the decision on ward placement.

issues. On the issue of pubs in the corporation housing estates, however, Progressive councillors are considerably more favourable than their constituents on a ward-by-ward basis and thus disagreements (43 per cent) are found to outnumber agreements (37 per cent) on this issue. For Labour councillors, the general level of agreement with their party supporters is lower on meters (44 per cent) and integration (63 per cent) than in Table 3.7 but somewhat higher on the issue of elimination of fee-paying schools (53 per cent). The real contrasts occur, however, over the pubs and rates issues. For the former issue, Labour councillors show considerably greater agreement with their supporters (70 per cent) than do their Progressive colleagues, but for the latter issue, there is an extremely high level of disagreement (84 per cent).

Why there should be such a great contrast in the level of agreement between Progressive councillors and their constituents and Labour councillors and their constituents on the rates issue has already been explained. Electors are rarely, if ever, favourably disposed towards a tax rise, no matter how vital that tax rise may be for maintaining government services. As members of the majority party, Labour councillors must accept responsibility for running the government. Therefore, even though they find their constituents oppose a tax or rate rise, they must still support it. Progressive councillors, being the minority opposition, can enjoy the freedom of agreeing with a majority of their constituents by opposing a tax rise while at the same time accepting little of the responsiblity for their action. Unfortunately, no similar readily available explanation can be proposed for the disagreement between Progressive councillors and their constituents over the disposition of pubs in the corporation housing estates.

A ward-by-ward examination of the agreements of councillors with their constituents taking account of councillors' own conception of their representative role produces disappointing results. For the purpose of this comparison councillors were divided between those emphasising the ward (pure *and* mixed ward roles of Table 3.2) and those emphasising the city (pure *and* mixed city roles of Table 3.2). On the pubs issue councillors with primarily ward orientations are more likely than councillors with primarily city-wide orientations to be in agreement with their constituents (61 per cent compared to 48 per cent), but for the problem of school integration the reverse is true (74 per cent compared to 86 per cent). For the fees, meters and rates issues, hardly a difference can be found between the levels of agreement or disagreement among the two groups of councillors and their constituents.

Our evidence thus far has indicated that Glasgow councillors tend to have opinions generally in agreement with those of their constituents over the five issues studied. We are interested in determining, however, whether these opinions can be characterised as having arisen from councillors' impressions of their constituents' opinions, and further, whether the impressions councillors have of their constituents' opinions are in fact accurate.

On all except the integration issue, for which no formal proposal was before the city council during the period of our data collection, councillors were asked for their impressions of the opinions of their constituents.

Table 3.8 indicates that these impressions were not formed as derivatives of the councillors' own opinions on the issues. On three out of four issues, in fact, the proportion of councillors who perceived their opinions to be contrary to those held by their constituents was greater than the proportion who saw their opinions as being in agreement with their constituents.

TABLE 3.8

Correspondence of councillors' own preferences and their appraisals of their constituents' preferences on four current issues (percentages of councillors)

	Appraisal same as own opinion (per cent)	Appraisal different from own opinion (per cent)	DK, NA (per cent)
Pubs	40	43	17
Fees	32	46	22
Parking	29	46	25
Rates	45	43	12

Nor were the impressions councillors had of their constituents' opinions very accurate. As indicated by the figures in Table 3.9, on all issues but rates for which appraisals of constituents' opinions were made, the modal appraisal was inaccurate. On the school fees and parking-meter issues, the ratio of incorrect appraisals is approximately

TABLE 3.9

Accuracy of councillors' appraisals of constituents' preferences on four current issues (percentages of all councillors and of councillors in each party group making accurate and inaccurate appraisals on each issue)

All (N = 80)	Pubs (per cent)	Fees (per cent)	Parking (per cent)	Rates (per cent)
Accurate	40	28	24	79
Inaccurate	44	50	55	19
DK, NA	16	22	21	3
Progressives (N = 37)				
Accurate	38	19	22	92
Inaccurate	46	49	54	5
DK, NA	16	32	24	3
Labour (N = 43)				
Accurate	42	35	26	68
Inaccurate	42	51	56	35
DK, NA	16	14	19	2

An appraisal is considered accurate when it mentions the category in which the ward has been placed by the procedure described in notes to Tables 3.7.

2 to 1, which (assuming a uniform distribution of outcomes) is just about the accuracy one would get guessing among three alternatives, i.e. constituents (1) favour proposal, (2) oppose it, (3) are split or have no opinion. On appraising constituents' opinions on the issue of pubs, councillors do better than chance but their level of accuracy never exceeds their level of incorrect appraisals. With the exception of the rates issue, Labour councillors show somewhat higher levels of accuracy than do the Progressives.

Role perceptions, however, do influence councillors' appraisals of their constituents' opinions. As indicated in Table 3.10, a greater proportion of councillors placing stronger emphasis on their ward roles perceive themselves as being of the same opinion as their constituents than do councillors who place emphasis on their city-wide roles.

TABLE 3.10

Correspondence of councillors' own preferences and their appraisals of their constituents' preferences on four current issues, by councillor role (percentages of councillors emphasising their ward role and percentages of councillors emphasising their city role, whose preferences are the same as or different from their own appraisals of their constituents' preferences, on each issue)

Ward emphasis	Appraisal same as own opinion	Appraisal different from own opinion	DK, NA	N
Pubs	42	42	16	38
Fees	37	39	24	38
Parking	37	39	24	38
Rates	55	37	8	38

City emphasis	Appraisal same as own opinion	Appraisal different from own opinion	DK, NA	N
Pubs	39	43	18	42
Fees	27	52	21	42
Parking	23	52	25	42
Rates	36	48	16	42
(N = 118)				

It is noteworthy that the rates issue, the only issue for which most appraisals are accurate, produces the largest contrast between the two groups. Clearly, a ward-role orientation helps produce for the councillor an illusion of greater agreement with his constituents' opinions, even though, as we have seen, greater agreement in fact does not exist.

Nor does having a ward as opposed to a city-wide representation role orientation make any difference in the accuracy of the appraisals councillors make of their constituents' opinions. Regardless of whether the role orientation held by councillors has primarily a ward or a city emphasis, the modal appraisals for all issues but rates are inaccurate, and the differences between the accuracies of the two groups of councillors are never greater than 5 per cent.

On a geographic basis, then, the opinions of Glasgow councillors can be described as representative of those of their constituents, but this representativeness does not appear to be based upon the councillors' awareness of their constituents' opinions. Opinions held by councillors do not necessarily correspond to the opinions they believe their constituents hold, and, in addition, the appraisals of constituents' opinions made by councillors are generally inaccurate.

CONSTITUENCY REPRESENTATION BY GLASGOW PARTYWORKERS

Party models of representation often suggest that partyworkers form an important link between the constituent and his representative. The geographic representation model suggests that in Glasgow partyworkers should form this link on a ward-by-ward basis. Let us see how well their preferences and appraisals fit a party-geographic model of representation.

Table 3.11 contains data comparing the opinions of partyworkers with the opinions of electors in their wards. The results are strikingly similar to those obtained for councillors in Table 3.7. In all cases in Table 3.11, including the rates issue, partyworkers are shown to be

TABLE 3.11

Correspondence of partyworkers' and ward electors' preferences on five current issues (percentages of partyworkers whose preferences are the same or different from the preferences held by the majority of their ward constituents on each issue)

	Pubs (per cent)	Fees (per cent)	Parking (per cent)	Rates (per cent)	Integration (per cent)
Same	57	47	43	57	75
Different	14	44	23	30	11
Indeterminate	29	9	34	13	3
(N = 118)					

modally in agreement with electors in their wards, although on the issue of school fees agreements exceed disagreements by a mere 3 per cent.

When the data are broken down by party it once again becomes apparent that agreement on the rates issue is primarily a Progressive phenomenon (83 per cent as opposed to only 31 per cent for Labour), but Progressives are no longer found to disagree so extensively with party supporters in their wards over the issue of pubs in the corporation housing estates (41 per cent are in agreement).

Once again Labour shows a higher level of agreement with their constituents on the pub issue (67 per cent), while on the issue of school fees Progressives now show a considerably higher level of agreement with their constituents than do Labour partyworkers (67 per cent compared to 47 per cent). The expansion of parking-meter areas, although still showing more agreements than disagreements in each party (55 per cent to 30 per cent for Progressives, 36 per cent to 19 per cent for Labour), also has a high number of indeterminate cases, stemming largely from the fact that a substantial number (34 per cent) of partyworkers do not have opinions on this issue.

Table 3.12, the analogue of Table 3.8, shows again the parallel trends of behaviour between councillors and partyworkers. Like councillors, partyworkers cannot be said to have formed their appraisals of electors'

TABLE 3.12

Correspondence of partyworkers' own preferences and their appraisals of the preferences of electors in their own wards on four current issues (percentages of partyworkers)

	Appraisal same as own opinion (per cent)	Appraisal different from own opinion (per cent)	DK, NA (per cent)
Pubs	42	42	16
Fees	42	36	25
Parking	23	27	50
Rates	59	26	14
(N = 118)			

opinions on the basis of their own opinions of the issues. Only for the rates issue is there any striking contrast between the proportion of partyworkers attributing to the electors opinions similar to their own, and those attributing to the electors opinions contrary to their own.

Turning to the data in Table 3.13, it becomes apparent that party-workers are no more accurate than councillors in gauging the opinions of electors within their wards. As was the case with city councillors, Labour partyworkers show more political acumen on the pubs, fees and meters issues, but their Progressive colleagues prove more adept at gauging opinion on the rates issue. The overall level of accuracy on fees and meters is lowest once again, but Labour partyworkers appear to have a more accurate picture of electors' opinions on fees than do Labour councillors.

Almost exactly as we did with councillors, then, we can describe the opinions of Glasgow partyworkers as generally representative of the opinions of the electors in their wards over the five issues studied. Yet there is precious little evidence that this representativeness is based upon any accurate picture of electors' actual opinions. Opinions held by partyworkers often do not correspond to the opinions they believe electors hold, and, in addition, partyworkers' perceptions of opinions held by electors in their wards are generally inaccurate.

POTENTIAL CONTROL OF ELECTORS OVER COUNCILLORS

What about the electors themselves? How much control do they have over their representatives? Even though Glasgow councillors may have inaccurate impressions of their constituents' preferences, electors, if they are aware of their councillors' positions or the positions of their councillors' parties, can exert some control over even the most Burkean or most party-oriented of councillors simply by refusing to re-elect those whose own or party's policies violate electors' preferences.

Glasgow electors were asked questions relating to their awareness of their representatives' positions on all but the integration issue. They were first asked if they knew the names of their councillors. Regardless of their knowledge of their councillors' names, they were asked the position their councillors held on each of the respective issues. Finally, regardless of their knowledge of the positions of their councillors, they were asked the positions of the Labour and Progressive parties on these issues.

The ability to give a representative's name when asked on the spur of the moment is by no means a necessary condition for a citizen to exert some control over that representative, but it does indicate the degree of closeness with which the citizen watches that representative. Glasgow electors were by no means closely watching their city council-lors. Of our 563 respondents 314 admitted outright to no knowledge

TABLE 3.13

Accuracy of partyworkers' appraisals of ward electors' preferences on four current issues (percentages of all partyworkers and of partyworkers in each party group making accurate and inaccurate appraisals on each issue)

	Pubs (per cent)	Fees (per cent)	Parking (per cent)	Rates (per cent)
All (N = 118)				
Accurate	41	28	18	74
Inaccurate	40	42	33	13
Indeterminate	19	30	49	13
Progressives (N = 54)				
Accurate	35	9	13	88
Inaccurate	39	46	37	6
Indeterminate	26	44	50	7
Labour (N = 64)				
Accurate	45	43	22	64
Inaccurate	41	39	30	19
Indeterminate	14	17	48	17

of their councillors' names. Another 77 guessed wrongly, while 59 others named their Member of Parliament. In other words, four out of five electors did not know the name of even one of their councillors. Only 22 electors, less than 4 per cent of our sample, correctly named more than one councillor.

Electors' knowledge of their councillors' positions on three of the four issues about which they were asked was as meagre as their knowledge of the councillors' names. Eighty-four per cent had no idea how their councillors stood on the pubs and school fees issues, while 78 per cent had no idea how their councillors stood with regard to the placement of additional parking-meters in the downtown area. Only on the rates issue did any substantial number of respondents (41 per cent) profess to have an idea where their councillors stood and of these respondents barely 55 per cent were correct in their appraisals. Clearly, then, close scrutiny of the issue positions of their city councillors is not a way Glasgow electors keep control of their representatives.

It is through their perceptions of the party positions on the issues studied that electors enjoy at least the possibility of controlling their representatives. In contrast to the eight out of ten electors who knew nothing about their councillors' positions on three out of four issues, at least six out of ten electors claimed knowledge of the Labour party's position on every issue, and at least five out of ten claimed knowledge of the Progressive party's position on three out of the four issues (see Tables 3.14 and 3.15). Furthermore, a comparison of Table 3.3 with

TABLE 3.14

Glasgow electors' perceptions of Labour Party position on four current issues (percentages of all electors and of Progressive and Labour electors)

(Perceived Labour Party position)

	For (per cent)	No position (per cent)	Split (per cent)	Against (per cent)	Don't know (per cent)
All (N = 563)					
Pubs	34	4	5	16	41
Fees	52	2	1	11	33
Parking	49	2	2	6	41
Rates	56	1	2	18	22
Progressives (N = 164)					
Pubs	39	2	6	20	34
Fees	65	—	2	6	27
Parking	56	3	1	4	37
Rates	75	1	1	8	15
Labour (N = 290)					
Pubs	33	4	5	16	42
Fees	50	2	1	14	33
Parking	46	2	2	7	42
Rates	48	1	2	25	24

Table 3.14 indicates that for every issue, the electors' modal impression of the Labour party's stand corresponds to the 'for' position actually held by the majority of Labour councillors on all four issues. With regard to the Progressive party's position the record is almost as good. The modal impression held by electors corresponds to the majority position of the Progressive councillors on all but the pubs issue, and for this issue, it is primarily Labour supporters who have the mistaken impression that Progressives oppose the legislation. In fact, by a bare percentage point, 21 to 20 per cent, the Progressive party supporters correctly discern their own councillors' position. One additional erroneous perception appears in Table 3.15. Labour supporters attri-

TABLE 3.15

Glasgow electors' perceptions of Progressive Party position on four current issues (percentages of all electors and of Progressive and Labour electors)

(Perceived Progressive Party position)

	For (per cent)	No position (per cent)	Split (per cent)	Against (per cent)	Don't know (per cent)
All (N = 563)					
Pubs	15	4	5	21	54
Fees	15	2	1	39	43
Parking	31	2	4	11	52
Rates	28	2	2	38	30
Progressives (N = 164)					
Pubs	21	3	6	20	49
Fees	13	1	3	52	31
Parking	33	2	7	11	47
Rates	13	2	2	62	20
Labour (N = 290)					
Pubs	13	4	5	22	55
Fees	19	2	—	33	46
Parking	32	2	2	12	51
Rates	38	1	2	25	33

bute support for the rate rise to the Progressives as well as to their own party.

Progressive electors, besides being somewhat more accurate in their perceptions than their Labour counterparts, also claim more knowledge of both parties' position. On all four issues, fewer Progressive than Labour supporters deny knowledge of either party's position. This greater level of accuracy and knowledge of Progressive party supporters as compared to Labour supporters is likely to be a consequence of their higher average level of education and political participation.[98]

POTENTIAL CONTROL OF PARTYWORKERS OVER COUNCILLORS

Although on a ward-by-ward comparison the opinions held by party-workers were no more similar to those of their constituents than were the opinions held by city councillors, and although on that same ward-

[98] *Class, Religion*, chap. 6, discusses the link between education, party support and election turnout in Glasgow.

by-ward basis partyworkers could make no more accurate appraisals of constituent opinions than could councillors, Tables 3.3 and 3.4 did indicate that the overall distribution of opinions of partyworkers, in accordance with our stratification model of representation, resembled more closely the distribution of electors' opinions than did the overall distribution of opinions of city councillors. Because of the more frequent communication postulated between partyworkers and councillors than between electors and councillors, it is expected that partyworkers will be more aware of councillors' names, and of individual and group opinions among the councillors. These expectations are borne out by the findings.

To begin with, in contrast to the mere handful of electors who could name their three councillors, fully 65 per cent (77 out of 118) of the partyworkers correctly named all three councillors. Only eight workers admitted to knowing no councillors' names, and only five who claimed knowledge failed to name at least one correctly. Thus, eight out of nine partyworkers, as opposed to 1 out of 5 electors, could name at least one councillor from their ward.

Information about councillors' stands on the four issues is also more abundant among partyworkers than electors. Partyworkers are least informed about the non-party issues, pubs and parking-meters, but even on these issues the 'don't knows' amount respectively to 53 and 61 per cent of the respondents in contrast to 84 and 78 per cent of the electors. Only 41 per cent of the workers claim no knowledge of their ward councillors' positions on pubs, and a mere 20 per cent have no ideas where their councillors stand on rates. On the rates issue, the one issue on which we can compare partyworkers with the electors, 69 per cent of those who professed knowledge of their councillors' positions were correct in their appraisals of that position. The comparable figure for electors was 55 per cent.

Finally, partyworkers have a better perception of the position of the majority of the councillors of each party. As can be seen from Table 3.16, partyworkers of both parties not only have accurate perceptions of the position of the majority of Labour councillors, but (comparing with Table 3.14) they have higher levels of agreement among themselves as to what that position is. Comparing Table 3.17 with 3.15, it is clear that on the two party-related issues, partyworkers in both parties have considerably higher levels of agreement as to where the parties stand than do electors. On the appraisal of the Progressive party's stand on pubs, Progressive partyworkers are more accurate than their

TABLE 3.16

Glasgow partyworkers' perceptions of Labour Party position on four current issues (percentage of all partyworkers and of Progressive and Labour party-workers)

(Perceived Labour Party position)

	For (per cent)	No position (per cent)	Split (per cent)	Against (per cent)	Don't Know (per cent)
All (N = 118)					
Pubs	62	4	14	9	11
Fees	81	1	4	3	11
Parking	62	8	3	2	25
Rates	78	3	3	6	9
Progressives (N = 54)					
Pubs	48	—	13	17	22
Fees	72	—	2	6	20
Parking	61	4	—	2	33
Rates	83	—	2	—	15
Labour (N = 64)					
Pubs	73	8	14	17	22
Fees	88	2	6	2	3
Parking	62	11	6	2	17
Rates	73	5	5	11	3

Progressive constituents, but Labour partyworkers (though less inaccurate than Labour electors) have incorrect impressions of the Progressive party position on this issue, and the overall accuracy rating for partyworkers (25 per cent) is not much better than 15 per cent for electors on this issue. With regard to the meters issue, although the modal appraisals of partyworkers are correct, the electors display higher levels of agreement as to the Progressive party position.

REPRESENTATION IN GLASGOW: SOME CONCLUSIONS

This completes the first segment of our analysis of representation in Glasgow. What has emerged thus far has suggested that no one of the simple models of representation discussed at the beginning of the chapter adequately describes the representative process with regard to the five issues studied. The generally inaccurate appraisals councillors

TABLE 3.17

Glasgow partyworkers' perception of Progressive Party position on four current issues (percentages of all partyworkers and of Progressive and Labour partyworkers)

(Perceived Progressive Party position)

	For (per cent)	No position (per cent)	Split (per cent)	Against (per cent)	Don't know (per cent)
All (N = 118)					
Pubs	25	7	10	25	32
Fees	3	1	2	81	14
Parking	25	—	2	22	51
Rates	4	—	—	87	9
Progressives (N = 54)					
Pubs	28	7	11	22	32
Fees	3	1	2	81	14
Parking	24	—	2	74	19
Rates	—	—	—	88	11
Labour (N = 64)					
Pubs	23	6	9	27	33
Fees	2	—	2	86	11
Parking	27	—	2	23	48
Rates	8	—	—	86	6

and partyworkers make of ward electors' opinions imply that a combination of party and microcosm models is the best simple description of the distributions of opinion over the five issues. On the rates issue, however, Labour councillors and partyworkers act in a most Burkean manner, defying what they know to be opposition to a rates increase on the part of their constituents and party supporters. Less well do the data fit the geographic model of representation. Although their actual opinions on issues tend to correspond to those of electors in their wards, as mentioned above, relatively few councillors or partyworkers have accurate perceptions of their constituents' opinions. In addition, few electors have any idea of who their ward councillors are, or of where their councillors stand on the issues studied. Electors appear aware not of their ward councillors' position, but rather of the positions of the Progressive and Labour parties, thus furnishing some further evidence of the party portion of the party-microcosm model of representation.

The evidence regarding the stratification model of representation is mixed. Within the parties, as the model predicts, workers and councillors are in greater agreement with each other than with electors, but the prediction that partisans of opposite parties within one stratum will be more in agreement with one another than with partisans of the same party in other strata does not hold across the five issues. On the other hand the theory as stated in Chapter 1 allows for the disruptive effects of party competition on the agreement of activists in relation to certain issues. To achieve a better test of the stratification model, therefore, additional evidence must be examined concerning the relationship between electors and activist strata in high- and low-turnout wards. The model predicts greater levels of agreement between strata in high- as opposed to low-turnout wards, and also greater levels of accuracy and information in the perceptions of opinions of members of other strata. To this further investigation of the stratification model then, the next section is devoted.

STRATIFICATION MODEL OF REPRESENTATION: WARDS WITH HIGH AND LOW TURNOUT

High- and low-turnout wards were determined by averaging the local election turnout rate in each ward for the municipal elections of 1962–6. The twelve wards with the highest turnout over this period were designated high-turnout wards while the twelve with the lowest turnout rates were designated low-turnout wards. The average for high turnout for the city over the five-year period 1962–6 was 36·1 per cent. The average for high-turnout wards over the same period was 44·0, the highest average turnout for any ward being 51·4 per cent and the lowest of this group being 38·3 per cent. The low-turnout wards had an average turnout of 26·4 per cent, the highest among the group being 31·2 per cent and the lowest 21·1 per cent. Interestingly, the sample of councillors from the low-turnout wards was heavily Labour – 18 Labour and only 3 Progressives, while the sample drawn from the high-turnout wards was heavily Progressive – 22 Progressives and 7 Labour.

Let us begin with the question of agreement of councillors with their constituents over the five issues studied. Table 3.18 contains data on the level of agreement between councillors and electors on a ward-by-ward basis for the high- and low-turnout wards.

The clear trend of the data indicates a disconfirmation of the prediction that levels of agreement will be higher in high-turnout wards. The

TABLE 3.18

Correspondence of councillors' and ward electors' preferences on five current issues in high- and low-turnout wards (percentages of all councillors in high- and low-turnout wards, of Progressive councillors in high-turnout wards and of Labour councillors in low-turnout wards whose preferences are the same as, or different from the preferences held by the majority of their ward constituents on each issue)

	Pubs (per cent)	Fees (per cent)	Parking (per cent)	Rates (per cent)	Integration (per cent)
High-turnout (N = 29)					
Same	62	38	45	65	90
Different	17	41	34	21	7
Indeterminate	21	21	21	14	3
Low-turnout (N = 21)					
Same	62	38	62	14	67
Different	24	38	38	67	29
Indeterminate	14	24	—	19	5
Progressives – High-turnout (N = 22)					
Same	36	59	59	82	77
Different	32	32	23	5	5
Indeterminate	32	9	18	14	18
Labour – Low-turnout (N = 18)					
Same	61	44	50	—	61
Different	22	28	44	78	11
Indeterminate	17	28	5	22	28

The method of determining high- and low-turnout wards is described in the text. Councillors representing medium-turnout wards are omitted from this analysis.

remarkable characteristics of the data are actually the similarity between the distribution of agreements in high- and low-turnout wards, and also the similarity of the distributions in Table 3.18 to those in Table 3.7. Looking first at the pubs and fees issues, there is virtually no difference between levels of agreement in high- and low-turnout wards, and the overall distributions are practically the same as those in Table 3.7 which include all wards. Contrary to the expectations of the model, the level of agreement between councillors and electors on the meters issue is higher in low-turnout wards than in high-turnout wards. Although, at first glance, agreement on the rates issue appears to be considerably higher in high-turnout wards than in low-turnout wards, the relationship is entirely spurious, a direct consequence of the fact that high-turnout wards have mostly Progressive councillors while low-turnout wards have almost entirely Labour councillors. Comparing data for 'Progressives only' and 'Labour only' gives an indication of the essential similarity within each party between the distribution of agreements on rates over high- and low-turnout wards and the distribution of agreements over all wards. Only on the integration issue do we get an affirmation of the prediction, and one out of five can hardly be attributed to anything but chance.[99]

When we look at the councillors' appraisals of constituents' positions on the issues (Table 3.19), the model fares a little better. On three out of four issues councillors in high-turnout wards make more accurate appraisals of their constituents' opinions than do councillors in low-turnout wards. On the pubs and meters issues, the two issues which are not party-related, the increases in accuracy are only slight compared to the average district (see Table 3.9), but they appear to be genuine. A comparison of the data in Table 3.19 with that for Progressive and

TABLE 3.19

Accuracy of councillors' appraisals of constituents' preferences on four current issues, by high- and low-turnout wards (percentage of councillors representing high- and low-turnout wards making accurate and inaccurate appraisals on each issue)

	Pubs (per cent)	Fees (per cent)	Parking (per cent)	Rates (per cent)
High-turnout (N = 29)				
Accurate	45	21	24	93
Inaccurate	41	55	41	3
DK, NA	14	24	34	3
Low-turnout (N = 21)				
Accurate	29	33	10	67
Inaccurate	33	62	62	33
DK, NA	38	5	29	—

Labour councillors in Table 3.9 suggests that the accuracy levels for the rates issue which appear to corroborate the model, and the accuracy

[99] In this and subsequent tables in the chapter, we consider absolute levels of agreement and accuracy exactly as tabulated. We do not consider the relative ratio of agreements to disagreements or accuracies to inaccuracies.

levels for the fees issue, which disconfirm the model, are both consequences of the over-representation of Progressive councillors in
high-turnout wards, and of Labour councillors in low-turnout
wards.

Turning our attention to the sample of partyworkers, we find that in
the twelve high-turnout wards, we have interviews with 18 Progressive
and 23 Labour partyworkers. In the twelve low-turnout wards, we have
interviews with 14 Progressive and 21 Labour partyworkers. Since we
have a better balance of both Progressives and Labour in high- and
low-turnout wards than we had with councillors in these wards, we
shall be able to do some comparisons between high- and low-turnout
wards of agreements on and appraisals of constituent opinions by
activists of the same party.

Looking first at all partyworkers in high- and low-turnout wards
(see Table 3.20) we find some slight evidence for the predicted relationship of high turnout and greater agreement with constituents' opinions.
On pubs and fees, those in low-turnout wards are more in agreement
than those in high-turnout wards; on meters, rates and integration
issues, the opposite (and predicted) case occurs. On all issues except
integration the difference in levels of agreement between high- and
low-turnout wards is a mere 6 per cent or less, however, leaving open
the possibility that the relationship may be random.

When we make comparisons of the levels of agreement within the
parties the stratification model's predictions hold nicely, especially
within the Progressive party. On all five issues Progressive partyworkers in high-turnout wards display higher levels of agreement with
party members on a ward-by-ward basis. For three of the five issues
(pubs, rates and integration) the differences in levels of agreement are
10 per cent or more. Within the Labour party the results are almost as
good. On four of the five issues partyworkers in high-turnout wards
display higher levels of agreement with members of their own party
than do workers in low-turnout wards. On two of the issues, fees and
meters, the differences are 13 per cent or greater, and for the exceptional
issue, pubs, the agreement levels differ by only 2 per cent.

As is shown in Table 3.21, the predictions of the stratification model
hold well for partyworkers' appraisals of ward opinion. On all four
issues for which appraisals were made, partyworkers in high-turnout
wards achieved a greater level of accuracy than partyworkers in low-
turnout wards. The differences are 10 per cent or larger on every issue
but parking-meters. Within the parties the predictions hold for three

TABLE 3.20

Correspondence of partyworkers' and ward electors' preferences on five current issues in high- and low-turnout wards (percentages of all partyworkers and of Progressive and Labour partyworkers in high- and low-turnout wards whose preferences are the same as or different from, the preferences held by the majority of their ward electors in each issue)

	Pubs (per cent)	Fees (per cent)	Parking (per cent)	Rates (per cent)	Integration (per cent)
High-turnout (N = 41)					
Same	54	39	56	59	83
Different	7	39	22	27	17
Indeterminate	39	22	22	15	—
Low-turnout (N = 35)					
Same	60	43	49	54	66
Different	17	37	34	31	34
Indeterminate	23	20	17	14	—
Progressives – High-turnout (N = 18)					
Same	39	67	44	78	67
Different	33	28	33	6	17
Indeterminate	28	6	22	17	17
Progressives – Low-turnout (N = 14)					
Same	29	64	36	57	36
Different	21	14	14	14	36
Indeterminate	50	21	50	29	29
Labour – High turnout (N = 23)					
Same	65	52	61	30	61
Different	17	13	13	43	9
Indeterminate	17	35	26	26	30
Labour – Low-turnout (N = 21)					
Same	67	33	48	24	57
Different	10	43	29	52	14
Indeterminate	24	24	24	24	29

out of four issues, the exceptions being meters for Progressives and pubs for Labour.

With regard to the usefulness of the stratification model for predicting the relationship between activists and electors on a ward-by-ward basis, therefore, we can say that the model provides a better description of the relationship between the lower activist stratum, the partyworkers,

TABLE 3.21

Accuracy of partyworkers' appraisals of ward electors' preferences on four current issues, by high- and low-turnout wards (percentages of all partyworkers and of Progressive and Labour partyworkers in high- and low-turnout wards making accurate and inaccurate appraisals on each issue)

	Pubs (per cent)	Fees (per cent)	Parking (per cent)	Rates (per cent)
High-turnout (N = 41)				
Accurate	49	24	17	80
Inaccurate	37	44	32	15
DK, NA	15	32	51	5
Low-turnout (N = 35)				
Accurate	37	14	14	66
Inaccurate	26	66	40	17
DK, NA	37	20	46	17
Progressives – High-turnout (N = 18)				
Accurate 56	56	17	11	94
Inaccurate	28	39	39	6
DK, NA	17	44	50	—
Progressives – Low-turnout (N = 14)				
Accurate	14	—	14	86
Inaccurate	29	64	29	—
DK, NA	57	36	57	14
Labour – High-turnout (N = 23)				
Accurate	43	30	22	70
Inaccurate	43	48	26	22
DK, NA	13	22	52	9
Labour – Low-turnout (N = 21)				
Accurate	52	24	14	52
Inaccurate	24	67	48	29
DK, NA	24	10	38	19

and the electorate, than it does of the higher activist stratum, the city councillors, and the electorate. An explanation of this finding can be advanced on the lines of our original reasoning. For the increased level of integrative behaviour produced by greater activism in high-turnout wards will of course emerge mainly between electors and those activists who lie at the least 'political distance' from them i.e. the partyworkers. The increment of activity implied by higher turnout will probably not be enough to bridge the two gradations to the level of councillors, except marginally. This marginal bridging of the gap with councillors can account for the slightly more accurate appraisals of constituent opinion in high- compared with low-turnout wards. But the very much greater increase in the level of interaction with the partyworkers would account for the very much greater preferential agreement and factual accuracy displayed in high-turnout wards compared with low-turnout wards.

Generally it can be said that the stratification model has more success predicting the accuracy of appraisals than predicting the correspondence of opinions; and in order for the model to be useful for predicting correspondence of opinions, party first had to be controlled. Finally, although a comparison of the levels of agreement on opinions and accuracy of appraisals between high- and low-turnout wards were, more often than not, in the predicted direction, comparing the data in the tables of this section with the analogous data in Tables 3.7 through 3.13 indicates that levels of agreement and accuracy in high-turnout wards were not consistently higher than the levels of agreement and accuracy over all thirty-seven wards. Likewise, neither were levels of agreement and accuracy in low-turnout wards consistently lower than the levels for all thirty-seven wards.[100]

The last test to which we want to put the stratification model is to re-run the data on knowledge of party stands on pubs, fees, meters and rates to see if partyworkers and electors in high-turnout wards have more accurate perceptions of the party stands. Tables 3.22 and 3.23 contain data on electors' knowledge of these stands broken down both by high- and low-turnout and by party.

For electors' estimates of the Labour party's position on all four issues (Table 3.22), the relationships predicted by the stratification model appear with a regularity that is almost startling. To begin with, for all breakdowns of the data, a greater percentage of electors in high-turnout wards than in low-turnout wards claim to have knowledge of the Labour party's position on each issue. In addition, with the exception of Progressive electors' estimates of the Labour position on rates, modal estimates in high-turnout wards are more accurate about what position the Labour party holds on each issue. Comparing the data in Table 3.22 with those of Table 3.14, it is clear that in high-turnout wards

---

[100] Comparisons on a ward-by-ward basis, while always hazardous given the unreliability of the small sample taken from each ward, are extremely hazardous concerning Progressives in low turnout wards for here the Progressive electors number only twenty-three.

TABLE 3.22

Glasgow electors' perceptions of Labour Party position on four current issues, by high-
and low-turnout wards (percentages of all electors, and of progressive and Labour
electors, in high- and low-turnout wards)

	High-turnout (Perceived Labour Party position)					Low-turnout (Perceived Labour Party position)			
	For (per cent)	No position or split (per cent)	Against (per cent)	DK (per cent)		For (per cent)	No position or split (per cent)	Against (per cent)	DK (per cent)
All (N = 203)					*All* (N = 118)				
Pubs	40	10	17	33	Pubs	31	11	15	43
Fees	61	4	13	22	Fees	40	2	11	47
Parking	55	3	4	37	Parking	46	3	7	44
Rates	62	3	19	16	Rates	48	3	2	31
Progressives (N = 73)					*Progressives* (N = 23)				
Pubs	38	8	27	26	Pubs	26	4	22	44
Fees	32	1	7	10	Fees	48	—	9	44
Parking	62	3	3	33	Parking	57	4	—	39
Rates	77	3	11	9	Rates	78	4	—	17
Labour (N = 89)					*Labour* (N = 73)				
Pubs	41	12	11	30	Pubs	36	11	16	37
Fees	54	5	20	21	Fees	44	3	11	43
Parking	53	3	7	37	Parking	43	3	10	45
Rates	52	3	26	19	Rates	41	1	26	32

modal estimates of Labour party position are generally more accurate
than the modal estimates for all wards combined. The only exception
is the nearly equal levels of accuracy reached by Progressives in high-
turnout wards (38 per cent) and by Progressives in all wards (39 per
cent) over the Labour position on pubs.

For electors' estimates of the Progressive party's position on these
same issues (Table 3.23), the results are nearly as good. In all comparisons except Progressive electors' estimates of their party's position on
the rates issue, a greater percentage of electors in high-turnout wards
than in low-turnout wards claim knowledge of the party's position.
As to the accuracy of the estimates, although the modal estimate of the
Progressive party position on pubs remains inaccurate for all except
Progressive electors in high-turnout wards, the general pattern is still
one of greater accuracy of the estimates in high-turnout than in low-
turnout wards. For instance, Labour electors in high-turnout wards do
not make the error of attributing support for the rate increase to the

TABLE 3.23

Glasgow electors' perceptions of Progressive Party position on four current issues, by high- and low-turnout wards (percentages of all electors, and of Progressive and Labour electors, in High- and low-turnout wards)

	High-turnout (Perceived Progressive Party position)					Low-turnout (Perceived Progressive Party position)			
	For (per cent)	No position or split (per cent)	Against (per cent)	DK (per cent)		For (per cent)	No position or split (per cent)	Against (per cent)	DK (per cent)
All (N = 203)					*All* (N = 118)				
Pubs	16	11	25	47	Pubs	13	8	25	55
Fees	18	3	47	33	Fees	14	1	33	53
Parking	32	6	13	49	Parking	33	3	8	56
Rates	24	4	46	26	Rates	32	3	29	36
Progressives (N = 73)					*Progressives* (N = 23)				
Pubs	23	12	22	43	Pubs	17	4	26	52
Fees	16	1	66	16	Fees	4	—	57	39
Parking	37	7	12	44	Parking	26	4	13	57
Rates	11	7	63	19	Rates	17	—	65	17
Labour (N = 89)					*Labour* (N = 73)				
Pubs	14	13	27	45	Pubs	12	7	25	56
Fees	21	3	36	39	Fees	19	1	29	51
Parking	32	5	14	51	Parking	36	3	7	55
Rates	34	3	36	27	Rates	41	3	18	38

Progressive party, an error found among Labour electors in low-turnout wards and among all Labour electors in Table 3.15. Also the modal estimates of party position on fees and rates are more accurate in high-turnout than low-turnout wards, for five out of six comparisons, the sole exception being a difference of 63 and 65 per cent accuracy for Progressive electors over the rates issue. For the meters issue, two out of three comparisons go against the predicted outcome, but the differences are trivial – 1 and 4 per cent respectively. For estimates among Progressive electors, the comparison is in the predicted direction, and the difference is 11 per cent: 37 per cent of those in high-turnout wards correctly estimate the party position while only 26 per cent in low-turnout wards are correct. Comparing the data of Table 3.23 with those of Table 3.15 in all cases the percentage of electors in high-turnout wards who correctly perceive the Progressive party position is equal to, or higher than, the corresponding percentage found for all electors in Table 3.15.

E

Turning our attention to the perceptions partyworkers have of the Labour party position, the expected relationships between partyworkers in high- and low-turnout wards generally occur. In ten out of twelve comparisons the percentage of workers in high-turnout wards who claim no knowledge of the Labour party position is smaller than or equal to the percentage in low-turnout wards. In nine out of twelve comparisons the partyworkers in high-turnout wards make as good or better estimates of the Labour party position than do workers in low-urnout wards. The record is not so good, however, when the data are compared with the data in Table 3.16. In only seven out of twelve comparisons do partyworkers in high-turnout wards make more accurate estimates than the partyworkers in all wards combined. Although the differences are never more than 3 per cent for Labour partyworkers, those in high-turnout wards make poorer estimates than the average for all Labour partyworkers on all four comparisons. Since the difference between high- and low-turnout wards relates mainly to electoral activity, it is of course to be anticipated that less difference will open up between partyworkers from these types of ward than between electors.[101]

The data on partyworkers' perceptions of Progressive stands indicate that once again the predicted pattern of outcomes generally occurs. In ten out of twelve comparisons a greater percentage of partyworkers in high-turnout wards than in low-turnout wards claim knowledge of the Progressive party's position on the issues. There is still a considerable amount of error in estimates of the party position on pubs and meters, but for fees and rates, the party-related issues, five out of six comparisons show that the workers in high-turnout wards have more accurate perceptions of the party position than those in low-turnout wards. In their estimates of the Progressive party's position on pubs and meters, workers in high- and low-turnout wards are about equally inaccurate. Comparing the data with those in Table 3.17, it becomes apparent that for the party-related issues workers in high-turnout wards have more accurate perceptions of Progressive party positions than those in all wards, for five out of six comparisons. On the pubs issue, Labour partyworkers in high-turnout wards have a more distorted picture of the Progressive party position than do the Labour partyworkers across all wards. Their counterparts, however, the Progressive

---

[101] Nevertheless some differences between partyworkers of the magnitude just encountered might still be expected on the argument that where electors are less active, partyworkers are likely to be less active too.

partyworkers in these same wards, have more accurate perceptions of the party position than do the Progressive partyworkers across all wards. For the meters issue, the estimates of Labour partyworkers in high-turnout wards show a slightly greater degree of accuracy than the estimates of Labour partyworkers across all wards, but the estimates Progressive workers make of their own party position remain confused, even in high-turnout wards.

SUMMARY

The functioning of a modern mass democracy is dependent upon a scheme of representation whereby major interests in the society can bring forth alternatives and policies they desire. In order for such a system to function successfully representatives must somehow be made aware of constituent opinions or interests. In this chapter we reviewed five basic models describing ways in which representatives could act in order to carry out this function, and we then checked to see how closely each of these models described the representative process in Glasgow.

It was discovered that no simple model described the process, but that the most economic description could be got by taking elements of what we called the party and microcosm models of representation. The party and stratification model discussed in our first chapter also functioned fairly well, although it provided a less close fit than the party-microcosm model. Nevertheless, for specific problems, such as positions on the rates issue, or accuracy of appraisals of constituent opinion, the Burkean and party-stratification models were more useful than the party-microcosm model for understanding the data. Also the stratification model was highly successful in explaining differences in perceptions of party positions held by electors and partyworkers in high- and low-turnout wards.

Measurement of the representatives' awareness of constituents' interests, opinions and problems, however, does not tell us everything about the representative process. Obviously, the channels by which electors, partyworkers, and councillors find out about each other's opinions, interests or problems will help to explain how or why the particular relationships between constituents and representatives measured in the chapter came into being. The vital process of communication between the political strata must be investigated. To this task Chapter 4 is devoted.

4. Communication

The information an individual possesses will to a great extent determine the decisions he makes. If the channels through which one group
of individuals receives information are characteristically different from
those of some other group, then the two groups are likely to possess
different perspectives and differing amounts of information over the
same decision areas. In the present study, we have already found that
Glasgow councillors, partyworkers and electors possess different perspectives and different amounts of information on a variety of current
issues. In this chapter we will try to determine whether the manner in
which Glasgow's three political strata receive information can explain
these differences.

To begin with, our stratification model suggests some relationships.
Councillors and partyworkers are characterised as exhibiting more
integrative behaviour over issues than are electors. This means that they
will communicate with one another concerning political matters more
frequently than will electors, and in the course of their communications
they will exchange more information. As a result, in comparison to
electors, a greater number of councillors and partyworkers will hear of
political events from one another, and will in fact rely upon one another
as their best sources of information, especially about local politics.
None the less, there will be barriers to communication between strata,
so relatively few members of each stratum are expected to be in frequent
contact with members of other strata concerning political issues. In
addition, despite sometimes extensive within-stratum communication,
members of all three strata are expected to be heavily dependent
upon the mass media as their best source of political information.

The type and quality of the media depended upon by each stratum
are also likely to differ. Previous research has led us to expect that
councillors and partyworkers more often than electors will rely upon
high-quality newspapers for their information.[102] Relative to electors

[102] The basic finding is that citizens with higher education, interest, and involvement in politics read better-quality newspapers and news magazines. Cf.

the active strata will more often choose printed matter as their best source instead of television or radio, and they will, in general, read about politics more broadly.

Although these expectations hardly appear startling, it should be noted that their emphasis is radically opposed to some widely-held conceptions of the flow of political communications. We have already (Chapter 1) contrasted the stratification model with the classical model of party structure, whereby workers gather information from the electorate and pass it up to the party representatives and organisers: at the same time transmitting central decisions downwards. Although the correspondence is by no means perfect, this party structure model of communication resembles many theories based on the so-called 'two-step flow of information'.[103] The general argument of such theories is that political ideas are seldom transmitted directly from élites and media to the mass public. Instead these ideas are assimilated in the first place by persons whose relatively high political involvement prompts them to pay exceptional attention to élite and media messages. These 'opinion leaders' are then consulted by other members of the population to whom they pass on the ideas they have taken from the media, thus helping to modify the behaviour and beliefs of the persons who consult them. Our stratification model suggests, on the other hand, that partyworkers, councillors (and by implication other opinion leaders) tend to talk to one another instead of to the general population. The general electorate gets most of its political information directly from the mass media, not filtered through the opinion leaders.

The Glasgow partyworkers with whom we will be particularly concerned in the subsequent analysis cannot be automatically identified with the 'opinion leaders' of these 'two-step' theories, since many such theories emphasise the similarity between opinion leaders and the people they influence, in terms of social and other characteristics. Partyworkers share many characteristics with residents of their own ward but obviously have idiosyncrasies which prevent them being

---

Rose, *Politics in England*, chap. 8; Colin Seymour-Ure, 'The Press', in D. E. Butler and Anthony King, *The British General Election of 1966* (London, 1966); Key, *Public Opinion*, chaps 14–15.

[103] Elements of this 'two-step flow' theory are presented in Elihu Katz and Paul F. Lazarsfeld, *Personal Influence* (New York, 1955) Part I, chaps 1 and 2, and Part II, chap. 14. See also Paul F. Lazarsfeld *et al.*, *The People's Choice* (New York, 1944) chaps 14 and 16. For some critical comments see Verling C. Troldahl, 'A Field Test of a Modified "Two-Step Flow of Communications Model"', *Public Opinion Quarterly*, XXX (1966–7) 509–24.

regarded as near-average members of the public.[104] (This is even more true of councillors.) The measurement of activity levels through differences between status groups is thus a limitation of our data which makes a direct test of these two-step theories difficult. But two strong arguments can be advanced for regarding the subsequent analysis as just as much a check of the two-step models as of the stratification model:

(1) Precisely because the stratification model is being tested the two-step models are being tested too. In terms of our argument in Chapter 1 any noticeable gradation in activity levels produces an interactional and communications hiatus between persons at different levels. Obviously the 'near-average' opinion leaders cited by the two-step theories are at a higher level of activity than the average member of the population, even if not quite at the level of our partyworkers or councillors: therefore they will not in terms of our argument pass on any significant flow of information or ideas to the population. The check against the reported behaviour of electors, partyworkers and councillors is quite capable of upholding or disconfirming the stratification model, but the very decision that the latter has been upheld casts doubt on the diametrically opposed two-step theories, and vice versa.

(2) Moreover, Glasgow partyworkers (and even more councillors) do display many characteristics which opinion leaders too are said to have – being highly involved, very active and talking about politics a great deal, often in order to influence someone's opinion. Party workers in fact are opinion leaders writ large, since their role involves them in exactly the same functions attributed to opinion leaders in general but in much intensified form. If therefore persons for whom giving political advice is a central function are found to hold very limited communication with electors, we can argue forcibly that communication between electors and near-average opinion leaders will also be severely limited, contrary to the expectations of the two-step theories.

Data against which the rival models can be checked come from reports of partyworkers and electors on their best sources of political information and on their reading and viewing habits, and from the responses of all three strata to more direct questions about communication on political issues. After examining the actual communication flow revealed through these responses, we shall make a final assessment of the standing of the different models in light of the empirical analysis.

[104] For comparisons of activists' social backgrounds with those of the population see *Class, Religion*, chap. 5.

QUANTITY OF INFORMATION AVAILABLE

The simplest expectation we derive from the stratification model is that activists actually absorb more political information than electors. The ability of partyworkers and councillors to give more specific and more accurate political appraisals than electors has been demonstrated in the previous chapter. We can amplify this finding here by examining the tendency of partyworkers to read, see and listen more than electors (councillors were not asked the appropriate questions). It is evident first of all that partyworkers generally read a greater number of daily newspapers than do electors. Some 55 per cent of the partyworkers read three or more dailies, while only 32 per cent of the electors are such prodigious readers. The average number of papers read by party-workers is 2·8 in contrast to an average of 2·2 for electors.[105] No similar relationship, however, is found with regard to Sunday papers. Both strata average slightly more than two Sunday papers for each member, and the only differences that can be found are at the extremes of no Sunday papers read or four or more Sunday papers read. Only 2 per cent of the partyworkers as opposed to 5 per cent of the electors read no Sunday paper, and 14 per cent of the partyworkers in contrast to 8 per cent of the electors read four or more Sunday papers.

Magazine readership among our respondents is limited, but the pattern of readership again shows evidence of partyworkers' greater interest in securing political information. Fifty-five per cent of the electors and 35 per cent of the partyworkers read no magazines at all. The reading habits of those who did read magazines tended to be somewhat narrow: out of eight types in a broad classification of magazines, only 11 per cent of the electors and 24 per cent of the partyworkers read more than one type. Even on this measure, however, it is noticeable that partyworkers read a greater variety of magazines – an average of 1·0 type as opposed to only 0·6 type for electors.

Turning to television and radio news programmes, we find that

[105] Readership was determined from replies to the question of which papers respondents read 'regularly'. Respondents were shown lists of daily and Sunday papers sold in Glasgow, so it is possible that the absolute number of papers named includes some papers with which the respondents were familiar but did not read regularly.

If respondents asked what 'regularly' meant, interviewers were instructed to reply three times a week or more often for dailies and twice a month or more often for Sundays.

Cf. Butler and Stokes, *Political Change In Britain* (London, 1969) chap. 10, for comparative figures on readership habits for Britain as a whole.

partyworkers also show more interest in acquiring information from these media. Only 15 per cent of the partyworkers fail to watch a television news programme as compared to 26 per cent for the electors. Nearly half the electors (47 per cent) see one or fewer programmes, but this is only true of one fourth (25 per cent) of the partyworkers. On the other end of the scale, 47 per cent of the partyworkers watch four or more programmes regularly while only 14 per cent of the electors are so attentive. The 118 partyworkers watch a total of 354 programmes, an average of 3·0 programmes each; in contrast, the 563 electors watch 1000 programmes, an average of only 1·8 each.

Radio news programmes do not have a very large audience among members of either stratum. None the less, the partyworker's average is 0·7 programmes each, while the electors average only 0·4. Although 57 per cent of the partyworkers listen to no radio news, this proportion is still smaller than the 69 per cent of the electors who listen to no radio news. Also, partyworkers show a slight edge at the top of the scale – 14 per cent listen to two or more programmes as opposed to 10 per cent for electors.

On every medium examined partyworkers seem to expose themselves to more information than electors, as anticipated. Still we can expect that the more educated and more partisan electors will also expose themselves more, thus lessening or obliterating the contrast since education and partisanship are two of the main characteristics distinguishing partyworkers from average electors. For this reason we have included in Table 4.1 averages for the separate party groupings of partyworkers and electors, and for electors of varying levels of education.

Partisanship and education have almost no effect on the number of newspapers read by electors. Progressives, Labour and independents all average approximately 2·2 daily newspapers, again precisely the average for all electors. Progressive and Labour electors also average 2·2 Sunday newspapers, again the same average as all electors taken together, but independents read slightly fewer Sunday papers, an average of only 1·9. Education makes no apparent difference – whether an elector ended his formal education at an age under 15, at age 15, or at an age over 15, the average number of either daily or Sunday newspapers read never varies beyond a lower limit of 2·1 and an upper limit of 2·3. Nor does partisanship make an impact on the number of daily or Sunday newspapers read by party workers – both Progressive and Labour workers average 2·8 dailies and 2·3 Sundays.

TABLE 4.1

Quantity of political information available to Glasgow partyworkers and electors (average numbers of newspapers, magazine types, radio and TV programmes read or watched by all partyworkers and electors, and by party and educational groupings)

	All party-workers read/watch (per cent)	Progressive party-workers read/watch (per cent)	Labour workers read/watch (per cent)	All electors read/watch (per cent)
Average number				
Daily newspapers	2·8	2·8	2·8	2·2
Sunday newspapers	2·3	2·3	2·3	2·2
Magazines	1·0	0·8	1·1	0·6
TV news programmes	3·0	2·9	3·1	1·8
Radio news programmes	0·7	0·7	0·7	0·4

	Progressive electors read/watch (per cent)	Independent electors read/watch (per cent)	Labour electors read/watch (per cent)	Electors who ended formal education at age of −15 (per cent)	15 (per cent)	15+ (per cent)
Average number						
Daily newspapers	2·2	2·2	2·2	2·1	2·3	2·3
Sunday newspapers	2·2	1·9	2·2	2·1	2·2	2·2
Magazines	0·8	0·4	0·4	0·5	0·6	1·0
TV news programmes	2·0	1·3	1·8	1·7	1·9	2·0
Radio news programmes	0·6	0·5	0·3	0·4	0·4	0·6

Types of magazine are coded as: news or news analysis (including *The Economist, Statist, Time, Newsweek, Statesman, New Statesman, New Society, Spectator, Tribune, Time and Tide*), union or party, Scottish, religious, general information (including *Punch, Life, Reader's Digest, Paris Match, Time*), trade or professional, Women's.

Although 55 per cent of the electors read no magazines at all, sharp differences emerge between Progressive and other electors. Only 37 per cent of the Progressive electors read no magazines at all in contrast to 63 per cent of the Labour electors and 70 per cent of the independents. Progressive electors read more widely also; they average 0·8 type of magazines each as compared to only 0·4 type for Labour supporters and independents. Education also makes a difference. Only 27 per cent of those electors who remained at school after 15 read no magazines in contrast to over 55 per cent of the other electors. Those with higher education also read more widely than other electors, averaging 1·0 type of magazines – about double the rate for the rest of the electors. The breakdown by party indicates that Labour partyworkers are more

avid magazine readers than Progressive partyworkers. Only one out
of four Labour partyworkers fails to read a magazine, but almost half
the Progressives do not read any magazines at all. In fact, the average
Progressive elector reads as many types of magazines as the average
Progressive partyworker, and the average elector with education over
15 years of age tends to read as much as the average partyworker. The
magazine readership of Labour partyworkers surpasses that of all types
of electors, except those with higher education, where the differences
are not very large.

Partisan electors tend to watch more news on television than do
independents. Progressive and Labour electors average 2·0 and 1·8
programmes respectively as compared to an average of only 1·3 for
independents. In addition, fewer than one quarter of the partisans
watch no news programmes in contrast to some 44 per cent of the
Independents. Education, on the other hand, appears to have little
effect on the number of programmes watched – from low to high
education the average number of programmes watched varies but 0·3.
Nor are electors with low education apt to ignore television news.
Only 27 per cent of those with low education levels watch no news
on television. This hardly differs from the corresponding figure of
24 per cent for those with higher levels of education.

The average partyworker in both parties watches more television
news than the average member of any of the groups of electors looked
at. While there is little difference between Progressive and Labour
partyworkers in the average number of programmes watched, Labour
workers report a less evenly distributed pattern of viewing habits.
At the low end of the scale, 19 per cent of the Labour partyworkers, in
contrast to only 11 per cent of the Progressives, watch no television
news programmes; but at the high end, 52 per cent of the Labour
workers, in contrast to 43 per cent of the Progressives, watch four or
more programmes.

As we have noted previously, radio news programmes do not reach a
majority of voters, and only a small percentage of voters rate them as
their best sources of political information. None the less, there are some
differences in listening habits among electors of different partisanship
and educational levels. Labour electors average fewer programmes
than either Progressives or independents, and fewer Labour electors
listen to programmes than do other electors. Electors with formal
education over 15 years tend to listen to more radio news programmes
than do other electors. Partyworkers of both parties listen more fre-

quently to radio news programmes than do any group of electors, but there are no significant differences in the listening habits of Progressives and Labour.

The averages of Table 4.1 thus demonstrate that the reading, viewing and listening habits of partyworkers give them more opportunity to assimilate political information than is enjoyed by any group of electors. Proof that the opportunity is actually taken, at least in regard to newspapers, is provided by reports on which part of the newspaper is read first, presented in Table 4.2. From these it appears that 60 per cent of the partyworkers as compared to only 17 per cent of the electors turn first to either local or national news, editorials, or law reports. When questioned further, 115 out of 118 partyworkers, fully 97 per cent of those interviewed, stated that they read at least one of the above-mentioned newspaper parts, but only 394 of 563 electors (70 per cent) stated that they read at least one of these parts. That leaves 30 per cent who seek virtually no political information at all from the newspapers. Progressive electors show the greatest interest in political news, some 21 per cent of their number stating that they turn first to local or national news or to the editorial pages. Labour supporters and independents show somewhat less interest with only 15 and 17 per cent of their number turning directly to one of these parts. Interest in news and editorials also increases with greater education. Thirty-two per cent of the electors with education over 15 years of age turn first to one of these parts in contrast to only 18 per cent of those with education to 15 years of age and 15 per cent of those with education under 15 years. Only 16 per cent of Progressive electors indicate seeking no political news at all from the papers, but 29 per cent of Labour electors and 33 per cent of independents freely indicate this. A similar pattern occurs for education: only 11 per cent of those with formal education beyond the age of 15 indicate seeking no political news from the papers, but 30 per cent of those with education to 15 years and 28 per cent of those with education under 15 years of age seek no political information from the newspapers. However, partyworkers show more interest than even the higher educated electors in seeking political information, since 63 per cent of the Labour partyworkers and 55 per cent of the Progressives turn first to political news or editorials.

QUALITY OF POLITICAL INFORMATION AVAILABLE

Partyworkers seem to use the media to garner political information to a greater extent than electors, as well as exposing themselves more to

TABLE 4.2

Parts of newspapers read first by Glasgow partyworkers and electors (percentages of all partyworkers and electors, and of party and educational groupings)

	All party-workers (per cent)	Progressive party-workers (per cent)	Labour party-workers (per cent)	All Elec. (per cent)	Prog. Elec. (per cent)	Lab. Elec. (per cent)	Ind. Elec. (per cent)	Electors who ended formal education at age of −15 (per cent)	15 (per cent)	15+ (per cent)
No papers read	—	—	—	1	—	1	—	1	—	1
Local news	9	9	8	2	2	3	—	2	3	2
National news, law reports	32	24	39	10	10	9	12	9	6	24
Editorials and letters	19	22	16	5	9	3	5	4	9	6
Finance and industry, agriculture, fishing	3	4	3	1	1	—	—	—	1	4
TV/Radio, books, theatre, arts	3	—	5	4	3	3	9	11	18	7
Accidents and crimes	3	4	2	12	9	15	9	6	2	1
Women's news, marriages, births	6	11	2	12	13	14	6	14	9	13
Sports, features, contests	12	14	9	23	14	27	24	25	27	8
Headlines, advertisements, other	14	11	17	28	35	22	32	28	20	34
DK, NA	—	—	—	2	2	2	3	2	4	—
Total	101	99	101	100	98	99	100	102	99	100

the media in the first place. The question also arises of the quality of the media available to them. Activists should rely on different types of media from electors, if their anticipated tendency to different kinds of interaction is to be confirmed. Moreover the distinctive types of media they patronise should provide better and more detailed news coverage than those favoured by electors: they should prefer quality to popular newspapers, BBC television to Independent, the Home and Third Services on radio compared to the Light.

These expectations are confirmed by the summary percentages given in Table 4.3. Although a large majority of the newspapers read by each stratum are of the popular variety, about one out of four papers read by the partyworkers are quality papers, while this is true of barely one out of sixteen papers read by the electors. In all, 118 partyworkers read 85 quality daily and 75 quality Sunday newspapers. Five hundred and sixty-three electors barely read more quality newspapers – 94 dailies and 77 Sundays. Differences are intensified when we come to magazines. Partyworkers read mostly news magazines, union or party magazines, and general information magazines (60 per cent of the types named). Electors, on the other hand, show little preference for news or party magazines (5 per cent); they read women's magazines (47 per cent) and general information magazines (17 per cent) instead. These differences cannot be attributed to the fact that 53 per cent of the electors in our sample are women, in contract to only 23 per cent of the party workers. Even if we eliminate women's magazines from consideration, 67 per cent of the remaining magazine types read by partyworkers are either news, party, or general information magazines. For the electors, the corresponding figure is still only 42 per cent, the bulk of which is composed of general information magazines alone.

The types of television programmes watched by members of each stratum are rather similar, but the networks to which they tune are not. For partyworkers, 40 per cent of the programmes watched are regular newscasts and 58 per cent are news features and analysis; for electors the corresponding figures are 42 per cent and 52 per cent. Despite these overall similarities in viewing habits, however, a closer look shows important differences. Partyworkers tend to favour the BBC for both regular newscasts and news features, but electors tend to favour only BBC news features, and they report watching STV news programmes more frequently than those of the BBC. The general pattern which emerges indicates that 59 per cent of the programmes watched by partyworkers are on BBC and only 39 per cent are on STV. Electors,

TABLE 4.3

Quality of political information available to Glasgow partyworkers and electors (percentages out of all newspapers, magazine types, radio or TV programmes read or watched by all partyworkers and electors, and by party and educational groupings)

	All party-workers (per cent)	Progressive party-workers (per cent)	Labour party-workers (per cent)	All electors (per cent)	Progressive electors (per cent)
Quality out of all Daily newspapers read	26	23	29	7	15
Quality out of all Sunday newspapers read	27	17	36	6	7
News/information out of all types magazines read	45	35	52	21	23
Union/party out of all types magazines read	15	2	22	1	—
BBC out of all TV news/ features programmes watched	59	60	58	47	58
Home/Third Service out of all radio news/features programmes heard	84	77	89	73	79

	Labour electors (per cent)	Independent electors (per cent)	Electors who ended formal education at age of		
			−15 (per cent)	15 (per cent)	15+ (per cent)
Quality out of all Daily newspapers read	3	6	4	5	24
Quality out of all Sunday newspapers read	5	7	3	5	20
News/information out of all types magazines read	19	24	16	17	36
Union/party out of all types magazines read	1	—	1	—	1
BBC out of all TV news/ features programmes watched	39	41	41	46	65
Home/Third Service out of all radio news/features programmes heard	68	65	73	62	91

Quality Daily newspapers are the (Scottish) *Glasgow Herald, Scotsman*, and (London) *Telegraph, Times, Guardian, Financial Times*: quality Sundays are the *Sunday Telegraph, Sunday Times, Observer*. In comparison with the popular press quality newspapers make a sharper separation between news reports and comment and give more detailed and greater background coverage of events. The same can be said of B(ritish) B(roadcasting) C(orporation) television in comparison to Scottish (Independent) television programmes and BBC Home and Third Service programmes compared to Light Service programmes.

on the other hand, watch both networks' news programmes with equal frequency – 47 per cent of the programmes named are on BBC and 47 per cent are on STV.

The types of radio programmes listened to by partyworkers and electors are almost identical. Sixty-four per cent of the broadcasts heard by electors are the Home news, and the corresponding figure for party-workers is 65 per cent. The only patterned differences appear to be that the electors tend to listen to Light Programme broadcasts more frequently than do partyworkers (20 per cent *v.* 11 per cent), while the partyworkers tend to listen more frequently to Home news features (15 per cent *v.* 7 per cent). Altogether 84 per cent of partyworkers' programmes originate on the Home or Third compared to 73 per cent of electors'.

Again we cannot discount the possibility that qualitative differences in media habits, even more than quantitative differences, may be affected by education and partisanship. These do in fact exert a considerable influence on the types of newspapers read. Among electors, Progressives are far more likely to read a quality daily than are either Labour supporters or independents: 15 per cent of the daily newspapers read by Progressives are quality papers as opposed to only 3 and 6 per cent of the dailies read by Labour supporters and independents. But the apparent lack of interest in quality dailies displayed by the latter groups is attributable in part to the fact that Glasgow's main quality Scottish daily, the *Glasgow Herald*, generally supports Progressive–Conservative measures, for upon turning to Sunday papers, we discover no significant differences in the frequency with which Progressives, Labourites and independents read quality newspapers. In contrast to partisanship, education shows a consistent relationship with electors' reading habits both for daily and Sunday newspapers. In both cases, the higher the elector's level of education, the more likely he is to read a quality newspaper.

When the data on partyworkers are assessed, it becomes clear that Labour workers tend to select quality newspapers more frequently than Progressive partyworkers. Unlike the party supporters among the general electorate, they are not put off by the conservative views of the *Glasgow Herald*, and they mention reading quality Scottish dailies (17 per cent), mostly the *Herald*, nearly as often as do Progressive party-workers (19 per cent). In addition, 12 per cent of the daily papers read by Labour partyworkers are quality nationals while this is true of only 4 per cent of those read by the Progressives. When it comes to Sunday papers, the differences between Labour and Progressive partyworkers are even stronger – 36 per cent of the Sunday papers read by the former group are quality papers while the same is true of only 17 per cent of those papers read by the latter. Electors with over 15 years' education, in fact, mention reading quality daily and Sunday newspapers with the same or greater frequencies than Progressive partyworkers.

When types of magazines are examined the differences among electors are somewhat surprising. Fourteen per cent of the magazines read by independent electors are news or news analysis magazines as opposed to only 3 and 2 per cent of the magazines read by Progressive and Labour partisans. The partisan electors make up this apparent lag in news interest by reading a larger proportion of general information magazines than do independents, but the independents also show less interest in women's magazines than other electors and more interest in Scottish magazines and residual types of magazines not read by a sufficient number of electors to be classified. It appears that the few independents who do read magazines generally represent those intelligent independent voters so often appealed to (especially by the underdogs) in the rhetoric of election campaigns.

Education affects magazine readership in the expected manner. The important differences, however, are between these electors with over 15 years' education and other electors. The former group reads more news and general information magazines than the latter and is also less prone to read women's magazines. But whether an elector finished his education at age 15 or before age 15 seems to make little difference.

In contrast to all other groups looked at, the majority of types of magazines read by Labour partyworkers are either news magazines or union and party publications. (Labour partyworkers are in fact the only group which reads a significant number of union and party magazines.) Labour partyworkers also read very few women's and very few Scottish magazines compared to other groups. Progressive partyworkers do not read nearly as many union and party magazines as their Labour counterparts. They do, however, read more news and general information magazines (35 per cent of total types) than any group of electors except the high education group, whose reading habits closely resemble their own. The only differences in habits are that Progressive partyworkers tend to read fewer women's magazines and more Scottish and religious magazines than the more highly educated electors.

The type of television news programmes watched by electors appears closely related to their party identification and their level of education. A firm majority (58 per cent) of the programmes watched by Progressive electors are on the BBC. In contrast, most news programmes watched by Labour party electors and independents are on STV. STV news, rather than news features, are most popular with the latter group. Electors' preferences for BBC news and features tend to increase with increasing levels of education. Those with education under 15 years of age report virtually the same viewing habits as Labour supporters and independents. Those with education to 15 years of age split their viewing about evenly between BBC and STV. But those with higher education prefer BBC even more strongly than do the Progressives (65 per cent).

There is little difference between the television habits of Progressive and Labour partyworkers – both strongly prefer BBC news and features. None the less, Progressive electors' preferences for the BBC are as strong as those of partyworkers, and the more highly educated electors favour BBC by an even larger margin than do workers for either party.

Regarding radio programmes, Progressive electors tend to devote smaller proportions of their listening time to the Light programme and to Home news features than do Labour electors and independents. Instead fully three-quarters of the programmes heard by them are regular newscasts on the Home service. Those electors with high education also concentrate on Home news, devoting but a small proportion of their listening time to the Light programme. Compared to other electors they manage to listen to as many or more Home features. The influence of education on the listening habits of less-educated electors is not so well patterned. Electors with low education listen to relatively fewer news broadcasts on the Light programme than do those with intermediate education. They also listen more frequently to the Home news, and contain the small proportion who listen to news on the Third programme.

Progressive and Labour partyworkers listen to news on the Home service with about the same frequency, but they differ in their choice of news features. Progressive partyworkers listen more frequently to the Light programme and less frequently to Home features than do Labour workers. In addition, Labour partyworkers are the only group which has any notable number (still only 7 per cent) of Third programme listeners. As compared with electors, partyworkers do not show any outstanding or unusual patterns. The listening habits of Progressive workers resemble those of electors with low education, and to a slightly lesser degree, those of Progressive electors. In contrast, the listening habits of Labour partyworkers do not closely parallel those of any group of electors investigated. Of all the groups of electors and partyworkers examined, Progressive electors and those with high education tended to concentrate the largest proportion of their listening on BBC Home news.

Overall there is less contrast between the quality of the media available to partyworkers and those available particularly to more highly educated electors than there was in terms of quantity. Nevertheless considerable differences remain between partyworkers and the average elector.

BEST SOURCES OF POLITICAL INFORMATION

While reading and listening habits offer a general guide to patterns of communication among the three strata, a more direct entry is offered by an examination of information-seeking habits themselves. We examine these habits as they emerge on politics in general, and local politics in particular, through questions on the best sources of political information: later we shall see how councillors, partyworkers and electors first heard of specific issues and how they would consciously seek additional information on these issues.

TABLE 4.4

Best sources of political information reported by Glasgow partyworkers and electors (percentages of all partyworkers and electors)

Sources	Politics in general		Local politics	
	Electors	Partyworkers	Electors	Partyworkers
Personal non-media sources	—*	—*	16	59
Daily newspapers	48	42	48	34
Sunday newspapers	9	19	4	—
Newspapers (unspecified)	—	4	2	4
Television	28	22	16	3
Radio	3	—	2	1
Magazines	2	9	2	—
Other	1	1	2	—
Not interested, no best source	8	3	7	—
DK, NA	2	—	1	—
Total	101	100	100	101

*On local politics a filter question was included, which asked the respondent if he used the media as his best source. No such filter was included for politics in general.

With regard to the best sources of information named for politics in general, there is, as anticipated in our initial argument, a tendency for partyworkers to rely more heavily upon printed media than electors. Seventy-four per cent of the partyworkers as opposed to 59 per cent of the electors rely on newspapers or magazines for most of their political information. But there is a qualitative difference as well: 28 per cent of the partyworkers name Sunday newspapers (19 per cent) or magazines (9 per cent) as their best sources, while only 11 per cent of the electors name these. Yet Sunday newspapers and magazines, rather than daily newspapers, are precisely where one is more likely to find in-depth analysis of the political news. This suggests that a greater proportion of partyworkers take the time to seek extended analyses of the news in the printed media. In addition (even though they watch more television and radio news than do electors) partyworkers are less likely to rely upon television and radio as their best sources of political information – 22 per cent of the partyworkers rely on these media in contrast to 31 per cent of the electors.

The sources relied upon for information about local politics, however, show the most contrast. Fully 59 per cent of the partyworkers name non-media sources to which they have personal access as their best sources of information. This contrasts with the mere 16 per cent of the electors who mention the same type of sources. Both strata also place heavy reliance on daily newspapers for local information, but partyworkers rely very little on television and radio (4 per cent) while 18 per cent of the electors still pick these media as their best sources of information.

A further breakdown of the data to indicate the specific sources other than the mass media which respondents relied upon for local political information produces additional evidence of the superior information of the partyworkers. The great majority (88 per cent) of the 70 partyworkers who do not get their best information from the mass media get their information directly from city councillors, officers or council minutes (24 per cent) or from party meetings, minutes or other partyworkers (64 per cent). Only a few rely on their friends (7 per cent), and all other sources are of negligible importance. In contrast to the partyworkers the 94 electors who do not get their best information on local politics from the mass media report a diverse set of alternative sources. Only 26 per cent get their information from city council or political party sources. Almost as many (23 per cent) rely upon their friends, and an additional 11 per cent upon their spouse or another relative, for local information. Even workmates and members of voluntary organisations other than the party provide the best information respectively for 7 and 6 per cent of these electors. Some 11 per cent are even unable to say where they got most of their local political information.

For best sources of information about politics in general, there is little difference between Progressive and Labour electors. Independents show slightly less interest: a smaller proportion of them rely on daily and Sunday newspapers than do partisan electors, and a larger proportion of them report that they are simply not interested in politics. Education also makes but a moderate impact on the choice of sources of information about politics in general. Those whose education extended past 15 years of age tend to rely more upon radio and magazines for political information than do other electors, but, somewhat surprisingly, electors with lower levels of education rely more heavily on Sunday papers than those of higher educational attainments. In contrast to 8 to 10 per cent of the electors with lower levels of education, however, none of the electors with over 15 years of education report taking no interest in politics.

Party affiliation makes a greater impact on the sources of political information cited by partyworkers than on those cited by electors. Labour partyworkers rely less on daily newspapers (34 per cent to 50 per cent) and much more upon magazines (16 per cent to 2 per cent) than do Progressive partyworkers. Workers of both parties choose Sunday newspapers as their best source on politics about twice as often as do partisan electors (19 per cent to 10 per cent), no partyworkers rely upon radio news, and only a negligible number say they are not interested in politics in general. With the exception of Sunday papers the sources of information cited by Progressive partyworkers do not greatly differ from those cited by Progressive electors, but in addition to Sunday papers, Labour partyworkers rely more on magazines and less on daily newspapers than do Labour party electors.

For local politics, there once again is not a great deal of difference between the best sources of information reported by Progressive and Labour electors. The former pay somewhat more attention to daily newspapers (58 per cent to 47 per cent) while the latter watch more television and more often rely on the Sunday papers. Sixteen per cent of supporters of both parties rely on non-media sources for their information. Independent electors show a somewhat different pattern from that of partisans. To begin with, a greater proportion of independents (21 per cent) than partisans (3 and 6 per cent) professes no interest in local affairs. Independents rely upon personal non-media sources, however, to a greater degree (20 per cent) than do Progressive and Labour electors, and their level of reliance on television resembles that of Labour electors more closely than it does that of Progressives. Education tends to have only a small influence over electors' choices of sources of information on local politics. Those with under 15 years of education rely less on daily newspapers and more on television than do other electors. They also rely somewhat more on personal non-media sources than do electors in the highest educational group. The best sources on local politics for such electors differ little from those of electors in the lowest grouping except that fewer of the former group report having no interest in local politics at all.

There are stark differences between Progressive and Labour party-workers on best sources of information regarding local politics. Almost three-quarters of the Labour partyworkers report personal non-media contacts as the source of most of their information about local politics. Virtually all the rest of the Labour partyworkers rely on daily news-papers. Progressive partyworkers also rely heavily on non-media sources (44 per cent), but they rely more heavily on daily newspapers (44 per cent) or newspapers in general (7 per cent). With the exception of 4 per cent who get their best information from television, Progressives choose no other best sources of information on local politics. Compared to electors, of course, partyworkers in both parties depend upon personal sources for their local information to a much greater degree.

Partisan affiliation does not make a great deal of difference to the nature of non-media sources employed by electors. Progressive electors (26 per cent) cite workmates and relatives more frequently than do Labour electors (11 per cent), and Labour electors tend to rely more heavily upon friends (26 per cent to 19 per cent) and miscellane-ous (other) sources (13 per cent to 0 per cent), but except for the miscellaneous category the differences are not more than 7 per cent. Education seems to have a similar moderate effect. Less-educated voters cite friends less often than do more educated electors, while the latter cite relatives and miscellaneous sources less often, but once again the differences are not great – 13 per cent at maximum.

In contrast virtually all the Labour partyworkers cite either council-lors and official council sources (22 per cent), or party sources (74 per cent) as the origin of their information. Progressive partyworkers rely less heavily on party sources (46 per cent), slightly more heavily on direct contacts with council sources (29 per cent), and a great deal more heavily upon friends (21 per cent). The concentration on council and party sources by workers of both parties, however, is vastly greater than that of any group of electors examined.

Before going on to information-seeking on specific issues our findings on the primary sources of political information of electors and partyworkers should be summarised. In general, partyworkers pay more attention to political news in the papers and on television than do electors, including partisan and more educated electors. The superior local party organisation of the Labour party is reflected in the greater proportion of Labour partyworkers compared to Progressive workers who read party and union publications and who receive their best information on politics from party sources. The mass media, as predicted by our model, play a vital role in purveying information about politics in general both to ordinary electors and to partyworkers. Only on matters of local political concern are partyworkers able to take advantage of their contact with party and governmental agencies to get their best information. The vast majority of electors, even for local matters, still rely upon the mass media for most of their information. We find little evidence of the two-step flow of communication.

LEARNING OF SPECIFIC ISSUES

If our observations thus far have been correct, we should when attention is turned to specific issues (the pubs, fees, parking-meters and rates issues which have already been introduced in the preceding chapters) find corroborating evidence of activists' use of more and better sources of information than are used by electors. We can, in addition, provide an extra dimension to the analysis, for questions concerning sources on specific issues were directed to councillors as well as to partyworkers.

The relevant data on how electors, partyworkers and councillors heard about each issue are found in Table 4.5. Those who had not heard about an issue are excluded from the calculations of percentages in the upper portion of the table.[106]

[106] Electors who said they had not heard of an issue were given a brief factual description of the proposals and then asked the same sequence of questions as those who had heard. The only issue where the addition of such electors' responses might seriously affect results is the question of fees, and here analysis shows that responses of those who had not heard of the issue hardly diverge from the responses of those who had. For a more detailed discussion of this question see Budge, 'Patterns of Democratic Agreement' (unpublished Ph.D. dissertation, Yale University Library) note to chap. 12, pp. 267-8: also H. Hyman, *Survey Design and Analysis* (New York, 1955) p. 343.

When the electors are asked how they first heard about each issue, sources other than the mass media are not often mentioned. A majority of electors, for instance, first heard about each issue in the daily newspapers. Although for pubs and fees word of mouth was the second most common means of hearing about an issue, this method was less common than radio/television for the meters and rates issues. Radio and television were the second most common method by which electors heard about meters, but receipt of official notices was a more common method for first hearing of the rate increase. With the exception of the high proportion who received official notices concerning rates, the proportions of electors indicating daily newspapers (54–62 per cent) and the proportions indicating word of mouth and radio/ television (6–21 per cent) tend to parallel the reports of best sources of information about local politics presented in Table 4.4. The political party organisation, we note, plays virtually no part at all in first apprising electors about any of the issues studied.

For partyworkers a different pattern emerges, which reflects the communication structures of the political parties. For pubs and fees the most common means through which workers heard of the issue was the political party organisation and its agencies (34 and 37 per cent), and for the latter issue ward agencies, where the municipal ward committees often serve as the Progressive party organisations, are the second most common means (26 per cent). Like electors a majority of partyworkers (59 per cent) heard about the meters from the daily papers, and a plurality (46 per cent) heard about rates from the same source. Unlike electors, however, only a few (5 per cent) of partyworkers cite official notices as their earliest source of information about the rate increase; instead over 30 per cent of the partyworkers cite political party agencies or city council agencies as their source on this issue. Radio and television are rated by workers as unimportant sources over all four issues, but daily newspapers are still the second most common means by which they heard about elimination of fees (14 per cent). The general pattern lends credence to the report (Table 4.4) that personal non-media sources are highly important sources for securing information about local politics for partyworkers.

The city council and its agencies are naturally the primary sources through which councillors report having first heard of the four issues. Only on school fees are any other sources – political party agencies and word of mouth – cited more frequently. For all other issues either political party agencies or word of mouth are the second most common means through which councillors report having heard of issues. The school fees issue is also the only issue which came to the attention of any notable proportion (15 per cent) of the councillors through the mass media, daily papers in particular. No sources other than the afore-mentioned are cited by more than 9 per cent of the councillors as their original source of information about any issue, and no councillors at all cite either Sunday papers or radio/television for any issue.

As predicted by our model, there are few reports of issues being made known by communication between the political strata. For such information, electors rely upon the mass media coupled with some word of mouth communication among themselves. Partyworkers rely more heavily on their own party contacts, but they also make heavy use of the mass media and some use of ward agencies. Councillors pick up their original information primarily through council agencies, but word of mouth and political party agencies do rank about evenly as the second most important sources, and they are especially important for the pubs and fees issues. In fact, their importance for the pubs and fees issues comprises the only evidence found of significant flows of com-munication between strata about new issues.

Neither an elector's party nor his level of education makes any important impact on the manner in which he heard of the issues. Regardless of affiliation or education, the proportions of electors naming each source of information is virtually identical to the pro-portions for all electors reported in Table 4.5.[107] The only noteworthy differences that can be found are in the proportions who heard of the issues, not in the pattern of how the issues were heard. For the pubs and fees issues, greater proportions of Progressives than of other electors report having heard of the issues. For the fees and parking issues, greater proportions of electors with over 15 years' education than other electors report having heard of the issues.[108]

---

[107] If one takes each possible combination, i.e. Labour-Progressive, Labour-Independent, Progressive-Independent, Over 15-Under 15, Over 15-15, Under 15-15 and compares the distribution of responses for each issue, the average least squares correlation (r) between distribution of responses is greater than 0·95.

[108] The percentages who have not heard of each issue are as follows:

	Affiliation			Education		
	Prog.	Lab.	Indep.	Over 15	15	Under 15
Pubs	10	16	21	14	14	16
Fees	45	66	65	38	71	60
Parking	24	27	23	22	21	30
Rates	5	5	12	6	10	4

TABLE 4.5

How electors, partyworkers and councillors heard of four current issues
(percentages of councillors, partyworkers and electors on each issue)

	Electors				Partyworkers				Councillors			
	Pubs (per cent)	Fees (per cent)	Parking (per cent)	Rates (per cent)	Pubs (per cent)	Fees (per cent)	Parking (per cent)	Rates (per cent)	Pubs (per cent)	Fees (per cent)	Parking (per cent)	Rates (per cent)
Daily newspapers	61	57	62	54	30	14	59	46	4	15	6	5
Sunday newspapers	1	1	—	1	—	3	2	—	—	—	—	—
Radio/TV	6	15	18	13	1	2	3	6	—	—	—	—
Word of mouth	21	17	15	10	8	9	9	6	21	24	4	18
Political parties	—	2	—	—	34	37	8	18	23	28	17	8
Ward agencies	5	—	—	—	14	26	3	3	5	—	1	8
Council and council agencies	—	—	—	1	5	2	11	13	33	23	60	49
Official actions	1	—	—	18	—	2	—	5	2	1	1	—
Through own efforts and dedication	—	—	—	—	1	—	—	3	9	4	5	8
Don't know	5	5	3	3	5	4	3	1	2	1	2	3
Not ascertained	1	2	1	1	1	2	—	—	1	4	4	3
Total	101	99	99	101	99	101	98	101	100	100	100	102
*Number who heard of issue**	479	230	410	529	118	114	112	118	82	82	82	82
Never heard†	15	59	27	6	—	3	5	—	—	—	—	—

*Percentages in upper portion of table are based upon this N.
†Percentages in lower portion of table are based upon 563 electors, 118 partyworkers, 82 councillors.

For partyworkers, in contrast with electors, the effects of party affiliation are very important (Table 4.6). Although daily newspapers are still the primary sources of information, Labour partyworkers tend to rely on the political party organisation and its agencies as sources of information while Progressives place heavier reliance upon ward agencies for their information. The most common means by which Labour partyworkers report hearing of the pubs and fees issues, for instance, is through the political party, and political party sources rank second to daily newspapers for Labour partyworkers on the parking and rates issues. For Progressive partyworkers both ward and political party agencies outrank daily newspapers as the original sources of information on the fees issue, but daily newspapers rank first on the

TABLE 4.6

How Progressive and Labour partyworkers heard about four current issues (percentages of Progressive and Labour partyworkers on each issue)

	Progressive				Labour			
	Pubs (per cent)	Fees (per cent)	Parking (per cent)	Rates (per cent)	Pubs (per cent)	Fees (per cent)	Parking (per cent)	Rates (per cent)
Daily newspapers	50	12	60	56	14	17	58	38
Sunday newspapers	—	6	4	6	—	—	—	—
Radio/TV	2	2	8	9	—	2	—	3
Word of mouth	6	4	13	6	11	14	7	6
Political parties	9	22	2	4	55	49	15	30
Ward agencies	19	49	2	4	11	6	3	2
Council and council agencies	9	2	10	17	2	2	12	9
Official actions	—	4	—	6	—	—	2	5
Through own efforts and dedication	—	—	—	—	2	—	—	6
DK, NA	6	—	2	—	6	9	3	2
	—	—	—	—	—	—	—	—
Total	101	101	101	102	101	99	100	101
Number who heard of issue*	54	51	52	54	64	63	60	64
Never heard†	—	6	4	—	—	2	6	—

*Percentages in upper portion of table are based upon this N.
†Percentages in lower portion of table are based upon 54 Progressive partyworkers, 64 Labour partyworkers.

three remaining issues. For Progressives, ward agencies rank second as original sources of information on the pubs issue, but word of mouth and contacts with council agencies respectively are the second most common sources of information about the parking and rates issues. For Labour partyworkers, general word of mouth is the third most common source of information on the pubs and fees issues, and contacts with council agencies are the third most common source on parking and rates. Only on the parking issue do a majority of Labour party-workers cite daily newspapers as their source; a majority of Progressives, however, cite daily newspapers on all but the school fees issue.

Party differences are also apparent in the councillors' reports of where they first heard about each issue (Table 4.7). Labour councillors show a much heavier reliance on the party organisation than do Progressives. The most common way in which Labour councillors report

TABLE 4.7

How Progressive and Labour councillors heard about issues (percentages of Progressive and Labour councillors on each issue)

	Progressive (N = 39)				Labour (N = 43)			
	Pubs (per cent)	Fees (per cent)	Parking (per cent)	Rates (per cent)	Pubs (per cent)	Fees (per cent)	Parking (per cent)	Rates (per cent)
Daily newspapers	5	28	13	15	2	2	—	—
Sunday newspapers	—	—	—	—	—	—	—	—
Radio/TV	—	—	—	—	—	—	—	—
Word of mouth	18	28	3	5	23	21	5	—
Political parties	8	5	8	—	37	49	26	30
Ward agencies	8	—	3	—	2	—	—	—
Council and council agencies	49	31	62	74	19	16	58	61
Official actions	—	3	3	3	5	—	—	—
Through own efforts and dedication	8	—	3	5	9	7	7	7
DK, NA	5	5	7	8	2	5	5	2
Total	101	100	102	100	99	100	101	100

having first heard of the pubs and school fees issues is through the party organisation – at council group meetings or at regular city or constituency party meetings. Party is the second most common way these same councillors heard of the other two issues, meters and rates. In contrast, for Progressive councillors, meetings or minutes of council bodies are the most common sources of information for every issue, while the party organisation is of little or no importance. For councillors in both parties, general word of mouth is an important source of initial information on the pubs and fees issues, and for Progressive councillors daily newspapers are cited as important sources of such information on the fees and parking issues. Daily newspapers are of only trivial importance to Labour councillors as sources of information.

GATHERING ADDITIONAL INFORMATION

The general thrust of the communication aspects of our model has thus far been confirmed by our data. The mass media provide most political information to electors and even to partyworkers. When the media do not provide this information alternative sources are usually found in a communications network within rather than between strata. Thus councillors, though not finding as much information as other strata in the media, find information from other councillors at least as often as they find it from contacts with members of other political strata.

Contrary to predictions, this pattern of information-seeking does not extend to electors' methods of gathering additional information about political issues nor to activists gathering information about the opinions other strata hold on such issues. Although the tendency is less pronounced among city councillors, the general pattern discovered is one of directly approaching members of other political strata. Let us now take a close look at the data.

In addition to being asked how they first heard about issues, for the pubs, fees and rates issues electors were asked how they might go about finding more information about the issue if they so desired. The results (Table 4.8) reflect a broad acceptance of the norms of participatory

TABLE 4.8

How electors would find out more about three current issues
(percentages of electors on each issue)

	Pubs (per cent)	Fees (per cent)	Rates (per cent)
Approach councillors	34	37	39
Corporation departments	9	22	13
Central government	3	4	3
Party association	1	2	2
Other associations	9	3	6
Public meetings	16	12	14
Individual research	18	15	15
Personal contact	9	6	7
	—	—	—
Total	99	101	99
Total number of responses★	536	543	575
Do nothing	6	5	4
Don't know	12	11	8
Not ascertained	1	1	2
	—	—	—
Total†	19	17	14

★Percentages in upper portion of table are based upon these totals.
†Percentages in lower portion of table are based upon 563 electors.

democracy on the part of electors, but they are somewhat incongruent with previous reports from electors on their sources of information.

As we discovered in the previous chapter, some 80 per cent of the electors have no idea who their councillors are. This does not stop them, however, from selecting direct approaches to councillors as the most common method by which they would attempt to find out more about each issue. From 34 to 39 per cent of the methods named for each issue cover approaches to councillors, about double the next most popular choice. Although over 60 per cent of the electors name the mass media as their best source of information about local politics, and a comparably high percentage name these media as the way they first heard of issues, when it comes to finding out more about these very same issues individual research (which includes perusing the newspapers and other media) ranks only second in popularity, comprising but 15 to 18 per cent of the methods chosen. Clearly, the democratic admonition to see one's representative overrides the inclination to use more thoroughly the means by which information ordinarily is gathered.

The third and fourth most common methods of gathering additional information also indicate an acceptance of participatory norms. Between 12 and 16 per cent of the responses suggest public meetings as the means to find out more about a given issue, and between 9 and 22 per cent of the responses suggest approaching corporation departments. The local party associations are rarely chosen as sources for additional information (only 2 per cent of the choices); other voluntary associations are far more common choices, and even approaching Members of Parliament or other representatives of the central government is a more popular method of gathering information. On average, only one elector in ten has no idea how to gather additional information about an issue, and only one in twenty admits to a preference not to seek any additional information at all.

Electors' widespread inclination to approach councillors directly or through public meetings stands in such striking contrast to their reported knowledge of councillors, and to the manner in which they report having actually acquired information, that it demands interpretation. The question posed was hypothetical, in that it asked how electors *would* acquire additional information if they wished to find out more about the issue. Interviewers moreover were instructed not to accept an initial response of 'nothing' or 'wouldn't want to', but to probe until some specific course of action was named. Thus while answers provide enlightenment on how electors *would* seek information once they were sufficiently roused, they do not reflect information-seeking behaviour on normal everyday issues. Our evidence on knowledge of councillors' names confirms this interpretation, for if 34 to 39 per cent of electors habitually approached a councillor direct, they might at least be expected to remember his name. Less than 20 per cent of our sample possessed this minimal information however, let alone knowledge of his position on current issues. We did not ask directly about electors' actual contact with councillors. But evidence from a 1965 survey of English local government electors reveals that only 17 per cent in county boroughs (most comparable with Glasgow) had ever in fact contacted a councillor.[109]

Certainly therefore electors' hypothetical modes of information-seeking reveal extensive acceptance of participatory norms, and also their potential for effective contact with other strata on an intensely-felt issue, like the important irreconcilable disagreements which we consider capable of shattering consensual processes of decision-making. But they do not seem to describe a present reality.

Instead of being asked how they would gather more information about issues, partyworkers were asked how they would gather more information about the opinions electors in their wards had about issues. Their replies (Table 4.9) reveal a penchant for direct informal contacts with electors as opposed to the formal mechanisms of the political party or other agencies. Between 41 and 47 per cent of the responses suggest asking citizens directly through canvassing, informal chatting and holding 'surgeries'; from 19 to 29 per cent of the responses suggest holding public meetings; but only 11 per cent of the responses suggest using the party agencies to find out about opinions. Similarly, going to a ward councillor, a city official or simply considering oneself an already knowledgeable political representative accounts for only 7 to 11 per cent of the responses. Practically every partyworker would actively solicit opinions; 4 per cent or fewer indicate that they would merely sit back and wait for constituents to come to them, and none is at a loss to say how he might proceed.

City councillors, in contrast to partyworkers, tend to rely more heavily upon formal channels of communication in order to assess constituents' opinions on the issues. The most frequently cited method, varying between 26 and 32 per cent of the responses, is finding out constituent opinions by conferring with other councillors, with corporation officials, or with activists with whom the city councillor

[109] *Maud Committee Report*, vol. 3, p. 52, Table 72.

TABLE 4.9

How partyworkers and councillors would find out more about constituents' opinions on four current issues (percentages of councillors' and partyworkers' responses on each issue)

	Partyworkers			Councillors			
	Pubs (per cent)	Fees (per cent)	Rates (per cent)	Pubs (per cent)	Fees (per cent)	Parking (per cent)	Rates (per cent)
Through being a political representative	11	7	10	26	32	31	30
Party agencies	11	11	11	10	10	10	8
Local leaders/people directly affected	3	1	—	2	4	2	2
Local organisations	5	5	6	22	14	12	16
Public meetings	19	29	23	20	22	19	20
See individuals directly	47	41	45	15	14	20	19
Mass media	—	1	1	1	2	2	3
Other personal contacts	5	5	5	3	2	2	2
Total	101	100	101	98	100	98	100
Total number of responses*	150	147	146	143	108	129	117
Do nothing	3	4	4	10	7	6	15
Don't know	—	—	—	1	—	1	1
No answer	1	—	—	—	—	2	1
Total†	4	4	4	11	7	9	17

*Percentages in upper portion of table are based upon these totals.

†Percentages in lower portion of table are based upon 118 partyworkers, 82 municipal councillors.

routinely has contact. An additional 12 to 22 per cent of the responses suggest going to local organisations, and 10 per cent of the responses suggest using the local party organisation. Direct contacts are still important, however. About 20 per cent of the responses for each issue cite public meetings as a method of finding out constituent opinion, and another 14 to 20 per cent of the responses recommend approaching constituents directly on a personal basis. Councillors are also more likely to say they would do nothing other than wait for constituents to approach them – the proportion adopting this position runs as high as 10 and 15 per cent respectively on the pubs and rates issues.

Differences in party affiliation are associated with some noteworthy variations in the patterns in which additional information is gathered by all three political strata. Among electors, Labour and Progressives both incline to approach councillors more directly than independents (Table 4.10). Independents, on the other hand, more commonly prefer

TABLE 4.10

How Progressive and Labour electors find out more about three current issues
(percentages of Progressive and Labour electors' responses on each issue)

	Progressive			Labour			Independent		
	Pubs (per cent)	Fees (per cent)	Rates (per cent)	Pubs (per cent)	Fees (per cent)	Rates (per cent)	Pubs (per cent)	Fees (per cent)	Rates (per cent)
Approach councillors	44	46	42	31	35	36	18	26	31
Corporation department or officials	4	20	13	11	21	13	16	21	15
Central government representative	3	3	3	3	3	3	2	10	2
Through parties	2	1	2	—	2	3	4	5	2
Local organisations	9	3	8	9	3	5	6	3	8
Public meetings	16	9	10	17	15	18	14	9	16
Individual research	13	12	16	17	15	15	33	19	20
Personal contact	8	6	8	11	5	7	6	7	7
Total	99	100	102	99	99	100	99	100	101
Total number of responses*	158	163	172	285	279	287	49	58	61
Do nothing	7	5	4	5	6	3	9	6	8
Don't know	8	10	5	12	10	9	26	17	14
No answer	1	—	1	1	1	2	—	1	3
Total†	16	15	10	18	17	14	35	24	25

*Percentages in upper portion of table are based upon these totals.
†Percentages in lower portion of table are based upon 164 Progressives, 290 Labour, 66 Independent-apolitical.

individual research as a method of seeking additional information than do partisan electors. Labour electors show a greater tendency than other electors to prefer public meetings as a method of gathering information, while Progressive electors prefer the direct approach to councillors more than any other group. In addition, Progressives are somewhat less likely to consider approaching corporation department officials than are other electors.

The differences between Labour and Progressive partyworkers are of a nature with which we are already familiar. Once again Labour partyworkers place more reliance upon party structure (Table 4.11).

TABLE 4.11

How Progressive and Labour partyworkers find out more about constituents' opinions on three current issues (percentages of Progressive and Labour partyworkers' responses on each issue)

	Progressive			Labour		
	Pubs (per cent)	Fees (per cent)	Rates (per cent)	Pubs (per cent)	Fees (per cent)	Rates (per cent)
Approach political activists	15	10	12	8	6	7
Party agencies	3	7	12	16	14	11
Local leaders/people directly affected	5	2	—	1	—	—
Local organisations	7	10	9	5	2	4
Public meetings	15	20	18	22	35	29
See individuals directly	54	48	49	42	36	41
Mass media	—	2	—	—	1	—
Other personal contacts	2	3	1	7	6	9
Total	101	102	101	101	100	101
Total number of responses*	61	61	70	88	86	76
Do nothing	4	6	2	2	3	5
Don't know	—	—	—	—	—	—
No answer	2	—	—	—	—	—
Total†	6	6	2	2	3	5

*Percentages in upper portion of table are based upon these totals.

†Percentages in lower portion of table are based upon 54 Progressive partyworkers, 64 Labour partyworkers.

F

From 11 to 16 per cent of the responses given by Labour partyworkers suggest using party agencies to gather information about electors' opinions while only 3 to 12 per cent of the Progressives suggest this method. Labour partyworkers are also more likely to suggest calling public meetings than are Progressive partyworkers. The Progressives, for their part, are more likely to name direct approaches to both electors and political activists in order to gain additional information about the opinions of electors in their wards.

The breakdown by party also reveals important differences between information-seeking habits of Progressive and Labour councillors (Table 4.12). In order to discover more about their constituents' opinions, Progressive councillors are more likely to favour conferring with other councillors and with corporation officials than are Labour party councillors. A minimum of one-third of the Progressive councillors' responses cite this method as compared to a maximum of one-fourth of the responses of Labour councillors.

Progressive councillors are no less likely to go directly to constituents than are Labour councillors (15 to 21 per cent of the Progressive responses v. 10 to 21 per cent for Labour) but on each issue a greater proportion of them (8 to 22 per cent v. 5 to 9 per cent) indicate that they would do nothing at all to find out more about their constituents' opinions. Labour councillors have a different pattern of responses. They tend to favour structured contacts with constituents. As a result, for every issue a greater proportion of Labour than Progressive responses fall into each of three categories – use of party agencies, contacts with non-political associations and summoning public meetings.

Breakdowns of the data by criteria other than party produce few interesting differences. As was the case with hearing about issues, electors classified by levels of education show no systematic differences in methods of finding out more about issues. Nor does being in high- rather than low-turnout wards make any systematic difference in the way electors seek more information about the issues.[110] Whether a

[110] The differences among electors by education are virtually nil. The average least squares correlation (r) of the distributions for each pairing (Over 15–Under 15, Over 15–15, Under 15–15) is once again over 0·95. For high- and low-turnout wards, however, the correlations are not so high – 0·65 for pubs, 0·86 for fees and 0·62 for rates. But the only systematic pattern to be found is that those electors in high-turnout wards suggest individual research more often than do electors in low-turnout wards. Those in low-turnout wards suggest using every other method more frequently than do those in high-turnout wards for at least one of the three issues, but never consistently for all three.

TABLE 4.12

How Progressive and Labour councillors find out more about constituents' opinion on four current issues (percentages of Progressive and Labour councillors' responses on each issue)

	Progressive				Labour			
	Pubs (per cent)	Fees (per cent)	Parking (per cent)	Rates (per cent)	Pubs (per cent)	Fees (per cent)	Parking (per cent)	Rates (per cent)
Through being a political representative	34	45	38	39	19	22	24	22
Party agencies	6	2	6	4	15	17	14	11
Local leaders/people directly affected	4	4	2	—	—	3	3	3
Local organisations	19	8	11	11	25	19	14	21
Public meetings	16	16	17	19	24	27	22	22
See individuals directly	15	28	21	17	15	10	19	21
Mass media	1	2	5	7	1	2	—	—
Other personal contacts	4	4	2	4	1	—	3	0
Total	99	99	102	101	100	100	99	100
Total number of responses*	68	49	66	54	75	59	63	63
Do nothing	11	11	8	22	9	5	5	9
Don't know	—	—	—	—	2	2	2	2
Not ascertained	—	—	—	—	—	—	5	2
Total†	11	11	8	22	11	7	12	13

* Percentages in upper portion of table are based upon these totals.
† Percentages in lower portion of table are based upon 39 Progressive councillors (including Dean of Guild and Deacon Convener) and 43 Labour councillors.

partyworker is from a high- or low-turnout ward also makes little difference to the ways in which he would seek to find out more about how electors in his ward think. Even for councillors every important difference associated with being in a high- or low-turnout ward can be attributed to the fact that most councillors in high-turnout wards are Progressives and most in low-turnout wards are Labour.[111]

A final breakdown of the data by self-ascribed representative roles yielded only one result worth discussing. For all but the rates issue, in comparison with councillors with primarily city-wide orientations, a smaller proportion of councillors with primarily ward orientations said they would do nothing to find out more about what their constituents were thinking. Actual percentages range from 3 to 5 per cent of ward-oriented councillors compared to 9 to 16 per cent of the city-oriented. When the manner in which councillors of each type said they would find out more about constituents' opinions was compared, however, there were practically no differences at all.[112]

PARTYWORKERS AND THE PROBLEM OF POLITICAL LINKAGE

Much has been made of the vital role that local party organisation can play in linking electors to their representatives. Among other things, it is argued that a good partyworker can sound out constituent opinion and relay this information to the electors' representatives. Relaying information in the other direction, he can offer advice on how to deal with the government and can help make government services more personalised and responsive to the problems of the citizens.[113]

[111] See Chapter 3 (Table 3.20) for the partisanship of activists in high- and low-turnout wards. The correlations between the responses of partyworkers in high- and low-turnout wards average 0·94 across the three issues about which partyworkers were asked. The correlations are equally high between the responses of Progressive party councillors and councillors in high-turnout wards. The average correlation between the responses of Labour councillors and councillors in low-turnout wards, however, is somewhat smaller: r equals 0·88 over all issues except rates, but it only equals 0·68 for this latter issue. The main differences on rates appear to be a greater willingness on the part of councillors in low-turnout wards to see individuals directly (33 per cent), accompanied by a lesser willingness to approach other activists (14 per cent) or local organisations other than the party (5 per cent).

[112] The correlations between the responses of councillors with ward-role orientations and those with city-role orientations is as follows: pubs, 0·92; fees, 0·91; parking, 0·92; rates, 0·96.

[113] Cf. Jean Blondel, *Voters, Parties and Leaders*, chap. 3; Peter G. J. Pulzer, *Political Representation and Elections*, chap. 3; Samuel J. Eldersveld, *Political Parties: A Behavioral Analysis* (Chicago, 1964) chaps 3, 4, 14; Frank Sorauf, *Political Parties in America* (Boston, 1964) chap. 6.

This sort of picture, however, does not coincide with stratification predictions. We expect instead that partyworkers will be more insular; that their communication will be mostly within, not between, strata; that usually, therefore, they will not perform the functions of an idealised partyworker like the one described above. Let us look at the relevant data.

Partyworkers were asked whether they had discussed each issue with anyone in the last few months. Only for rates did a majority report having had a recent discussion in the past months (Table 4.13), but a substantial portion of workers (35-43 per cent) had also discussed either the pubs, fees or meters issues.

TABLE 4.13

Partyworkers' discussion of four current issues (percentages of all partyworkers, of Progressive and Labour partyworkers and of partyworkers in high- and low-turnout wards reporting discussion in past month on each issue)

	Pubs (per cent)	Fees (per cent)	Parking (per cent)	Rates (per cent)
All (N = 118)	36	43	35	55
Progressives (N = 54)	30	22	33	55
Labour (N = 64)	41	61	36	55
High-turnout wards (N = 41)	54	59	51	54
Low-turnout wards (N = 35)	20	37	20	54

Two interesting breakdowns in the data can be made. First, on all issues Labour partyworkers reported as great or greater frequency of discussion in recent months than did their Progressive counterparts; and second, for high-turnout wards on all issues over 50 per cent of the partyworkers indicate having had a discussion, while for low-turnout wards, with the exception of the rates issue, less than 37 per cent of the workers report having had such discussions. The first set of findings is consistent with our previous observations that Labour partyworkers rely more heavily upon non-media sources for their political information; the second is consistent with expectations of our theory that interested and active electors (found more frequently in high-turnout wards) will stimulate more political communication between strata.

Additional information indicating whether discussions take place within or between strata is included in Table 4.14. Looking first at the data for all partyworkers, it is clear that most workers who did have

TABLE 4.14

Persons with whom partyworkers discussed four current issues (percentages of all partyworkers, of Progressive and Labour partyworkers and of partyworkers in high- and low-turnout wards)

	Pubs (per cent)	Fees (per cent)	Parking (per cent)	Rates (per cent)
All (N = 118)				
Discussion only with activists*	28	32	25	42
Discussion only with electors	6	3	6	8
Discussion with activists and electors	2	7	3	6
Progressives (N = 54)				
Discussion only with activists*	21	17	23	40
Discussion only with electors	7	—	9	7
Discussion with activists and electors	2	6	2	7
Labour (N = 64)				
Discussion only with activists*	34	45	30	43
Discussion only with electors	5	6	3	8
Discussion with activists and electors	2	8	3	5
High-turnout wards (N = 41)				
Discussion only with activists*	44	36	33	39
Discussion only with electors	7	5	12	12
Discussion with activists and electors	2	17	5	5
Low-turnout wards (N = 35)				
Discussion only with activists*	15	35	11	38
Discussion only with electors	6	—	6	9
Discussion with activists and electors	—	3	3	9

*Activists are councillors, corporation officials, partyworkers, and friends and family of partyworkers.

discussions in recent months communicated with members of active or more active political strata – their own primary groups and friends,[114] fellow partyworkers, councillors and corporation officials. Even although we have included the leaders of community organisations among electors contacted by partyworkers, only a small proportion of partyworkers have engaged in such discussions. The average proportion performing a linkage function – talking with both higher activists and electors – is even smaller. Although a majority of workers in both

[114] Our presumption is that relatives and associates of workers are themselves likely to be politically active.

parties reported discussion with activists, for each issue the proportion of Labour workers mentioning such discussion was greater than of Progressives. (This more frequent within-stratum communication appears to reflect the stronger more integrative structure of the Labour party.) The greater proportions of workers reporting discussion on all issues with electors, or with electors and activists, in high-turnout compared with low-turnout wards, is again consistent with expectations.[115]

Only one in four partyworkers of either party report never having had any contact with the councillors from their ward (Table 4.15). Labour partyworkers, however, report more frequent contacts – 60 per cent report having contacts 'often' or 'very often' as opposed to only 45 per cent of the Progressives. The content of the contacts also differs

TABLE 4.15

Partyworkers' contacts with ward councillors (percentages of all partyworkers, of Progressive and Labour partyworkers, and of their contacts with councillors)

| | Frequency of Contacts | | | | |
	Very often (per cent)	Often (per cent)	Occasionally (per cent)	Never (per cent)	Total (per cent)
All (N = 118)	34	19	20	27	100
Progressives (N = 54)	30	15	30	26	101
Labour (N = 64)	38	22	13	28	101

| | Content of Contacts | | | | | |
	Current services and general problems (per cent)	Specific political problems (per cent)	Electoral matters (per cent)	Organisation (per cent)	Ward committee (per cent)	Other (per cent)	Total (per cent)
All (N = 134)	44	31	7	5	11	2	100
Progressives (N = 52)	50	25	8	4	10	4	101
Labour (N = 82)	40	35	6	6	12	—	100

[115] A breakdown of our data by both party *and* high- and low-turnout wards shows however that the contrast between high- and low-turnout wards in regard to the proportions discussing issues with electors does not appear with regard to the parking and particularly the rates issue (9 per cent compared to 10 per cent and 9 per cent compared to 19 per cent respectively). More important, the proportion of workers discussing the issue exclusively with activists is greater than the proportion contacting electors in only three out of the eight comparisons possible with Progressives in high- and low-turnout wards over the four issues.

slightly by party. Labour partyworkers are more likely to discuss specific problems of political policy while Progressives tend to discuss city services and politics in general more frequently. The frequency of contact is not greater for partyworkers in high- as opposed to low-turnout wards. In fact, only 23 per cent in low-turnout wards report no contacts with councillors as compared to 32 per cent of the partyworkers in high-turnout wards. Similarly a greater percentage of workers in low-turnout wards (69 per cent) than in high-turnout wards (49 per cent) say they have contacts 'often' or 'very often'. Nor does the content of the contacts differ greatly in high- v. low-turnout wards. The only notable differences are that workers in high-turnout wards tend to have fewer contacts concerning current services and a greater number of contacts concerning electoral matters than do partyworkers in low-turnout wards. Since these contacts take place among activists and not between activists and electors these findings have no direct bearing on our stratification model.

Only 14 per cent of the partyworkers report never having had any contact with the city party organisation, but there are large differences by party with regard to this behaviour (Table 4.16). Only 5 per cent

TABLE 4.16

Partyworkers' contacts with city party organisations (percentages of all party-workers, Progressive and Labour partyworkers, and of their contacts with city party)

	Very often (per cent)	Often (per cent)	Occasion-ally (per cent)	Never (per cent)	Total (per cent)
All (N = 118)	31	19	36	14	100
Progressives (N = 54)	22	15	39	24	100
Labour (N = 64)	38	23	34	5	100

Frequency of Contacts (header spans Very often, Often, Occasionally, Never, Total)

	Policy matters (per cent)	Elec-tions (per cent)	Organi-sation (per cent)	Help consti-tuents (per cent)	Other (per cent)	Total (per cent)
All (N = 147)	35	29	21	7	7	99
Progressives (N = 54)	26	43	7	9	15	100
Labour (N = 93)	41	20	29	6	3	100

Content of Contacts

of the Labour partyworkers as opposed to 24 per cent of the Progressives report no contacts, and over six in ten Labour workers as opposed to fewer than four in ten Progressives described the frequency of their contacts as 'often' or 'very often'. The content of the contacts also differs. Labour party contacts most frequently concern matters of policy or of political organisation while the most common subjects of Progressive party contacts are elections. In response to a related question, 60 per cent of the Labour partyworkers in contrast to only 9 per cent of the Progressive partyworkers report having sent a resolution to the city party at one time or another.

Except for the fact that relatively fewer partyworkers in low-turnout than in high-turnout wards report never having had any contact with the city party organisations, frequency of contact does not otherwise seem affected by high- or low-ward turnout. But both policy and election matters are discussed more frequently in high- as opposed to low-turnout wards; in contrast, organisational matters are discussed more frequently in low-turnout wards.

Seven out of ten partyworkers report having given advice or help to their constituents (Table 4.17). There are no significant differences between the parties with regard to this. Seventy-seven per cent of the advice concerned legal matters, and another 18 per cent dealt with putting electors in contact with councillors, corporation officials or the ward committee (representative functions). Only 5 per cent of the contacts concerned political advice. Progressive partyworkers tended to give a little more political advice and a little less legal advice than did Labour partyworkers, but the differences are not great.

Voting turnout is associated with some systematic differences with regard to the frequency with which political advice is given and the content of that advice. Only 24 per cent of the partyworkers in high-turnout wards as compared to 34 per cent of those in low-turnout wards report never having given any help or advice to a constituent. This finding ties in with a difference in the role-perceptions of workers in high-turnout as opposed to low-turnout wards: 39 per cent in high-turnout wards as opposed to 37 per cent in medium-turnout wards and only 13 per cent in low-turnout wards saw contact with constituents as a major task. The content of the advice actually given in high-turnout wards was almost all legal, but in low-turnout wards significant portions of the contact involved performance of representative functions, or political advice.

In considering the relevance to our model of activists' contacts with

TABLE 4.17

Partyworkers – help or advice given electors (percentages of all partyworkers, of Progressive and Labour partyworkers and of partyworkers in high- and low-turnout wards, and of their contacts with electors)

	Gave advice (per cent)	Occurrence of Contacts Never gave advice (per cent)	Total (per cent)
All (N = 118)	70	30	100
Progressives (N = 54)	69	31	100
Labour (N = 64)	72	28	100
High-turnout wards (N = 41)	76	24	100
Low-turnout wards (N = 35)	66	34	100

	Legal advice (per cent)	Content of Contacts Concerning representative functions (per cent)	Political advice (per cent)	Total (per cent)
All (N = 166)	77	18	5	100
Progressives (N = 64)	70	20	9	99
Labour (N = 102)	80	17	3	100
High-turnout wards (N = 63)	83	11	6	100
Low-turnout wards (N = 35)	49	37	14	100

electors, and the relationships just discussed of partyworkers with electors and councillors, we must again attempt to reconcile seemingly conflicting evidence. On the one hand we have electors' testimony (Table 4.8) that even when sufficiently roused by an issue to seek additional information they would tend to consult councillors or to attend public meetings, all but ignoring workers staffing the party agencies. If this pattern of information-seeking would prevail on intensely-felt issues it is plausible to assume that contacts are even less on day-to-day issues. On the other hand (Table 4.9) partyworkers much more than councillors incline to approach electors directly to find out about their opinions. And (Table 4.17) two-thirds of partyworkers recall actual advice given to electors. (It also appears however that much of this advice related to constituents' personal problems and not to wider political issues.)

The divergent testimony of electors about their contacts with party-workers and of partyworkers about their contacts with electors can be reconciled by presuming, in line with initial expectations, that electors in contact with partyworkers are a minority more oppressed by problems and therefore more politically active than average. Probably this is also the case with electors in contact with councillors on a day-to-day basis. Activists' appraisals of constituency opinion formed from these contacts would thus tend to inaccuracy when applied to the mass of constituents – as in fact we have found them to be (Tables 3.9 and 3.13). Seen in this light the findings on contacts between strata fit the actual patterns of information-giving and receiving found on current issues, which we discussed in the earlier part of the present chapter. It also fits general expectations, in that information-exchanges between activists and electors are limited and subject to error.

On looking back it is nevertheless clear that our model tended to underrate the ability of partyworkers to provide linkage between electors and their representatives. Most partyworkers have reasonably frequent contacts with both councillors and electors. Moreover, a substantial portion of these contacts concern the representation of constituents' problems or opinions to councillors or the explanation and adjustment of governmental regulations for constituents.

SUMMARY

In this chapter we have looked at the manner in which members of our three political strata receive and relay political information. As predicted by our model, the ordinary channels through which both electors and partyworkers receive information about politics in general are the mass media, but the quantity and the quality of the sources differ between strata. As expected, partyworkers seek more and better information than do electors – they read a greater number of newspapers and magazines, and they tune in to more television and radio news; they read the better-quality press, and they watch the BBC. And when it comes to seeking information about politics, partyworkers again differ from electors: to get their information they call upon personal contacts with the party organisation and with municipal councillors while electors tend still to rely upon the mass media.

When electors and partyworkers are asked about how they first heard of four current issues, the predicted patterns again appear. A majority of electors report having first heard of each issue in the media, and in spite of their general reliance upon the media, a majority of partyworkers report having first heard of the pubs and fees issues through personal contacts with party, ward or council agencies. In contrast to both electors and partyworkers, hardly any municipal councillors report having first heard of the pubs, meters or rates issues through the mass media; and even for fees, the mass media still rank behind party and council agencies and word of mouth in order of importance.

Among none of the strata do we find evidence of opinion leaders customarily funnelling information from the mass media or other sources to the general electorate.

In terms of its ability to predict how electors, partyworkers and councillors attempt to find out more about issues or about each other's opinions our model is less successful. Despite their general reliance upon the mass media for political information, most electors declare themselves ready to approach councillors or corporation departments or to attend public meetings when they want to find out more about local issues. Far from talking just among themselves and to other activists, most partyworkers propose summoning public meetings, seeing individual electors directly, or approaching non-party organisations in order to seek out constituents' opinions. None the less, the stratification model did successfully predict more frequent discussion of issues by partyworkers and more frequent contacts between partyworkers and electors in high- as compared to low-turnout wards.

Throughout the chapter the effects of party affiliation and of education on communication patterns were also discussed. Among electors, the information-seeking habits of Progressive and of the more educated tended to resemble the habits of partyworkers more closely than did the information-seeking habits of other electors. Among partyworkers and councillors, however, Labour party members appeared better informed on the issues and more in touch with their constituents. In addition, Labour partyworkers and councillors report using the party organisation as a source of information far more frequently than do Progressive partyworkers and councillors.

5. Differentiated Agreement

Our initial concern with the support given to democracy prompted us in Chapter 3 to a further analysis of fundamental procedural relationships as they manifest themselves in Glasgow, this time an analysis of relationships between electors and elected. Although representation gains a key interest from the light it sheds upon the functioning of democracy, the investigation led to a test of many predictions about the agreement of political strata. These derive from assumptions in the right-hand chain of Fig. 1.1, which relate less to the democratic nature of the polity than to the conditions necessary for the continuance of democratic practices. The reasoning summarised in the assumptions leads to the expectation that political activists will display more integrative behaviour than other groups, in the absence of salient and irreconcilable disagreements, and that they will consequently agree more than other groups in their issue-preferences and general political appraisals. This is not to say that activists will agree more on *every* such preference and appraisal – on the contrary we assume that they will agree less than other groups on issues related to party competition. But it is to say that they will agree more than other groups on the *majority* of preferences and appraisals.

In the last two chapters these predictions have had fair success. Certainly on the prior assumption that integrative behaviour is necessary to promote agreement, the main thrust of the communication data is to confirm that activists interact more within their own strata, and that under normal circumstances contacts between activists and electors are limited. These patterns of communication seem to affect factual appraisals: in Chapter 3 we discovered that councillors, partyworkers and electors hold very inaccurate ideas about each others' opinions, but that activists' perceptions at any rate are more accurate in high- than in low-turnout wards where they are in closer contact with electors (Tables 3.19 and 3.21). And on all five current issues examined electors agreed on preferences more with each other across party than with members of other strata. However there is one inconsistent finding: activists agreed across party only to the same extent as they agreed with other strata, and then only on three out of the five issues (Tables 3.5–3.7). It is true our model anticipated that activists would agree more only on a majority of issues – on a minority, party competition would divide activists more than electors. But even on the three where such activist agreement existed it was not uniquely high.

The tests of the agreement hypotheses carried out in Chapter 3 are not conclusive, for two reasons. First, the technical constraints necessitated by concise comparisons of activists' and electors' opinions through product-movement correlations prevented us utilising the full information at our disposal, even about preferences on the five issues examined. In order to reach final conclusions about relative agreement we must consider the intensity as well as the direction of these issue-preferences. Secondly, much other Glasgow data about both preferences and appraisals exist in a form which makes correlation analysis difficult. Other techniques can however be evolved to assess relative agreement and in this chapter we will try to apply them to all data at our disposal. Here therefore we attempt an answer to two questions central to our model. Is political agreement differentiated in the way we anticipate – that is to say do councillors agree more than party-workers than electors? And have relative prosperity and declining socioeconomic division in Glasgow really served to eliminate important, irreconcilable disagreements among all these groups, as must be the case if our assumptions are valid?

The type of agreement examined here differs from that discussed in the previous chapters. In comparing agreement on democratic procedures we looked at the excess of support for such procedures over the opposition they evoked. In examining representation we noted the majority opinion of each group and saw if they were all the same. These other discussions are thus concerned not only with the varying tendency of different groups to give a common response but also with the nature of that response – the extent to which the most popular responses are the same. Their concern is with agreement *on* some point, what we term directed agreement. Here on the other hand the interest is with agreement pure and simple, what we term non-directed agreement; that is, with the varying tendency of different groups to give a common response, which need not be the same for each group. For example, if one group is 70–30 in favour of some procedure while another is 70–30 against we shall in this discussion count them as equally agreed. For the percentage difference between majority and minority endorsements in each case is 40 and this indicates that both groups cluster to the same extent on a common response. All the techniques employed in this chapter attempt to estimate this tendency to group on a single reply. But some are necessarily more complicated than others because of the greater complexity of the data used as the basis for estimation.

Our discussion begins with the most straightforward responses (dichotomised issue-preferences with intensity rankings) which permit a relatively simple comparison of non-directed agreement. We then discuss the estimation of such agreement on preferences or appraisals where each respondent makes one choice out of a number of broad alternatives. We go on from this case to one where a single respondent makes several choices out of eight to eleven broad alternatives; first, second and third choices being noted as such.[116] In both cases we illustrate the technique by presenting a particular distribution and using the method discussed to estimate agreement. However, because of the sheer amount of data relevant to this analysis it will be possible to present separate tables only for these examples and for distributions of particular interest. Our conclusions about the ordering of agreement among councillors, partyworkers and electors will be based on summary tables, which record the final results of estimations, made through the methods described on various appraisals and preferences.[117] Discussion will be aided by use of the summary statistic we have termed a success ratio. For in estimating the success of the agreement hypotheses over a variety of responses all regarded as indicators of the two underlying phenomena of preferential and factual agreement, we face the same problem of summarising the main trends in our findings as confronted us in Chapter 2. Tests of the Representation and Communications models, being focused on a narrower set of data, did not present the same problem: nor will the discussion of politicians' autonomy and party competition in Chapter 6. In Chapter 2 we made use of the success ratio as a summary measure of the model's success over all data. This gave a fraction produced by subtracting the number of predictive failures from the number of predictive successes, and dividing by their sum. A predictive failure is any comparison on which councillors,

[116] Comparisons of non-directed agreement on a variety of data are discussed in detail in Budge, *Agreement*, chaps 3 and 12.

[117] Many of the distributions of appraisals and preferences mentioned in these summary tables have been presented in full in preceding chapters. The others are presented in full or summary form, and their substantive implications for Glasgow politics discussed, in chaps 6 and 7 of *Class, Religion*.

Fig. 5.1 Preferential Agreement on Five Current Issues (Percentages of Councillors, Partyworkers, Electors And Non-voters)

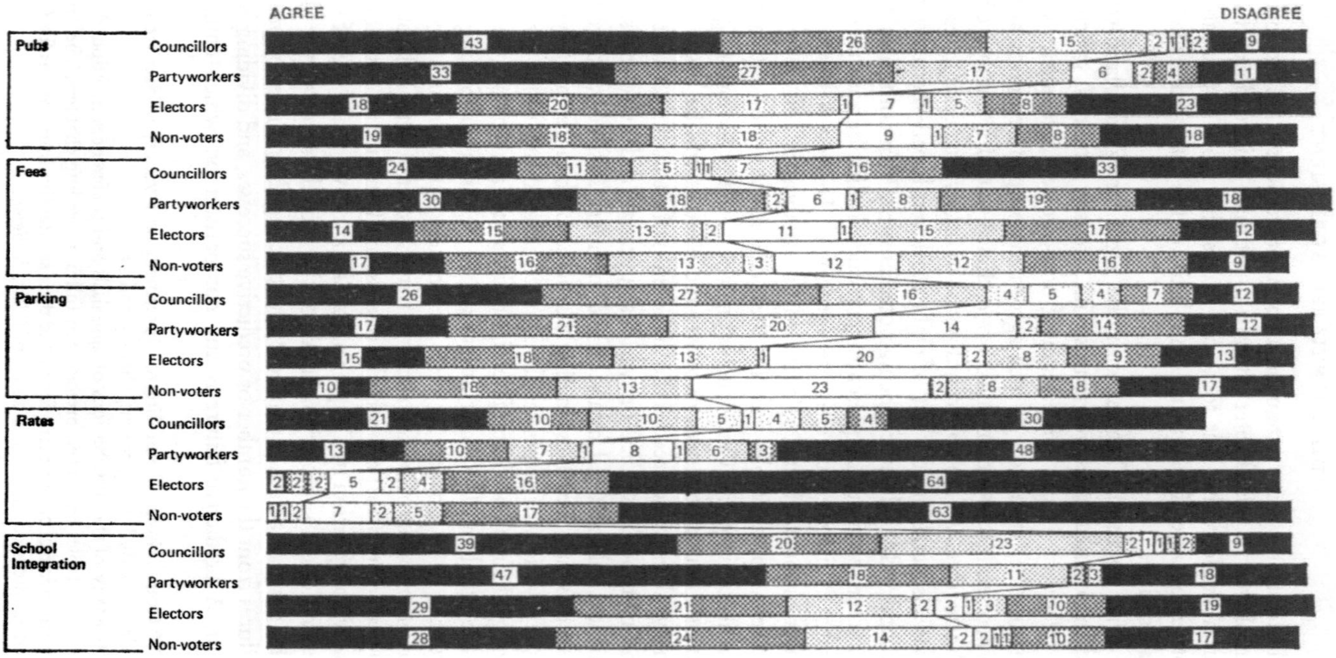

AGREE — DISAGREE

Pubs
- Councillors: 43, 26, 15, 2,1,1,2, 9
- Partyworkers: 33, 27, 17, 6, 2,1, 11
- Electors: 18, 20, 17, 1,5,1,1, 8, 2,4, 23
- Non-voters: 19, 18, 18, 9,1,7, 8, 18

Fees
- Councillors: 24, 7, 16, 33
- Partyworkers: 30, 18, 2,6,1, 8, 19, 18
- Electors: 14, 15, 13, 2, 11, 1,15, 17, 12
- Non-voters: 17, 16, 13, 3, 12, 16, 9

Parking
- Councillors: 26, 27, 20, 16, 4, 12
- Partyworkers: 17, 21, 20, 14, 2,1, 14, 12
- Electors: 15, 18, 13, 1,1, 20, 2, 8, 9, 13
- Non-voters: 10, 18, 13, 23, 2,1, 8, 8, 17

Rates
- Councillors: 21, 10, 10, 5,1,4, 5, 4, 30
- Partyworkers: 13, 7, 8, 1,6, 3, 48
- Electors: 16, 4, 64
- Non-voters: 17, 5, 63

School Integration
- Councillors: 39, 20, 23, 2,1,1,2, 9
- Partyworkers: 47, 21, 18, 11, 2,3, 18
- Electors: 29, 12, 2,3,1, 3, 10, 19
- Non-voters: 28, 14, 2,1,1, 10, 17

The survey questions which prompted respondents' preferences reported in Fig. 5.1 were as follows: Would you say that you agreed or disagreed with this proposal?

Introduction of pubs into corporation housing estates; stopping the payment of fees in some corporation schools; extension of parking-meters all over the city centre; increase in rates; mixing of Catholic· and Protestant children together in the same schools.

Would you say that this is an issue you felt very strongly about, fairly strongly about, or not strongly at all? In the figure very strong feeling is signified by the solid block.■■■ : fairly strong feeling by the heavily-toned block ▨▨▨: not strong feeling by the medium-toned block ⋯⋯; uncertain feeling (don't know how strong) by the lighter block ⋮⋮ . Those endorsing the proposal with these various degrees of feeling are placed on the left of the zigzag line which divides the figure. Respondents on the right-hand side of this· zigzag line either reject the proposal with similar gradations in feeling or adopt a neutral position signified by the unfilled block ▭ which is always placed between those who agree and those who disagree. The figures which appear in the middle of each block are the percentages of respondents in each sample who adopt that position. Percentages in this and following figures do not always add to 100 percent, partly because of rounding, but also because the figure does not report the varying (but small) percentages of respondents from whom no relevant answer could be obtained. On the increase in rates 10 per cent of councillors and 3 percent of partyworkers replied that the increase was inevitable and so agreement or disagreement was irrelevant. Since this response was peculiar to the rates issue it is not shown in the figure.

partyworkers and electors do not fall into the order anticipated: a predictive success is any comparison on which these groups do fall into the theoretically anticipated order; and the sum of failures and successes is the total number of unambiguous comparisons. Success ratios are of course simply a textual aid to estimating the success of our model, which readers can assess for themselves from the summary tables.

Following the general discussion of non–directed agreement centring around the summary tables we shall consider two topics of exceptional theoretical interest. One is the determination of whether in fact irreconcilable disagreement is absent from preferences on the most important problem facing Glasgow – the assumption on which analysis has been proceeding up to this point.[118] The second is a comparison between the views of municipal correspondents and of councillors, designed to reveal whether their agreement is indeed closer than that of

[118] Empirical confirmation of the assumption had to be delayed to this chapter because the technicalities of assessing agreement have to be discussed first.

correspondents and partyworkers, or correspondents and electors, as postulated by the stratification model.

PREFERENCES ON FIVE CURRENT ISSUES

We make a detailed estimate of non-directed agreement on the five current issues presented in Fig. 5.1 because these constitute the main data-set for which we have information about the intensity with which issue-preferences are endorsed, and because findings here link up with previous chapters where responses on these same issues were examined from the viewpoint of procedures, representation and communication.

It is immediately obvious from the distributions of opinion that the predicted order of agreement – councillors, partyworkers, electors – holds on pubs and parking and is diametrically reversed on rates. The decisions about agreement on fees and school integration are less clear. All groups show extensive internal disagreement on fees but electors clearly show most – almost equal numbers agree strongly and fairly strongly, as strongly and fairly strongly disagree. The opposition of fairly equal numbers with strong feelings is much less marked among partyworkers and councillors.[119] Both these groups can be regarded as more agreed than electors, therefore. The difficulty arises when we try to decide whether councillors are more agreed than partyworkers. Councillors with the strongest feelings split more evenly between agreement and disagreement than do comparable partyworkers. But councillors with reasonably strong feelings and councillors as a whole split less evenly than do their counterparts. This inconsistency is summarised in the percentage differences which exist between those with strong feelings, strong and fairly strong feelings, and all those who agree and disagree (Table 5.1).

We are forced to take all these differences into account because we do not know whether the views of all persons in each group count equally in the resolution of the issue, or whether the major influence rests with those who feel reasonably strongly or simply with those who feel most strongly. Where a vote is taken all persons will count equally. But where the decisions are those of a restricted committee or where lobbying assumes prominence the more intensely motivated are likely to press

[119] The absence of any strong feeling among larger numbers of electors might of course eventually cushion the effects of the more marked disagreement in their ranks (V. O. Key, *Public Opinion*, p. 71). But the possible ultimate cushioning effect of apathy does not affect the finding that when interviewed they were less agreed, in our sense of agreement.

TABLE 5.1

Preferential agreement on five current issues (percentage differences between the proportion of councillors, partyworkers, electors and non-voters, agreeing and disagreeing, agreeing and disagreeing very strongly and fairly strongly, agreeing and disagreeing very strongly)

	Percentage difference between proportions agreeing/disagreeing	Percentage difference between proportions agreeing/disagreeing very strongly and fairly strongly	Percentage difference between proportions agreeing/disagreeing very strongly
Pubs			
All councillors	73	57	34
All partyworkers	60	45	22
All electors	20	8	—4
All non-voters	23	11	1
Fees			
All councillors	15	13	9
All partyworkers	3	11	12
All electors	—2	—	2
All non-voters	12	8	8
Parking			
All councillors	48	33	13
All partyworkers	31	12	5
All electors	15	11	2
All non-voters	8	3	—7
Rates			
All councillors	—3	3	9
All partyworkers	28	29	36
All electors	80	76	62
All non-voters	82	77	62
Integration			
All councillors	71	48	31
All partyworkers	53	44	30
All electors	30	21	10
All non-voters	38	25	11

Table 5.1 should be read in conjunction with Fig. 5.1, whose bearings on agreement it elucidates. Entries consist of percentage differences between various proportions reported in Fig. 5.1. The larger the percentage difference the greater the tendency for respondents' answers to cluster on one of the preferences under review. The negative signs attached to particular entries signify that the difference on this comparison is in the opposite direction to the difference on the two other comparisons. Thus negative signs are one indication of low agreement.

their points with greater effect. Not knowing which way the question will be resolved we must take all splits equally into account. Thus if all percentage differences for one group are higher than those for another we can safely decide that the first group is more agreed. If some differences are higher for one contrast and some for the other – as for councillors and partyworkers on fees – we must regard the comparison as inconclusive.[120]

The percentage differences for school integration show councillors as more agreed than partyworkers in spite of the fact that more party-workers than councillors agree strongly with the proposal. For more partyworkers also disagree strongly. Both groups agree more than do electors on this proposal.

On all issues but parking non-voters agree more than electors as a whole – and therefore more than voters. This result is the opposite of the expected ordering. However it must be qualified in view of the known inaccuracy of replies to the question on voting. The group of nominal voters contains many actual non-voters, whose presence must on our assumptions weaken the agreement of the group.[121] Thus the fact that self-admitted non-voters agree more than nominal voters, although it suggests a weakness in our model, is not wholly conclusive. For this reason we shall not include the comparisons of other groups with non-voters in our estimates of success ratios.

With this omission the success ratio for the predicted order of agree-ment on these five issues comes to 0·57, which is not exceptionally high. On this occasion however a crucial point is concealed by the use of a statistic which summarises the success of the model over all issues. The point is that the predicted ordering emerges on all conclusive compari-sons on four out of five of the issues. It is the complete reversal of the prediction on rates that depresses the value of the success ratio. Now we have already noted that on our assumptions councillors should agree more than partyworkers, and partyworkers than electors, on the majority but not all of their issue-preferences, and so the undoubted emergence of this order on four out of five issues suffices to uphold the prediction.

A similar consideration applies to comparisons of agreement under party controls. No definite decision can be made on the agreement of Progressive councillors compared with partyworkers on fees, of

---

[120] Alternative measures of agreement on these issues are discussed and results compared with those from the method of proportions in Chapter 6 n. 157.

[121] For this finding see Appendix A, Table A.1.

TABLE 5.2

Preferential agreement on five current issues among Progressives (percentage differences between the proportion of councillors, partyworkers and electors, agreeing and disagreeing, agreeing and disagreeing very strongly and fairly strongly, agreeing and disagreeing very strongly)

	Percentage difference between proportions agreeing/disagreeing	Percentage difference between proportions agreeing/disagreeing very strongly and fairly strongly	Percentage difference between proportions agreeing/disagreeing very strongly
Pubs			
Prog. councillors	55	42	29
Prog. partyworkers	39	26	13
Prog. electors	—13	3	13
Fees			
Prog. councillors	71	63	53
Prog. partyworkers	83	69	31
Prog. electors	28	15	7
Parking			
Prog. councillors	24	18	—
Prog. partyworkers	34	14	6
Prog. electors	12	8	1
Rates			
Prog. councillors	79	66	60
Prog. partyworkers	80	78	78
Prog. electors	91	88	74
Integration			
Prog. councillors	87	58	39
Prog. partyworkers	39	28	13
Prog. electors	37	26	8

Table 5.2 summarises distributions of issue preferences for Progressives similar to those reported for total strata in Fig. 5.1. Its other features are described in the notes to Table 5.1.

Progressive councillors compared with either partyworkers or electors on parking, or of Progressive partyworkers compared with electors on rates, because the various percentage differences support different conclusions. All the comparisons that can be undertaken on pubs, fees, parking and school integration fall into the predicted order of councillors–partyworkers–electors. On the two comparisons possible on rates

TABLE 5.3

Preferential agreement on five current issues among Labour (percentage differences between the proportion of councillors, partyworkers and electors, agreeing and disagreeing, agreeing and disagreeing very strongly and fairly strongly, agreeing and disagreeing very strongly)

	Percentage difference between proportions agreeing/disagreeing	Percentage difference between proportions agreeing/disagreeing very strongly and fairly strongly	Percentage differences between proportions agreeing/disagreeing very strongly
Pubs			
Lab. councillors	88	70	37
Lab. partyworkers	78	61	30
Lab. electors	23	14	—
Fees			
Lab. councillors	40	33	30
Lab. partyworkers	80	78	48
Lab. electors	14	9	7
Parking			
Lab. councillors	70	44	26
Lab. partyworkers	28	11	5
Lab. electors	20	15	4
Rates			
Lab. councillors	77	53	37
Lab. partyworkers	8	12	—
Lab. electors	72	69	58
Integration			
Lab. councillors	56	37	23
Lab. partyworkers	65	58	40
Lab. electors	25	17	11

Table 5.3 summarises distributions of issue preferences for Labour similar to those reported for total strata in Fig. 5.1. Its other features are described in the notes to Table 5.1.

councillors again appear as less agreed than partyworkers or electors.

Comparisons between Labour partyworkers and electors on parking, and between Labour councillors and electors on rates, are inconclusive. The remaining comparisons fall into a slightly different pattern from that which emerges for the total groups and for Progressives. Labour councillors agree more than partyworkers on rates. And they agree less than partyworkers on both fees and school integration. In so far as any general tendency can be discerned over all comparisons it is however for the predicted order of agreement to hold.

The success ratio for the predicted ordering over all definite comparisons in Tables 5.1, 5.2 and 5.3 is 0·58, practically the same as for comparisons of the total groups alone. It is more illuminating however to note that the predicted ordering holds for almost all possible comparisons over four issues: it consistently fails on rates. On the majority of issue-preferences compared here, therefore, councillors do emerge as more agreed than partyworkers, and partyworkers than electors, and this is all that the model anticipated.

APPRAISALS OF GROUPS WITH UNDUE INFLUENCE IN GLASGOW: ESTIMATION OF NON-DIRECTED AGREEMENT WHERE A SINGLE CHOICE IS MADE OUT OF A RANGE OF ALTERNATIVES

Agreement on appraisals (i.e. factual judgements) of politics is important because it can affect both preferences and action on issues. We have already seen that a political representative's desire to reflect the preferences of his constituents can be quite vitiated by an inability to ascertain accurately what these preferences are. Similarly even where there is preferential agreement, a disagreement on appraisals (e.g. of the order of priority in which problems should be tackled) can be sufficient to destroy any possibility of united action.[122]

Non-directed agreement on dichotomised appraisals of the current issues just discussed,[123] especially on party stands in relation to these issues, can be estimated in exactly the same way as it was for preferences on the issues. Table 5.7 will summarise the bearing of agreements actually discovered on these appraisals on our expectation that activists will agree more than electors.

There are many other sets of data from which agreement on appraisals can be estimated, which are not related to these issues and which require somewhat different methods of estimation. Many of these data relate to more general appraisals of Glasgow politics than the issue-appraisals mentioned above, and some have already been encountered in Chapter 2. There they provide indications of the support given by activists and electors to democratic procedures. Here in the discussion

---

[122] For an extended argument on these lines see Budge, *Agreement*, chap. 2.

[123] Dichotomised in the sense that respondents were asked in relation to each party whether it was for or against the stated proposal on each issue.

of non-directed agreement we are not concerned with the pro- or anti-democratic nature of appraisals but simply with the extent to which each group makes the same appraisal.

The employment of different methods of estimation is necessitated by the form in which appraisals have been given. Up to this point we have been dealing with a limited range of reactions to a stated proposition, e.g. do you agree or disagree with the proposal to introduce pubs into corporation housing estates? Does the Labour party agree or disagree with this proposal, or has it no opinion? The distributions resulting from these questions cluster on agree or disagree or neutral, with the intensity of agreement or disagreement added on occasion.

One criterion for the ranking of councillors, partyworkers and electors on their agreement about groups exercising undue influence in Glasgow is indeed provided by a dichotomised distribution of the kind described. For it is apparent from Table 2.11 where the full distribution is presented, that sizeable numbers in each stratum think no group exercises undue influence. Thus we cannot assess agreement solely on the basis of the proportions naming each specific group. Equally however it would make little sense to assess agreement on a combined distribution where 'none' was regarded as an answer equivalent to naming a specific group. The relevant initial comparison is between the proportions saying 'no group' and those naming 'some group'.

Never the less we cannot fully decide who agrees most on these appraisals without going on to look at the various substantive appraisals separately, and seeing which group clusters its replies most markedly upon one such appraisal. Only if a group emerges as more agreed on initial comparisons of naming 'no group' or 'some group' in Table 2.11 *and* on the comparison of proportions making the most popular substantive replies in Table 5.4 will it be counted as more agreed on its total appraisals of groups exerting undue influence. Should the two comparisons support different conclusions the decision as to which is more agreed must be abandoned as inconclusive.

The question remains however of how to estimate agreement from the proportions in each stratum naming about twelve specific groups as exercising undue influence. The point of real interest – just as with the previous distributions – is the extent to which larger numbers in one group than in another focus upon one specific group to the exclusion of others. Any estimation procedure must also guard against the possibility that one group's answers do cluster more than another's, but in relatively equal numbers upon two different appraisals; for in

TABLE 5.4

Agreement on appraisals of groups with undue influence in Glasgow (percentages of councillors, partyworkers, electors and non-voters saying no such groups exist and saying that some do: percentages of councillors, partyworkers, electors and non-voters naming either of the two groups most popular in each group and the difference between these percentages)

Group	Per cent saying no group exists	Per cent making any positive appraisal	Order of popu- larity	Substantive appraisal	Per cent endorse- ment	Per- centage differ- ence
All councillors	48	52	1	Labour Party as a whole	17	
			2	Labour Council group	10	7
All partyworkers	31	55	1	Labour Party as a whole	14	
			2	Economic interests	11	3
All electors	19	43	1	Economic interests	10	
			2	Friends, relatives of councillors	4	6
All non-voters	15	40	1	Economic interests	11	
			2	Friends, relatives of councillors	5	6
Prog. councillors	26	74	1	Labour Party as a whole	29	
			2	Labour Council group	21	8
Prog. party- workers	15	70	1	Labour Party as a whole	30	
			2	{ Labour Council group	13	17
				Economic interests	13	
Prog. electors	19	44	1	Economic interests	11	
			2	Labour Council group	5	6
Lab. councillors	65	35	1	Labour Party as a whole	7	
			2	{ Corporation officials	5	
				{ Economic interests	5	2
				{ Religious groups	5	
Lab. partyworkers	44	46	1	Religious groups	17	
			2	Economic interests	9	8
Lab. electors	19	42	1	Economic interests	10	
			2	Friends, relatives of councillors	5	5

Table 5.4 summarises the bearings of Table 2.11 upon the non-directed agreement of the various strata. Non-directed agreement on this appraisal is estimated both on the initial proportions saying that groups with undue influence do or do not exist and in regard to the difference between the two largest proportions naming different groups as exercising that undue influence. All proportions are presented as percentages of the total number of councillors, partyworkers, electors and non-voters or as percentages of the number in each party group of councillors, partyworkers and electors.

such a case the first group cannot be said to agree more. A measure which records the tendency to cluster while reflecting an even split in the group between two different appraisals is the percentage differences we have previously been using: calculated in this case however as the difference between the proportions of a group endorsing the most popular and the second most popular appraisals in the group. Only two percentage differences need thus be considered in estimating agreement on appraisals of groups with undue influence: the difference between the proportions replying 'no group' or 'some group' in Table 2.11 and between the proportions endorsing the two most popular appraisals in Table 5.4.

In actual fact percentage differences between the substantive appraisals are so nearly equal, at any rate for the total groups, that decisions should be made mainly on the initial comparison. Here the predicted order is completely reversed, with electors agreeing equally with partyworkers and both more than councillors. (Non-voters agree slightly more than electors and hence than voters.) Among Progressives, partyworkers agree more than councillors and councillors than electors. The comparisons of Labour councillors and partyworkers and Labour electors and partyworkers are inconclusive because of the substantial contradiction between the two percentage differences. But Labour electors can be judged to agree more than the corresponding partyworkers. The success ratio for comparisons on this appraisal is really a failure ratio, since it assumes the negative value of -0.30. On this appraisal we should have had more predictive success had we proceeded at random rather than on our theoretical assumptions.

Non-directed agreement can be assessed by the method just described for other appraisals of Glasgow government already encountered in Chapter 2, such as appraisals of who runs Glasgow, and the existence of favouritism. The method can also be applied to likes and dislikes about the Glasgow parties, where agreement on substantive likes and dislikes is considered alongside the tendency to like or dislike 'nothing' as opposed to 'something' (Table 2.7). The relative agreement of councillors, partyworkers and electors on these appraisals is reported in Table 5.8 below.

APPRAISALS OF EFFECTS FROM THE DISAPPEARANCE OF GLASGOW PARTIES:
ESTIMATION OF NON-DIRECTED AGREEMENT WHERE SEVERAL CHOICES ARE
MADE OUT OF A RANGE OF ALTERNATIVES

The question of what would happen if there were no parties on the corporation nominally relates to future changes in procedures. Actually, as we emphasised in Chapter 2, it brings out views on the part presently played by the parties in city government.

Although the appraisal has much the same substantive import as those just considered it raises additional methodological problems. On the question of which groups have undue influence we estimated agreement on answers where each respondent had the opportunity to mention as many definite appraisals as he wished but where the great majority only mentioned one. We were thus able to ignore the slight overlapping of answers introduced by second appraisals and after-thoughts since these could not materially affect the conclusions reached from comparing the mutually exclusive first responses. But on the changes resulting from the disappearance of parties many if not most interviewees contributed two or three appraisals. We could of course still decide the ordering of agreement as we have with the previous appraisals – on initial answers only. But this would be throwing away valuable and necessary evidence by ignoring the possibility that respondents who had given initially different appraisals might converge towards each others' viewpoint on later replies. Such a tendency, besides showing a greater clustering of responses than was originally apparent, also indicates that for respondents the different appraisals initially endorsed are not so very far apart – are in fact quite compatible and capable of being advocated simultaneously. And this additional consideration must also be brought into the assessment of agreement.

One way of handling a number of replies given consecutively by the same respondents is to throw them into a multiple-response distribution from which we can retrieve the tendency of different groups to give two mutually exclusive sets of replies, or to focus on the same set.[124] A negative objection to proceeding this way stems from the danger – with our data – of double-counting. In order to facilitate analysis by other investigators who are bound to have different interests, we grouped replies initially into a large number of detailed categories, as close as possible to the answers framed by respondents themselves. But any set of answers must appear as a more or less random scatter when a large number of detailed categories are used. Besides, many of the detailed categories are closely related so that it is unrealistic to regard them as entirely different. Consequently we combine them into broader and more sharply distinguished groupings for presentation in the tables and for estimating agreement. But if we then throw first and second responses into the same distribution, a person who has been coded as endorsing two of the separate detailed categories which now form the same broader appraisal will be recorded twice as supporting that broader appraisal.

[124] Two procedures by which this could be done are discussed in Budge, *Agreement*, chap. 3 and Appendix B.

A more positive objection to the combination of all replies into one multiple-response distribution relates to the wastage of information entailed in such a procedure. Such analysis ignores the distinction between answers given first, second and third. It is important to discover whether group-members who give initially different responses converge in their subsequent replies. But it is equally important to discover if they diverge in their first and possibly most salient response, for this divergence may have equal importance for agreement.

On the basis of all these considerations the best initial approach to data where second and third replies occur in large numbers seems to be that adopted for appraisals of groups with undue influence on Glasgow government. The distribution of first replies must be examined to discover the extent of clustering on the two most popular appraisals, and the percentage difference between these two clusters must be estimated. However the decision as to which group is in greater agreement should not be made simply on the basis of these figures but also on the tendency of persons making the most popular and the second most popular replies to mention the other as a second or third alternative. This tendency can be measured by proportions for 'degree of overlap' – i.e. the proportions of all those making the most popular and the second most popular reply on their initial response who name the other reply on their second and third responses.

The appearance of the first table (5.5) reporting these summary statistics (percentages in each group endorsing the most popular and second most popular replies on their initial response, the difference between them, and the 'degree of overlap') can be compared with the full distributions for both the first and second replies on which it is based, since these have already been presented in Table 2.8. The estimation of agreement on the basis of these summary statistics can thus be compared with the results which would be obtained by detailed examination of all pertinent distributions relating to changes if parties disappeared.

The figures of Table 5.5 are contradictory for the comparison of all councillors and all electors since councillors split more evenly between two different initial appraisals, but unlike electors have some members who endorse both of the two most popular initial appraisals at some point. This applies also to comparisons between both sets of Progressive activists and their electors, and to Labour partyworkers and electors. In these cases comparisons must be abandoned as inconclusive. All councillors appear less agreed than all partyworkers and similarly

TABLE 5.5

Agreement on appraisals of changes if there were no parties on Glasgow corporation (percentages of councillors, partyworkers and electors naming the changes most popular among each group on first mention and the differences between these percentages: proportions of those in each group out of those naming either of the two most popular changes on first mention who name the other most popular change on their second mention, i.e. degree of overlap)

Group	Order of popu- larity	Substantive appraisal	First- mention per cent endorse- ment	Per- centage differ- ence	Second- mention degree of overlap
All councillors	1	Parties promote efficiency	33	5	0·16
	2	Parties are inevitable	28		
All partyworkers	1	Without parties politics more disinterested	30	14	0·20
	2	Parties necessary to democracy	16		
All electors	1	Without parties politics more disinterested	34	23	0·00
	2	Parties are inevitable	11		
Prog. councillors	1	Without parties politics more disinterested	45	19	0·11
	2	Parties are inevitable	26		
Prog. partyworkers	1	Without parties politics more disinterested	54	28	0·21
	2	Without parties government more businesslike	26		
Prog. electors	1	Without parties politics more disinterested	45	34	0·00
	2	Parties are inevitable / Parties necessary to democracy	9 / 9		
Lab. councillors	1	Parties promote efficiency	53	23	0·22
	2	Parties are inevitable	30		
Lab. partyworkers	1	Parties necessary to democracy	27	7	0·20
	2	Parties promote efficiency	20		
Lab. electors	1	Without parties politics more disinterested	26	12	0·00
	2	Parties are inevitable	14		

Table 5.5 summarises the bearings of Table 2.8 upon the non-directed agreement of the various groups, which is estimated here through the percentage differences and degree of overlap on the second mention. (Third mentions are very few and can be ignored.) Non-voters' agreement can be roughly estimated from Table 2.8.

among Progressives; among Labour the reverse is the case. Labour councillors, both in their initial appraisals and in their tendency to overlap appear more agreed than Labour electors – indeed are most agreed of all groups. Not surprisingly in view of these mixed results the success ratio for our model over all conclusive comparisons is zero.

The responses on which non-directed agreement must be assessed, through the percentage differences and degrees of overlap just mentioned, constitute the bulk of the evidence we shall present in the summary tables immediately below. They include preferences on two potential issues, i.e. topics on which no proposals for immediate action were being made but which could move later to the centre of political debate. The actual responses classed below as potential issues are preferences on changes in Glasgow government (Table 2.5) and on the roles of councillors (Table 3.1). Non-directed agreement was ascertained by the same method on a whole sequence of appraisals and preferences on the most important problems seen as facing Glasgow – the types of problem, more exact appraisals of their nature, preferences for action upon them.[125]

Agreement on the action respondents would take to gain their political demands (Table 6.8) is also considered, for a group may agree on most other aspects of an issue and yet be paralysed between the different strategies considered appropriate to realise its common goals. A last group of appraisals on which agreement is assessed relate to voting behaviour, a very central topic for activists whose own political potency is bound up with the electoral success of their party.[126] The voting appraisals consist in part of assessments of class structure and of the constitution of the social classes, on which agreement is estimated through percentage differences and degrees of overlap in the manner just described, and in part of dichotomised appraisals of the party most class members and most Catholics and Protestants will support,[127] on which agreement is assessed through the simple percentage differences employed in Tables 5.1, 5.2 and 5.3.

OVERALL ANALYSIS OF NON-DIRECTED AGREEMENT AMONG COUNCILLORS, PARTYWORKERS AND ELECTORS

Having specified the three differing but related methods through which we have assessed the comparative agreement of councillors, partyworkers and electors, we now present the final results of these assessments over all relevant data from our Glasgow surveys. Our discussion concerns itself with two points: first, the usefulness of the

[125] The substantive bearings for Glasgow politics of these appraisals and preferences are discussed in *Class, Religion*, chap. 7.

[126] This in fact is Assumption X of our model: a test of this assumption is presented in Chapter 6 below.

[127] A full discussion and analysis of perceived class structure in Glasgow is presented in *Class, Religion*, chap. 2: voting appraisals are considered in chap. 7.

TABLE 5.6

Success of the Stratification Model in predicting the ordering of non-directed agreement upon current issue preferences

Issues	Ordering of agreement for:		
	Total groups	Progressive groups	Labour groups
Pubs	3/3	3/3	3/3
Fees	2/2	2/2	2/3
Parking	3/3	1/1	2/2
Rates	0/3	0/2	1/2
School integration	3/3	3/3	2/3
Housing problem	0/1	—	0/1
Finance problem	0/1	1/1	0/1
Traffic problem	0/1	0/1	0/1
Education problem	1/1	1/1	1/1
Most important problem facing Glasgow	4/5	—	—

Success ratio over all current issues = 0·41
Number of issues where the results of all, or all but one, comparison are as predicted = 6/10

Table 5.6 summarises the emergence of the predicted order of agreement for all conclusive paired comparisons carried out on the five sets of issue preferences presented in Fig. 5.1 and Tables 5.1, 5.2 and 5.3 and for preferences on the important problems seen as facing Glasgow. The first entry in each cell of Table 5.6 is the number of successes: the second is the total number of conclusive comparisons. Blank entries result from inconclusive comparisons or comparisons not carried out under a party control.

The questions and procedures which elicited the types of important problems facing Glasgow are as follows: In general, what do you think are the most important problems facing Glasgow corporation at the moment? Which of these do you think is the most important problem, the one the corporation should try to take care of first? Which do you think is the second most important problem? Which do you think is the third most important problem, etc.? In coding types of problems named, responses were coded into thirty-five detailed categories which were, however, so grouped as to facilitate easy grouping into eleven broader categories used in the estimation of general agreement. For example, 'housing, redevelopment' groups – problems of housing upkeep, administration of housing lists, corporation rents, rehousing, slum-clearance, overpopulation, overspill, planning, redevelopment; 'Finance' groups — money, debts and economics of city, rates; 'Education' groups — educational administration, classroom over-crowding, quality, etc.; 'Traffic' groups – street congestion, road-planning, etc. These four areas were the ones identified by most councillors, partyworkers and electors as containing important problems facing Glasgow.

Once the type of problem was identified in an answer to any of the questions mentioned above, respondents were asked, 'What would you like to see the corporation do about that?' Regardless of whether any problem was named as first, second or third most important, preferences were combined and used to estimate non-directed agreement. Preferences were coded into thirty detailed categories which were the same for all types of problem mentioned (i.e. finance, traffic, education, housing) and these were subsequently

combined into fourteen broader categories for the purpose of estimating general agreement. For example, 'expand programmes' includes expressions of satisfaction with present
policy (which is directed to expansion), demands to increase expenditure, subsidise,
extension of existing programmes and initiation of new programmes. 'Get other sources
of revenue' embraces suggestions that the central government should help alleviate the
problem, financially and materially. 'Improve administration' refers to reviews of old
procedures and adoption of new procedures, better co-ordination, planning and service,
revision of priorities, provision of more power to personnel and improvement of the
qualifications of administrators. Only partyworkers and electors are compared on preferences about important problems, since councillors were not asked for their preferences on
the second and third most important problems.

stratification model of relative agreement, with and without a party
control: second, the extent to which ties of party increase agreement
within the different political strata, since party loyalties constitute the
most plausible alternative explanation of agreement to that provided by
activism.

We have supposed that the absence of irreconcilable important disagreement increases agreement among politically active groups,
relative to other groups, upon current issue-preferences generally. We
shall inquire whether such disagreement is actually absent below. On
the assumption that it is absent the success ratio of 0·41 over all current
issue-preferences is moderately good – it is much more useful in predicting agreement to have the model than to be without. Moreover
this value is pulled down by the fact that the model obviously does not
apply to preferences on rates, nor on the housing, finance and traffic
problems where partyworkers (the only activists involved in the comparison) show notably less unanimity than electors. The model does not
of course need to cover all issues in terms of our assumptions – which
are that political activity will, under prevailing conditions, be associated with relative preferential agreement only on a majority of current
issues, as in fact it is.

The success of the model on preferences about current issues is
paralleled by its ability to predict the ordering of agreement on appraisals of current issues. The ordering on most of these appraisals falls
into the expected pattern and this is reflected in a high success ratio of
0·62. The better performance of the theory on issue-appraisals as compared to issue-preferences bears out one finding from the analysis of
representation.

We anticipated however that political activity would be associated
with relative agreement not only for issue-appraisals but for a majority
of all political appraisals. However on general appraisals of parties and
government the success ratio falls to 0·19. The assumptions of the model

are still helpful here, but to a limited degree that points to the necessity of further explanations of these patterns. One point to note is that on

TABLE 5.7

Success of the Stratification Model in predicting the ordering of non-directed agreement upon appraisals of current issues

| | Ordering of agreement for: | | |
Appraisals of:	Total groups	Progressive groups	Labour groups
Existence of four current issues	4/4	4/4	4/4
Party stands on four current issues	6/8	7/8	6/8
Types of important problem	3/3	3/3	3/3
Nature of important problems	6/9	7/10	8/12
Popular preferences on the most important problem	1/1	—	—
Strategic action on four current issues	2/2	2/3	3/3

Success ratio over all current issues = 0·62
Number of appraisals where the results of all, or all but one, comparisons are as predicted = 4/6

Table 5.7 summarises the emergence of the predicted order of agreement for all conclusive paired comparisons carried out on the appraisals specified. The four current issues are the pubs, fees, parking-meters and rates issues, already considered. Existence of the issue was ascertained by the question: 'Have you heard of the (proposal)?' The question on party stands is described in n. 123 and text above. Strategic action on these four current issues is described in the notes to Table 6.8 below.

Types of important problem were ascertained through the questions mentioned in notes to Table 5.6. Besides naming the types of problem they considered important, respondents were encouraged to comment on the circumstances which made the topic a problem. These comments were taken verbatim and subsequently coded into twenty-nine detailed categories separate from those used to describe the type of problem. These categories were the same for all types of problem and thus the eleven broader categories used to estimate agreement are the same for the nature of the housing problem, for the nature of the finance problem, for the nature of the traffic problem, and for the nature of the education problem. Up to three responses (as distinguished by our detailed codes) were reported for each respondent. No distinction was made in estimating agreement between comments of respondents who regarded housing, finance, education or traffic as the most important problem, second most important problem, third most important, etc. Broad categories are, for example: 'Insufficient expenditure', which refers to shortages of personnel and equipment as well as purely monetary shortfalls; 'Planning and administration bad', which includes references to the necessary powers which personnel in the area lack; 'Discrimination', which in this area refers mainly to the fact that certain people, e.g. persons with large families or old-age pensioners have no provision made for them; 'Other sources of revenue', which consist largely of comments that the central government should give more aid to the corporation.

Appraisals of popular preferences on the most important problem are described in the text of Chapter 6.

G

TABLE 5.8

Success of the Stratification Model in predicting the ordering of non-directed agreement upon general political appraisals

	Ordering of agreement for:		
Appraisals of:	Total groups	Progressive groups	Labour groups
Glasgow parties	3/3	1/2	3/4
Glasgow government	2/6	3/6	4/6

Success ratio over all appraisals = 0·19

Table 5.8 summarises the emergence of the predicted order of agreement for all conclusive paired comparisons carried out on the responses reported in Tables 2.7, 2.8, 2.9 and 2.11.

appraisals of parties the model is quite successful, the success ratio being 0·55. Its inadequacy relates almost entirely to appraisals of government where the success ratio is 0·00. Political activity appears insufficient to explain non-directed as well as directed agreement on those topics.

TABLE 5.9

Success of the Stratification Model in predicting the ordering of non-directed agreement upon appraisals related to voting behaviour

	Ordering of agreement for:		
Appraisals of:	Total groups	Progressive groups	Labour groups
Religious voting	3/6	2/6	4/6
Class voting	2/6	1/6	2/6
Class description	6/7	6/7	5/7
Types of classes	2/3	2/3	2/3

Success ratio over all appraisals = 0·22
Number of appraisals where the results of all, or all but one, comparison are as predicted = 0

Table 5.9 summarises the emergence of the predicted order of agreement for all conclusive paired comparisons carried out on responses to the following questions: 'In local elections which party would you say most Protestants (Catholics) are likely to vote for?' (religious voting); 'In local elections which party would you say most working-class (middle-class) people are likely to vote for? (class voting); 'Do you ever think of yourself as being in a (social class)?'; (if yes) 'What class is that?'; (if No) 'Well, if you had to make a choice what class would you call yourself? What other classes would you say there were?' (types of classes); 'How would you describe people in the . . . class?' (class description). Responses to all these questions are discussed in detail in *Class, Religion*, chaps 2 and 6.

Other general political appraisals on which we predicted the association of activity with agreement were those related to class and voting. The moderate success ratio of 0·22 over all these appraisals masks the total failure of the model over direct appraisals of class and religious voting for the parties (where the success ratio is —0·17).

We expected the relative agreement of councillors and partyworkers on current issue-preferences and appraisals to lead to their greater agreement on potential issues, i.e. topics not yet current. This expectation was handsomely confirmed by a success ratio of 0·80 on the two potential issues examined.

TABLE 5.10

Success of the Stratification Model in predicting the ordering of non-directed agreement upon potential issue preferences

| | | Ordering of agreement for: | |
Issues	Total groups	Progressive groups	Labour groups
Changes in Glasgow government	2/2	2/2	2/2
Responsibilities of councillors	2/2	2/2	2/3

Success ratio over all preferences = 0·85
Number of issues where the results of all, or all but one, comparison are as predicted = 2/2

Table 5.10 summarises the emergence of the predicted order of agreement for all conclusive paired comparisons carried out on the responses reported in Tables 2.5, 2.6 and 3.1.

Overall therefore our model can be regarded as confirmed in its assertions about issue-preferences. In a strictly formal sense it is also confirmed in what it says about councillors' and partyworkers' greater agreement on appraisals, for on the majority of all appraisals considered here it performs quite adequately. However it is obvious that its success is heavily concentrated in the area of issue-appraisals, while in other areas such as government and voting behaviour it is positively misleading. The result of these tests must be to limit the assertions of the model on political appraisals, while preserving the main thread of the argument which runs from greater agreement on current issue-preferences and issue-appraisals to greater agreement on potential issues and hence to fewer irreconcilable disagreements in the future.

The evidence points clearly to the model's inability to predict and explain the pattern of agreement on the minority of political issues and

TABLE 5.11

Non-directed agreement among party groups compared with total groups on preferences on nine current issues and two potential issues

	Current issues									Potential issues	
	Pubs	Fees	Parking	Rates	School integration	Housing problem	Finance problem	Traffic problem	Education problem	Changes in Glasgow government	What councillors should do
Prog. councillors	−	+	−	+	+					○	○
Prog. partyworkers	−	+	+	+	−	○	+	−	−	+	○
Prog. electors	−	+	+	+	+	○	−	○	−	○	−
Lab. councillors	+	+	−	−	−					○	○
Lab. partyworkers	+	+	−	−	+	−	−	+	+	×	○
Lab. electors	×	+	+	−	−	○	−	+	+		+

Entries compare non-directed agreement inside each party group with agreement inside the total groups: + indicates that party agreement rises; − that it falls; ○ that it remains the same; × that the comparison is inconclusive. Blank cells result from the fact that no data existed on councillors' agreement on the current issues reported here.

on some general political appraisals. Can an alternative explanation be found in the influence of party? One way to find out is to see if non-directed agreement is greater within each party grouping compared with agreement among the total strata.

Among the five current issues originally considered (Tables 5.1, 5.2, 5.3) party exerts its most consistent effects on agreements on fees and rates. In the case of fees the ordering both within the parties and without them is consistent with the stratification model, increasing with activity. Party increases agreement inside each stratum but does not cut across the ordering. On rates it is the Progressives who consistently increase their agreement but again this overall increase leaves the original ordering as it was.

Examination of preferences on the remaining issues reveals no tendency for party to increase agreement consistently where the predicted ordering breaks down (that is to say, on the housing, finance and traffic problems). The sharpest effects of party are seen on traffic and education equally, but in fact education is the issue where the actual ordering of agreement corresponds perfectly to political activity.

TABLE 5.12

Non-directed agreement among party groups compared with total groups on appraisals of current issues

	Existence of issue	Party stands on issue P.F.		PG.		R.		Types of important problem	Nature of important problems				Strategic action on issues
	P	P	LP	L	PL	P	L		H.	F.	T.	E.	
Prog. councillors								−	−	+	−	−	+
Prog. partyworkers	O	+	−	−	−	O+	++	−	−	+	O	−	−
Prog. electors	O	−	O+	+	++	+	+	−	−	−	O	−	O
Lab. councillors		+	++	+	O+	−	+	+	+	+	O	O	+
Lab. partyworkers	O	+	++	+	O+	−	+	+	+	−	O	+	+
Lab. electors	O	+	OO	+	O−	+	−	+	O	+	O	+	O

Entries under 'Existence of Issue' summarise results for all four issues. Under 'Party Stands on Issue' P. = pubs, F. = fees, PG. = parking, R. = rates. The sub-title P stands for Progressives and L for Labour. Under 'Nature of Important Problems' H. = housing, F. = finance, T. = traffic, E. = education. Actual cell-entries are explained in the notes to Table 5. 11.

The same is true of issue-appraisals. Party certainly increases agreement in four out of six cases on the nature of the finance problem, where our model does poorly, but also on many appraisals of party stands on issues where it did well.

TABLE 5.13

Non-directed agreement among party groups compared with total groups on general political appraisals

	Appraisals of Glasgow parties				Appraisals of Glasgow government			
	Like Progs.	Like Lab.	Dislike Progs.	Dislike Lab.	Influence of groups	Job Favour- itism	Who runs Glasgow	If no parties
Prog. councillors					+			+
Prog. party- workers	+	−	−	−	+	−	+	+
Prog. electors	−	×	+	+	O	+	+	+
Lab. councillors					+			+
Lab. party- workers	−	+	+	×	−	+	−	−
Lab. electors	×	+	×	×	O	O	−	−

See notes to Tables 5.11 and 5.12.

Even in the area of general political appraisals where our model did least well, the effects of party are as often to decrease as to increase agreement; and this conclusion applies also to appraisals of voting behaviour. These appraisals constitute an interesting example, for it is obvious from the original responses[128] that party affects answers by making councillors and partyworkers particularly unwilling to concede groups to their political opponents. Progressives in the case of the working class and Catholics, and Labour with the middle class, are more likely to say that the group splits its vote. Thus the direction of agreement is powerfully affected by party. Its effect is however to increase non-directed agreement where adherents are laying claim to a group which actually does support them, but simultaneously to decrease agreement among the opposing adherents, some of whom realistically acknowledge that the group in question does support the other side while others refuse to cede it even verbally. Party as such is, in short, not as good a general predictor of non-directed agreement as political activity.[129]

[128] Reported in full in *Class, Religion*, chaps 7 and 8.

[129] A further control – very relevant to our model – which can be imposed upon councillors' preferences on the issues in Tables 5.1, 5.2, 5.3, relates to the length of time they have served upon the council. On the assumption that integrative behaviour promotes agreement, one can reason that the longer-serving members will be more integrated and therefore will be more agreed than those who have served for a shorter time. When preferences on four of these current issues were analysed we discovered the agreement of the longest-serving councillors – those who had entered in the 1930s and 1940s – decreased on pubs and fees although it

This conclusion helps counterbalance the mixed findings of Chapter 3 on directed agreement among the activist strata and the negative findings of Chapter 2 on activist support for democratic procedures. It is now possible to argue that Glasgow democracy works because of the general agreement of activists on the problems they face, rather than

---

increased on parking and rates: the agreement of the shortest-serving councillors – those entered in the 1960's – decreased on pubs, fees and parking although it increased on rates: while the agreement of the medium-serving councillors – those entered in the 1950s – increased on pubs, fees and parking and decreased on rates. The evidence thus supports the idea that shortest-serving councillors agree least over all the issues, but hints at the existence of a curvilinear rather than a purely linear relationship between length of council service and agreement, since the agreement of medium-serving councillors increases slightly more than that of longest-serving councillors over all issues. This pattern is still susceptible to interpretation in terms of the effects of integrative behaviour. The less extensive agreement of shortest-serving councillors may be attributed to their relatively fewer contacts and exposure to their fellows. We can also argue that the longest-serving councillors, being physically older and less able to keep up with affairs, may actually be reducing contacts with their fellows. The medium-serving councillors may well be the persons who have not only made their contacts but preserve the energy and desire to follow them up: they may perhaps be the most integrated group on the council and hence the most agreed.

Comparisons between the undifferentiated groups of councillors who have served varying periods may prove misleading. For the party balance shifts sharply inside each service group, reflecting the predominance of Progressives or Labour at the particular time of entry. Comparisons of agreement between the various service groups inside each party reveals that the less extensive agreement of shorter-serving councillors is evident only among Progressives (on pubs, fees and parking their agreement decreases, only on rates does it increase). Too few Progressives in our sample entered the Council in the thirties or forties to say whether the contrast between longest- and medium-serving councillors holds. Agreement among the shortest-serving Labour councillors actually increases on pubs, fees and rates and decreases only on parking, by comparison with longer-serving Labour councillors. It may be that corporation experience exposes councillors more and more to conservative influences – reluctance to disturb the established routine, financial constraints. In the party more attached to ideals of the extension of services and higher expenditures these influences may with time provoke greater discord, as some councillors stick to their original ideas and others succumb to council influences. The younger Labour councillors would in this case exhibit greater agreement precisely because they have been exposed for a shorter time to these inhibiting influences. Among Progressives however the conservative atmosphere of the corporation may simply reinforce existing ideas, so that longer-serving members show stronger agreement.

This discussion bears only peripherally upon the effect of integrative behaviour on agreement, since results are open to several interpretations. For more direct tests see Chapter 6.

TABLE 5.14

Non-directed agreement among party groups compared with total groups on appraisals related to voting behaviour

	Working-class vote	Middle-class vote	Protestant vote	Catholic vote	Appraisal of: People in working class	People in middle class	People in upper class	Types of class
Prog. councillors	−	+	−	−	+	−	−	−
Prog. partyworkers	−	+	+	+	+	−	−	−
Prog. electors	−	+	+	+	O	+	−	−
Lab. councillors	+	−	+	+	−	−	−	+
Lab. partyworkers	+	−	+	−	−	×	−	+
Lab. electors	+	O	O	+	+	+	−	+

See notes to Tables 5.11 and 5.12.

through their direct support for governmental procedures. Such a view has many difficulties, however, and these will be considered fully in our conclusions.

Irreconcilable disagreement: preferences on the problem considered most important

In analysing preferences on the four problems regarded as important by most respondents we found no tendency to disagreements which could be regarded as irreconcilable. Different alternatives were endorsed by activists in the two parties but these alternatives could, without difficulty, be combined as aspects of a common programme. Even on finance, which offers a potential arena for the most bitter clash, opposition developed between Progressive partyworkers' preference for straight cost-cutting and Labour partyworkers' endorsement of roundabout cost-cutting through government subsidies. Although these alternatives obviously differ the difference is entirely susceptible to negotiation and compromise; and over these problems electors' preferences commonly emerged as more uniform than those of partyworkers.[130]

The absence of irreconcilable disagreements within each of these issues is not however strong enough proof for its complete absence among Glasgow population and activists. Given the pervasive scarcity of resources and the fact that most preferences ultimately entail an

[130] For more extended discussion of substantive preferences on these problems see *Class, Religion*, chap. 7.

TABLE 5.15

Agreement on preferences on the Glasgow problem which is considered most important (percentages of councillors, partyworkers, councillors and partyworkers, electors naming the preferences most popular among each group on first mention of their preferences on the problem considered most important, whatever that problem is, and the difference between these percentages: proportions of those in each group out of those naming either of the two most popular preferences on first mention who name the other most popular appraisal on their second and third mentions, i.e. degrees of overlap)

Group	Order of popularity	Substantive preference	First-mention percentage endorsement	Percentage difference	Second-mention degree of overlap	Third-mention degree of overlap
All councillors	1	Expand housing programme	32	8	0·11	0·09
	2	Improve aspects of administration	24			
All party-workers	1	Expand housing programme	27	9	0·11	0·00
	2	Get other sources of revenue	18			
All councillors all party-workers	1	Expand housing programme	29	11	0·15	0·12
	2	Improve aspects of administration	18			
All electors	1	Expand housing programme	27	6	0·10	0·01
	2	Improve aspects of administration	21			

Table 5.15 takes advantage of the standardised coding of preferences on all types of problem to compare preferences elicited by the questions: 'Which do you think is the most important problem, the one the corporation should try to take care of first?' 'What would you like to see the corporation do about that?' [regardless of the type of problem named]. The competing preferences are thus more numerous than where preferences relate only to one type of problem. For example, support for expanding the housing programme must be compared with support for expanding the education, traffic and other programmes. However, certain preferences are grouped no matter what type of problem they refer to: e.g. cutting costs or improving administration. General agreement on the priority preferences considered in the table is therefore estimated on the basis of an array consisting in part of generalised preferences (such as improve aspects of administration or get other sources of revenue). It should be noted that the third most popular substantive preference on first mention among electors was one which is difficult to reconcile with extension of the housing programme: that is the proposal to cut some costs, endorsed by 16 per cent of electors. Base numbers for percentages in Table 5.15 (except degrees of over-lap) are those for the total samples.

increased or decreased allocation of resources to a particular use, the demand for increased expenditure on housing rapidly implies that expenditure must be held down on education, and vice versa. Similarly a desire of those primarily concerned with finance to cut costs will rebound on plans for other areas. Consequently all these preferences must be considered in relation to each other. Moreover they must be the preferences of overriding priority. Many people no doubt wish to expand the housing programme and to cut financial costs. But the interesting point – and the one which indicates what action will ultimately prevail – is which of these preferences is given priority by the greatest number. So we shall consider preferences on all issues not only contextually but also in relation to the issue – whatever it was – considered most important of all by the respondent.

It is a reflection of the overriding importance of the housing problem in Glasgow that for all groups its direct resolution is the most popular preference. Neither of the second most popular preferences expressed by electors or activists are necessarily incompatible with this: improvement of administration and the tapping of other revenues would in fact both facilitate expansion and not absorb resources to an extent that would seriously hinder it. The third most popular preference among electors – to cut some costs (endorsed by 16 per cent of electors) – is potentially irreconcilable with expansion of housing, but the relatively small number endorsing this course of action means that we are not confronted with a clash of relatively equal numbers of electors and hence there is no irreconcilable disagreement in our sense of the term.[131] This discovery that irreconcilable disagreement on important issues is absent among the body of electors and activists, no matter how the data are examined, assumes great importance in light of our theoretical assumptions. Our reasoning has been that such a salient split among activists would smash any tendency to agree more on issue-preferences and appraisals, with consequent fatal effects upon the politicians' ability to settle issues by compromise and negotiation, and hence upon the stability of their polity. Since we have already unearthed a substantial body of preferences and appraisals where politicians agree more (along with some where they agree less) the emergence of irreconcilable disagreement upon these important preferences would have disconfirmed the connection central to our whole chain of reasoning. Conversely this demonstration of the absence of irreconcilable disagreement strongly reinforces the argument of the model.

[131] Appendix B, Definition 1.3.

AGREEMENT OF MUNICIPAL CORRESPONDENTS AND COUNCILLORS

Our model also anticipates that correspondents will agree more with councillors than with any other group, since they are both regarded as engaging in the same rate of political activity. In testing this assertion we are limited by the small number of correspondents – only six in Glasgow. Because of this limitation we are unable to combine councillors and correspondents and to compare them with other groups, for the much greater numbers of councillors would determine the overall state of agreement within the combined group without much weight being given to the correspondents' position. We therefore treat correspondents as a separate group. The extent to which they agree with councillors as opposed to partyworkers and electors is estimated here with reference to their preference on the current proposals relating to pubs, fee-paying schools, parking and rates and on the proposal to integrate the separate school system, their view on whether the majority or minority should prevail on four of these proposals, their appraisals of important problems facing Glasgow, and appraisals of and preferences on Glasgow government, the strategic action they would take on issues and their estimates of how likely they are to get their way by such action. These comparisons parallel those between councillors, partyworkers and electors discussed in Chapter 2 and the present chapter. To add another group to those examined previously would have confused the presentation of findings, and so the whole question of correspondents' agreement with other groups is examined here.

1. *Preferences on five current issues*

Table 5.16 presents the full distribution of correspondents' issue-preferences which can be compared with those of the other groups in Fig. 5.1.

TABLE 5.16

Glasgow correspondents' preferences on five current issues

| | Agree | | | | | Disagree | | | |
	Very strongly	Fairly strongly	Not strongly	DK how strongly	DK neutral	DK how strongly	Not strongly	Fairly strongly	Very strongly
Pubs	2	2	1	1	—	—	—	—	—
Fee-paying	1	1	1	—	—	—	1	2	—
Parking	2	1	1	—	1	—	—	—	1
Rates	1	1	—	—	—	—	—	3	1
School integration	2	1	1	—	1	—	—	1	—

From the comparison correspondents can be seen to agree more with councillors than with others on pubs, parking and school integration, with electors on fee-paying and with partyworkers on rates.

2. Majority v. minority rule on four current issues

On the question of whether the majority of people in Glasgow or the particular group affected should decide four of the above proposals, all correspondents agree that people in corporation housing should decide whether they wish to have pubs or not: on school fees they are evenly split with three for the majority and three for parents: on parking five favour the majority in Glasgow with one neutral and qualified: on the rates four favour the majority, one is for private householders and one is qualified and neutral. It is obvious that correspondents' support for majority rule is far from being unqualified but this of course is true also of councillors, and on comparison with Table 2.2 correspondents' preferences on all four cases marginally resemble councillors' more than those of any other group.

3. Appraisals of Glasgow government

There are two appraisals on which we can compare the agreement of correspondents with that of councillors, partyworkers and electors. First on the question of groups exercising an undue influence on corporation affairs, five correspondents agree that such groups exist and one disagrees. This agreement resembles that of partyworkers rather than councillors. On the further point of what groups do exercise influence two mention Labour councillors, two the City Labour Party and one religious groups. This concentration upon Labour – councillors and party – resembles the replies of councillors more than those of other groups. There is a third aspect to this comparison of agreement. In Chapter 2 these same appraisals are examined to see who are most inclined to reject the idea that any minorities not regularly elected exercise an undue influence on Glasgow politics – that is to say, to see who are most inclined to view Glasgow as the functioning democracy which we consider it to be. On this view of the appraisal correspondents are evenly split – three either not agreeing that any minority exercises undue influence or placing this influence with the electorally victorious Labour party, while three regard forces outside the electoral competition as having influence. This even split is again very like that encountered among partyworkers. Over all aspects of the appraisal therefore correspondents' views seem to resemble those of partyworkers rather than those of councillors.

On the question of what would happen if there were no parties on the corporation – in effect, whether party competition is beneficial or harmful – three correspondents consider that parties promote efficiency (two adding that parties are therefore inevitable); one correspondent that there would be less sectionalism without parties, one that things would be more businesslike without parties. This distribution, with its concentration upon the point that parties promote efficiency and are inevitable resembles that of councillors more than those of the other groups, as can be seen by examination of Table 2.8.

4. Preferences about Glasgow government

Five correspondents favour changes in Glasgow government designed to promote the efficiency of councillors, mainly by recruiting younger men, paying them and making them full-time. One of these five also favours regional local government. The remaining correspondent does not state a preference. A comparison with Table 2.5, which gives the preferences of councillors, partyworkers and electors, shows that the most popular changes among both the former groups are ones which would promote the efficiency of councillors, but that councillors are slightly more in favour of this proposal than partyworkers and also favour regional government to a greater extent than partyworkers. Hence their preferences are nearer those of correspondents.

One correspondent endorses only a ward role for councillors, one mentions committee work first and then ward duties, one names the task of governing the whole city exclusively, while three mention both tasks of serving the ward and governing the city (all mentioning the city role first and the ward second). This array of preferences – especially the dominant tendency to mention both city and ward role – again resembles the replies of councillors somewhat more than those of other groups (Table 3.1).

5. Appraisals of important problems facing Glasgow

Four correspondents mention housing and redevelopment as the most important problem facing Glasgow, three stressing planned housing rather than a simple increase in the number of houses. The other two mention finance as the initially most important problem. Both of these subsequently mention housing and redevelopment as problems, one stressing the planning aspect. Two of those who first mentioned housing subsequently mention finance. The numbers mentioning housing generally compare with both councillors and partyworkers. Three per cent more partyworkers than councillors make an initial mention of finance. However, the heavy stress on planning and re-development among those who mention housing initially is shared by 17 per cent of councillors compared to 3 per cent of partyworkers.

An incidental point is that correspondents' appraisals of newsworthy topics broadly resemble their appraisals of important Glasgow prob-lems. All five who answered this question regarded finance as more newsworthy: four mentioned housing (two stressing its planning and development aspects) and three each education and transport.[132] Because of this natural connection between their appraisals of import-ant problems and their criteria of newsworthiness it follows that if interaction with councillors shapes correspondents' views on important problems it will also affect their appraisals of what topics to give coverage to. This influence on priorities is important in a situation where three correspondents say they cannot get all they want into their paper for reasons of space and time.

6. Appraisals of strategic action on current issues

Naturally enough four out of the six correspondents would seek to gain their way on issues by giving them prominence in the mass media. Two would take informal group action and one would additionally seek to work through the council. Only about 10 per cent of councillors and partyworkers in each case would seek to gain their way by pub-licity, so the comparison is inconclusive. Correspondents do not really resemble any of the other groups on this appraisal. This is what might be expected since they possess different political resources from any of the other groups.

Three correspondents think they are reasonably likely to succeed in getting their way on issues and three feel they are not likely. Here the correspondents are much more like councillors, 46 per cent of whom feel they are reasonably likely to succeed, compared with 37 per cent for partyworkers and 18 per cent for electors.

7. Conclusion

On three out of five current issues (pubs, parking and school integra-tion) correspondents' preferences are closest to councillors, and on one

[132] Four mentioned cleansing as less newsworthy, and two each the Parliamen-tary business of the corporation and health and welfare.

each to partyworkers and electors. On both potential issues (changes in government and councillors' duties) and all questions of majority $v.$ minority rule correspondents most closely resemble councillors. On factual appraisals of important problems in Glasgow and of the role of parties the conclusion holds, although on the question of group influence on the corporation partyworkers are closer to correspondents and no group much resembles them on their appraisal of strategic action on issues.

Thus the prediction of the model that correspondents would agree more with councillors is upheld on the majority of comparisons. Moreover it does seem clear from the discussion that the actual overlap of views is reasonably substantial. It is not the case that correspondents agree *more* with councillors when these are compared with the other groups but have really quite a different group view. The discussion has shown that their outlook is the same in more cases than not. This congruence of opinion between correspondents and councillors has important bearings on the discussion of politicians' autonomy in the following chapter.

6. The Politicians: Autonomy and Competition

A further question carried over from the analysis of the relationship between ward politicians and their constituents is how far politicians as a body can act without reference to outsiders: in effect, how far the council itself is a free agent, and how far it is constrained – for example by the competition between parties – to follow electoral or other leads. In seeking an answer to this point we can draw upon the study of representation undertaken in Chapter 3 but much other evidence has to be considered. For constituency pressures are not the only constraints which might be felt by councillors. And their attitudes towards each other could have an independent effect in tilting the role of the council towards party arena or collegial body.

IMPLICATIONS OF POLITICAL STRATIFICATION

Two aspects of our model (checked against survey data in Chapters 3 and 4) bear upon the discussion of politicians' autonomy. The first relates to communication. Considered as a whole our assumptions describe a situation where the flow of information between councillors, partyworkers and electors is much impeded, where appraisals of many other groups' opinions and actions are therefore inaccurate and where many politicians suspect their inaccuracy. Whatever the modifications enjoined on our predictions by the actual findings these do confirm the general picture of limited contact between political strata – particularly between electors and activists.

The second aspect of our model relevant here concerns the greater agreement of the higher political strata over all aspects of current issues and on some long-term political appraisals. Such agreement is postulated to follow from the more extensive interaction assumed to take place within the top strata – certainly when this is contrasted with the minimal contacts between electors and activists and between electors themselves. The evidence so far examined has confirmed these expectations to the extent of showing that councillors and partyworkers tend to agree more than electors not only on many factual appraisals of politics but also on many issue-preferences, both current and potential.

These substantive agreements may counterbalance the procedural disagreements discovered earlier.

Combined, the assumptions about discontinuous communication and differentiated agreement specify a state of affairs in which politicians collectively enjoy extreme freedom of action. Whether or not electors have strong issue-preferences – a point to be examined presently – they do not appear to be well communicated to politicians under the general conditions we assume and which appear to exist in Glasgow. There remains the possibility that decisions may be affected by what politicians *think* are electors' preferences, and we have assumed that most appraisals made by politicians of the opinions of large groups of electors will be reasonably accurate. This possibility, that in spite of limited direct communication politicians may still follow electors' preferences, is however theoretically vitiated by the exception of some politicians' appraisals from this overall expectation of accuracy – for example, their appraisals of the preferences of small groups of electors. It certainly appears that ward activists have very inaccurate perceptions of constituency preferences (Tables 3.9 and 3.13).

Of course impediments to communication not only introduce uncertainty into politicians' appraisals about electors but affect electors' appraisals of politicians even more powerfully, as we saw in the analysis of electors' potential control over councillors (Chapter 3). What is more we assume that most politicians realise electors have very little information about their doings and that the knowledge frees many of their decisions from fears of popular loss of votes.

If we are correct in these views, discontinuities in the flow of communication will cushion politicians from most popular movements of opinion. However this in itself only forces politicians to act in ignorance of popular feeling. It does not safeguard them from the fear of future sanctions at elections or through other channels. For – to take the Glasgow case – lively party competition in a democracy implies the close scrutiny of all actions by opponents and the press. Such scrutiny could prevent politicians from presuming on a uniform and invariant absence of popular attention to their actions. With the prospect of erratic and unexpected publicity added to the other uncertainties surrounding their decisions politicians might well shrink from the least controversial initiative.

But we are ignoring other factors in the situation if we anticipate that the clouds of popular apathy are liable to completely random dispersal. The first of these factors is the considerable agreements anticipated and actually discovered to exist among councillors. Where agreement on preferences exists, party rivalry should not influence the handling of the issue by revealing affairs to the public or preventing discreet co-operation between the rival groups of politicians. Thus politicians' anonymity and autonomy should be preserved from disruption by the parties at least on these matters. And this freedom from party disruption implies that the threat of disruption by the press and other mass media must also be absent on these issues. For our model expressly precludes the mass media from acting as communicators independently of councillors. The issues to which the media devote coverage are the issues which the close associates of politicians – the political reporters – consider worthy of promotion and their appraisals here are anticipated to be close to those of politicians, since the appraisals of both reporters and politicians are formed out of the integrative behaviour of persons on their common level of political activity. The evidence we have supports this assumption of similarity between correspondents' and councillors' appraisals by demonstrating that over all responses to our questions, correspondents' views were closer in most cases to those of councillors than to those of partyworkers and electors.

As with prior assumptions, our attribution of substantial freedom of action to politicians derives from much previous discussion and research. For example, R. A. Dahl and V. O. Key assert that it is the agreement of American politicians on the procedures which they observe that enable such procedures to persist in the face of widespread disagreement upon them among the American population.[133] J. Blondel, in a discussion of British voting behaviour, speculates on the influence of politicians' initiatives in polarising electoral competition between the solid middle class and the unionised working class.[134] The curious hiatus between widespread popular support for home rule and the past failures of home rule parties in Scotland has been attributed to the playing down of the home rule issue by the established politicians.[135]

In contrast other writers have emphasised the responsiveness shown by democratic politicians to popular preferences and demands. On the assumption – which also appears in our model – that one of their leading concerns is to gain more votes at elections than their opponents, it is often expected that parties will generally shift their policy positions so

[133] R. A. Dahl, *Who Governs?*, chap. 28; V. O. Key, *Public Opinion*, pp. 536–43.
[134] Blondel, *Voters, Parties*, p. 68.
[135] Budge and Urwin, *Scottish Political Behaviour*, chap. 10.

as to be closest to the largest electoral opinion cluster on any given issue. Thus Anthony Downs concludes that 'both parties in a two-party system agree on any issues that a majority of electors strongly favour'.[136] A critic has pointed out that such postulation of a relatively straightforward link between electors' opinions and politicians' actions is tenable only on the further implicit assumption that the perceptions and preoccupations of electors and politicians are necessarily the same, and that such an implicit assumption is unrealistic in the great majority of cases. Electors may evaluate parties on several different criteria and these may differ for politicians and electors.[137] The assumptions embodied in our own model would further stress the likelihood of different judgements being made by politicians and electors as a result of imperfect communication between them and the highly integrative behaviour of politicians among themselves.

None the less it is obvious that democratic politicians divide themselves into different parties and that these parties do compete, sometimes bitterly, for votes. But since our model seeks to explain broader political processes than the election strategies emphasised by Downs there is no need to accept politicians' quest for votes as a given end in itself. And in fact Assumption XII of our model explicitly postulates that politicians see party vote–maximisation only as one means to the satisfaction of their political demands. If demands can be satisfied in other ways – for example by negotiation with other activists, or collective agreements and action by the council as a whole – politicians would see no need to make them subjects of their electoral appeals. As we have already noted, the extensive agreements on issue-preferences discovered among councillors would thus remove many topics of potential controversy from electoral competition.

High agreement might further prevent an electoral free-for-all from engulfing councillors' generally consensual actions by extending to appraisals of paying electoral strategies. While the different groups of politicians compete for votes, we assume that they all regard such competition as attracting votes only when initiated in regard to some issues: competition on others might produce negative effects. The incessant interchange of views and close contact which we attribute to politicians are likely to affect each others' appraisals of issues ripe for competition to the extent that they become closely similar, even for

136 Downs, *An Economic Theory of Democracy*, p. 297.
137 D. E. Stokes, 'Spatial Models of Party Competition', *APSR* LVII (1963) 368–77.

adherents of rival parties. Thus the same issues are likely to be selected by opposing partisans as the venue for combat while others are not mentioned by tacit agreement.

Of course the argument for politicians' agreement on the issues selected for party-competition is of significance only if we go on to say that politicians themselves pick out the issues on which they are going to compete, and those to which they will not draw popular attention. If extraneous forces set the terms for party competition politicians would be forced to respond whatever their own tentative judgements of where they ought to stand.

Now our model states that the most general and minimal condition for attracting votes on an issue is that the issue be widely known. Electors' voting is not likely to be affected by party postures on issues of which they have never heard.[138] The model assumes also that the only way in which issues do become known at the popular level is through the mass media and that most politicians know this. But the persons who immediately give or deny coverage are the correspondents who form part of the same integrated group of high-level activists as the councillors and who tend as part of that group to form similar appraisals as its other members of what issues would be brought to, or kept from, public notice.

The specific issues chosen for competition we anticipate to be those on which politicians see a fairly even division of popular preferences. Generally speaking parties should be sufficiently adroit to avoid endorsement of policies perceived to be hopelessly unpopular where their opponents support the side perceived as overwhelmingly popular. Hence parties will provide an opening to their opponents only on questions where the electoral result appears sufficiently in doubt for each to feel it can attract enough votes to win. This implies that popular preferences are seen as fairly evenly divided on competed issues.

To summarise, our model does recognise party competition and tries to account for the form it takes and its effects on politicians' strategies. But it regards such competition as being largely shaped by

---

[138] We do not of course assume that all issues publicised in the mass media are automatically made the subject of party competition, but we do expect that no issue not publicised through the mass media will form the subject of a party split. Coverage is regarded as a necessary but not sufficient cause of party competition. We therefore expect to find party division on a proportionately higher number of publicised than of unpublicised issues.

politicians' – or at any rate high-level activists' – preferences and appraisals. No matter what the clustering of popular preferences on some issues, they will not be reflected in politicians' behaviour or opinions under the prior conditions we have specified because politicians agree upon them internally. Only on issues where the parties actually divide will the distribution of electoral preferences influence that of politicians, and then only if politicians' appraisals of electoral preferences are accurate. In this view there is no automatic convergence of electors' and politicians' preferences, as anticipated by Downs. It follows that the independence and autonomy of politicians are the overriding factor we take into account. The response to electoral preferences enforced by party competition is limited and subject to many checks. Autonomy is thrust upon politicians whether they wish it or not. The individual politician may look to his fellows for guidance but as a body politicians must in many cases rely upon themselves and top activists whose views resemble their own.

AN EMPIRICAL EVALUATION OF DIFFERENCES AND SIMILARITIES IN THE POLITICAL CRITERIA USED BY POLITICIANS AND ELECTORS

Although not implied by our model, Stokes' suggestion that politicians apply a different frame of reference to politics from that used by electors strengthens the argument for their autonomy by pointing to reasons for politicians' actively desiring freedom from electoral prompting. If politicians tend to act on other considerations than those which prevail with electors – perhaps merely on the simple necessity for co-ordination and consistency between different spheres of policy – they will have good cause not to open many issues to party competition and consequent popular debate. For such debate might force simplistic decisions which could prove immediately embarrassing and even in the long run electorally unprofitable if they turned out to hamper the conduct of affairs.

Paradoxically (since it disproves other assertions of our model) the finding that councillors ignore clearly stated majority opinions on issues where these contradict their own preferences also strengthens the argument for politicians' autonomy.[139] It demonstrates an indifference to popular feeling which could well stem from politicians' consciousness of their superior sophistication.

Assessments of the important problems facing Glasgow provide data through which the political criteria used by councillors, party-

[139] See Tables 2.2 and 2.4.

workers and electors can be compared.[140] In their ordering of priorities – the importance assigned to each problem – there was little difference between the appraisals made by different strata. A sizeable majority of each group named housing-redevelopment as most important, and comparable minorities in each named finance. Descriptions of four leading problems given by the majority in each group also coincided, on the whole: housing and education get insufficient expenditure; the finance problem was a matter of high costs; traffic was hindered by bad planning and administration. Generally, leading minority appraisals of problems also coincided between the three strata. In their suggested strategies for the total array of important problems the largest cluster in all three cases supported straight expansion of the housing programme. And the next largest support from both electors and councillors came for administrative improvements.

This coincidence between their priorities and grand strategies seems to designate Glasgow politicians and electors as inhabitants of the one-dimensional world of Anthony Downs rather than of the multi-faceted environment of D. E. Stokes. Hints of longer-range preoccupations of councillors can however be discovered in the stronger emphasis of some among them upon the planning and redevelopment of housing rather than its simple expansion.[141] Moreover in their appraisals of and preferences about the actual operation of government, councillors display a more complex appreciation of political circumstances than electors. Thus those who think that some groups in Glasgow exercise an undue influence are able on the whole to name that group as the Labour party instead of retiring into the answer that such groups do exist but cannot be named. Councillors are able to name the specific changes in local government which they desire, in marked contrast to electors.[142] On a wider social plane councillors are somewhat less disposed than electors to employ social stereotypes, although the difference is not great. Asked to indicate a preference between a person of the same class and religion as themselves, or of different classes and religions, 48 per cent of councillors said their choice would depend on the person himself, compared to 45 per cent of partyworkers and 41 per cent of

[140] For these assessments see Tables 5.6 to 5.15 and the related discussion in Chapter 5.
[141] Seventeen per cent of councillors named planning and redevelopment of housing as an important problem compared to 3 per cent of party workers and 1 per cent of electors.
[142] See Tables 2.6 and 2.7.

electors. Further proof of their more complex appreciation of political realities comes from the recognition of the mixed nature of their own roles (Table 3.1). All this evidence points to the possibility that councillors differ from electors not so much in the objects of their preoccupations as in the quality of the appraisals they bring to bear on their preoccupations.

A direct qualitative comparison of appraisals made by the different strata can be undertaken through a supplementary coding of responses to the questions on important Glasgow problems. In addition to placing responses in substantive categories such as 'build more houses' we expressly noted whether the respondents' discussion was clarified by reference to a broader theoretical, historical, geographical or political context, or whether the problem was tackled in isolation from ongoing social processes as a difficulty without precedents and parallels. Conceptions of the problem as unique and isolated seem likely to impoverish any consideration of policy and to underestimate the difficulties involved in its solution. Wider perspectives on the problem were in fact adopted by 55 per cent of the councillors and 35 per cent of the partyworkers compared to only 7 per cent of electors on the most generous interpretation. These striking results indicate that in spite of politicians' and electors' adoption of the same broad lines of policy the way in which these common preferences are interpreted and applied seem likely to diverge rather widely. A decision to expand the housing programme means for electors simply the building of more houses. For councillors it is more likely to involve considerations of planning and layout which simply do not occur to most electors, but which councillors feel bound to compare with the experience of other cities and to co-ordinate with other activities of the corporation and with the plans of the central government. With such problems in mind the politician has an obvious reason for wishing to enjoy a reasonable discretion in executing the simple popular imperatives – even if, in Glasgow, he happens to share them.

TESTS OF THE PREDICTIONS ON POLITICIANS' AUTONOMY DERIVED FROM THE MODEL

Politicians may desire autonomy but do they really attain it? Here we return to our predictive model. While it is silent on how far politicians desire freedom of action it unequivocally asserts that they enjoy great independence in a mass democracy, whether they desire it or not. The remainder of this chapter is devoted to testing the validity of derivations from the model which are concerned with politicians' autonomy and the limits which these impose upon party competition.

We must first consider if councillors do show up as autonomous on our data. If they are, their issue-preferences should vary quite independently of those of electors. There should in addition be a closer correspondence between their preferences and those of partyworkers, with whom we assume they are in closer touch.

If politicians' issue-preferences are independent of those of electors and closer to those of partyworkers, our model would attribute the finding to the more integrative behaviour of councillors and partyworkers and the comparative absence of communication between activists and electors. Can this be regarded as the real explanation? An examination of the promotion of agreement by integrative behaviour among councillors (the only group for which we have data) provides one test of the effects its presence or absence have on general agreement and thus on politicians' autonomy.

Party competition is also predicted by our model to affect politicians' agreement and cohesion – and hence their freedom for collective action – but only over a limited range of issues. We anticipate that competition is limited because the politicians through their associates the correspondents are able to focus attention upon some issues and exclude others from popular debate. We can test these predictions against the direct replies of Glasgow councillors, partyworkers and municipal correspondents to questions on their ability to bring issues to public attention and to keep issues from public attention.

Finally we shall examine the party competition itself to see if it conforms to our picture of it. Do councillors in fact divide by party only on issues that are known and which they have helped make known, with the correspondents? Does Glasgow party competition in fact focus around issues on which the populace is evenly divided because competition on other issues is recognised as hopeless by one side or the other? The answers given to these questions by our data will all test the adequacy of our model.

COINCIDENCE AND DIVERGENCE BETWEEN CURRENT ISSUE-PREFERENCES OF COUNCILLORS, PARTYWORKERS AND ELECTORS

The degree of convergence between issue-preferences is in one sense an unsatisfactory probe of the autonomy of councillors from the other two groups. Even if convergence were high it might derive from electors' response to the councillors' lead rather than vice versa. Our model however assumes that politicians' freedom of action stems largely from impediments to free communication between strata, and on these grounds we should expect independent variation of the opinion distributions rather than a flow of influence in either direction.

In Chapters 3 and 5 we have already compared preferences on the introduction of pubs into council estates, abolition of fee-paying in corporation schools, extension of parking-meters through the city centre, increase in rates and integration of Catholic and Protestant schoolchildren. At this point we need only review these discussions from our present concern with autonomy.

The overall correlation between the issue-preferences of councillors and electors was found to be 0·44.[143] The value is sufficiently high to indicate some degree of correspondence between preferences on the two sides, but it is not very high. Differences between the two groups are more apparent than similarities. The correlation between the preferences of councillors and partyworkers was 0·92. The stronger resemblance of councillors' and partyworkers' views again fits with our expectations. For if we suppose councillors and partyworkers to inter-act more extensively than councillors and electors they must according to our model show greater agreement.

The substantive import of these summary statistics is illustrated in Fig. 5.1 and Tables 5.1, 5.2 and 5.3, which graph the spread of council-lors, partyworkers and electors over different stands on the five issues. A loose general fit emerged between all three groups on pubs, school fees, parking and school integration. On fees a similar split existed among all groups and on the others majority preferences were the same. The value of the overall correlation was lowered in two ways. On all issues mentioned above the councillors' majority preference was endorsed more overwhelmingly and with less dissent than was the case among electors. And on the question of rates the majority of councillors supported an increase which was strongly opposed by most partyworkers and electors. (These differences between councillors and electors appeared also but with less force between partyworkers and electors, a finding which explains the higher correlation between councillors' and partyworkers' preferences and upholds our predictions.)

The rates distributions most strikingly demonstrate that there is no automatic adjustment between politicians' and electors' preferences. Strictly speaking, only Labour councillors show themselves independ-ent of electors' views on rates, but the Downsian model would expect

[143] See Table 3.4.

politicians of both parties to conform. Only on fee-paying is a strong party split among electors paralleled by a similar division among councillors. Evidence from the other issues is ambiguous: the tendency for councillors to pile up more on the preference endorsed also by the majority of electors could be explained by Downs as the result of an acute sensitivity to electoral opinions, and by Downs' critics as an example of the politicians' initiative giving a lead to electors.

We can supplement this discussion by considering convergences of preference on two potential issues – changes in Glasgow government and the job of councillors. The most salient preferences for change emerged from Table 2.5 as different for councillors and electors. The most salient and popular preference which they did share – for more efficient councillors – was endorsed much more heavily by councillors than would be justified by its support among electors if that were their prime consideration. Partyworkers here occupied a position midway between councillors and electors in that the proposals for making councillors more efficient were endorsed by a proportion almost equal to that for councillors, but their second most popular preference was for more powerful officials as among electors but not councillors. On the further question of what councillors should do, identical preferences were shared by the largest clusters of electors and councillors (and partyworkers). But councillors emphasised mixed ward and city roles to a much greater extent.[144]

Particularly on these potential issues which had not yet emerged for public debate the impression grows that councillors' greater agreement would set a lead for electors if the issue ever did emerge. This may well be the sequence of events on the current issues where evidence was absent on who influences who.

The possibility still remains that councillors may adopt the positions they do because they *think* that these represent electors' preferences. However, we have traced a low correspondence between councillors' own opinions and those they attribute to their constituents (Table 3.8). We have no direct evidence on councillors' appraisals of the preferences of electors as a whole on the five current issues just discussed. However their appraisals of popular preferences on the issue they consider most important do give a general indication of what their appraisals are likely to be over all issues. For if councillors see no very clear preference existing among electors on the most salient and urgent issue they are

[144] See Tables 3.1 and 3.2 and associated discussions.

not likely to see one on lesser issues. In fact 38 per cent of councillors find popular preferences divided on the most important problem facing Glasgow. Another 14 per cent saw only apathy and indifference among the population. Only a quarter of councillors correctly identified the leading popular preference for expansion of the housing programme. It is likely therefore that on most issues a sizeable number – even a majority – of councillors feel that they cannot guide themselves by non-existent or divided electoral preferences. It is irrelevant that these beliefs are wrong, in that few electors were either apathetic or undecided on the problem they consider most important, and they tended to be fairly highly agreed on the important problems.[145] Worth noting however is the fact that such appraisals would approach accuracy on the five current issues of main concern. On parking, one fifth of electors have no opinion and on fee-paying one tenth; and on both issues moreover only a quarter had strong feelings. The level of electoral agreement on all issues but rates is low. Additionally, proportions of electors ranging from 15 per cent on pubs to 59 per cent on fees had not heard of issues in the first place. Again the exception is rates: electors had heard of this issue and reacted extremely strongly.

Even when strong feeling is roused its translation into action requires a considerable effort. Asked what they would do if they felt strongly about any of four current issues, 26 per cent of electors said they would do nothing. Since people are naturally readier to say they would do something than to take real action (especially when they are subjected to strong probing) it will be appreciated that 26 per cent is a highly minimal estimate of the extent of popular apathy. If therefore a body of councillors do go their own way on the assumption that electors will not penalise their initiative they seem unlikely to face popular reactions or reprisals. And this freedom must operate to promote the autonomy we have discussed.

INTEGRATIVE BEHAVIOUR AMONG AND BETWEEN COUNCILLORS, PARTY-WORKERS AND ELECTORS

One feature of councillors' autonomy is their tendency to agree more than electors over most issues. We assume that the tendency to agree derives from another tendency for councillors to seek each other out and discuss politics to a greater extent, to support each others' actions

[145] See Table 5.15 and the supporting discussion. It is noteworthy that a larger proportion of partyworkers (58 per cent) than of councillors were unclear about popular preferences, in spite of their reported contacts with electors.

more strongly over a wider range of issues – generally to interact more
positively and frequently. The expectation that such integrative behaviour is more frequent among councillors but rare between councillors and electors is examined here through a reappraisal of the data on
communication discussed in Chapter 4.

One indicator of integrative behaviour is the sheer volume of discussion inside each stratum. On three of the current issues previously
considered proportions of electors ranging from 8 to 30 per cent said
they had discussed the issue with someone else. From 35 to 55 per cent
of partyworkers discussed them.[146] On the other hand proportions of
councillors from 66 per cent to 80 per cent were able to name specific
persons on the corporation with whom they would discuss topics
related to these issues.

Again, in considering how our respondents heard of four current
issues (Table 4.5), it is clear that most electors depend on the mass media
for information (an average of 52 per cent compared with 45 per cent
for partyworkers and 7 per cent for councillors). This orientation to the
media contrasts sharply with councillors' reliance upon their colleagues
and corporation officials. No electors report hearing the issue from other
electors or from partyworkers, and an average of 11 per cent only
learned in their primary groups: 48 per cent of councillors on average
heard from colleagues and officials, 17 per cent from partyworkers and
13 per cent in their primary groups (probably activist). Partyworkers'
chief source was other partyworkers: an average 22 per cent had heard
from fellow workers compared to 9 per cent who heard from councillors and officials. These replies confirm that little communication normally takes place between strata but that what there is flows chiefly
between partyworkers and councillors. They again demonstrate that
the total volume of communication among councillors is greater than
among the other two strata.

A further sideview at patterns of interaction is provided by councillors' descriptions of how they would set about discovering constituents'
opinions if they wished to do so, reported in Table 4.9. Never more than
a quarter of councillors on any issue would contact electors face to face.
Their heaviest reliance is placed on the party organisation, i.e. the
partyworkers and on routine or specially summoned meetings. But the
people who attend either type of meeting are not on our evidence

[146] An average of 3 per cent mentioned discussion with electors, 8 per cent with
councillors and officials. All other discussion was carried on in primary groups and
with fellow partyworkers.

typical of ordinary electors. Only five per cent of the latter, even if they felt strongly about an issue, would organise or attend public meetings. Only 1 per cent would work through the municipal ward committee. For that matter only 6 per cent mention the possibility of working through any aspect of the party organisation. Certainly 23 per cent mention an approach to councillors. And, as emerged in Chapter 4, roughly a third of electors would contact councillors if they wanted to discover more about an issue. We have already pointed out that these impulses to see their representatives constitute more of an acceptance by electors of the norms of participatory democracy, than an everyday political process. In fact, electors' reports of the actual ways they heard of issues stress their very infrequent contact with councillors. On the whole the communication data uphold our expectations about the more extensive interaction of councillors among themselves and the absence of interaction with other strata.

INTEGRATIVE BEHAVIOUR AMONG COUNCILLORS

The predictions we have advanced are upheld simply if most councillors communicate with other councillors and do not communicate to any marked extent with non-councillors. However we do assume that the generally closer identity between the views of councillors as a whole is due to integrative behaviour which should extend to the whole group. If very marked discontinuities appear in the interactions between different sub-groups they must cast doubt on the association of integrative behaviour with general agreement. The present attempt to discover if discontinuities of this type exist among councillors is based on responses to a question asked at the end of a sequence on the previously discussed issues of pubs, fees, parking and rates: Which other members of the council do you normally go to when you wish to discuss something concerning (corporation housing estates, corporation schools, traffic problems in Glasgow, city rates)? The data on discussions thus relates to the broad policy areas out of which these four specific issues rose. Fig. 6.1 presents the patterns of contact on all four topics. The data are summarised in Table 6.1, which should be read in close conjunction with the matrix.[147]

Traffic attracts least discussion among the topics (81 consultations in all and 48 between interviewed councillors). Housing is most

[147] We owe a considerable debt to M. J. Taylor for suggesting the formation of this matrix and table, supervising their construction and suggesting many of the points on which this section of our discussion is based.

FIG.6.1. COMMUNICATION AMONG GLASGOW COUNCILLORS ON FOUR POLICY AREAS

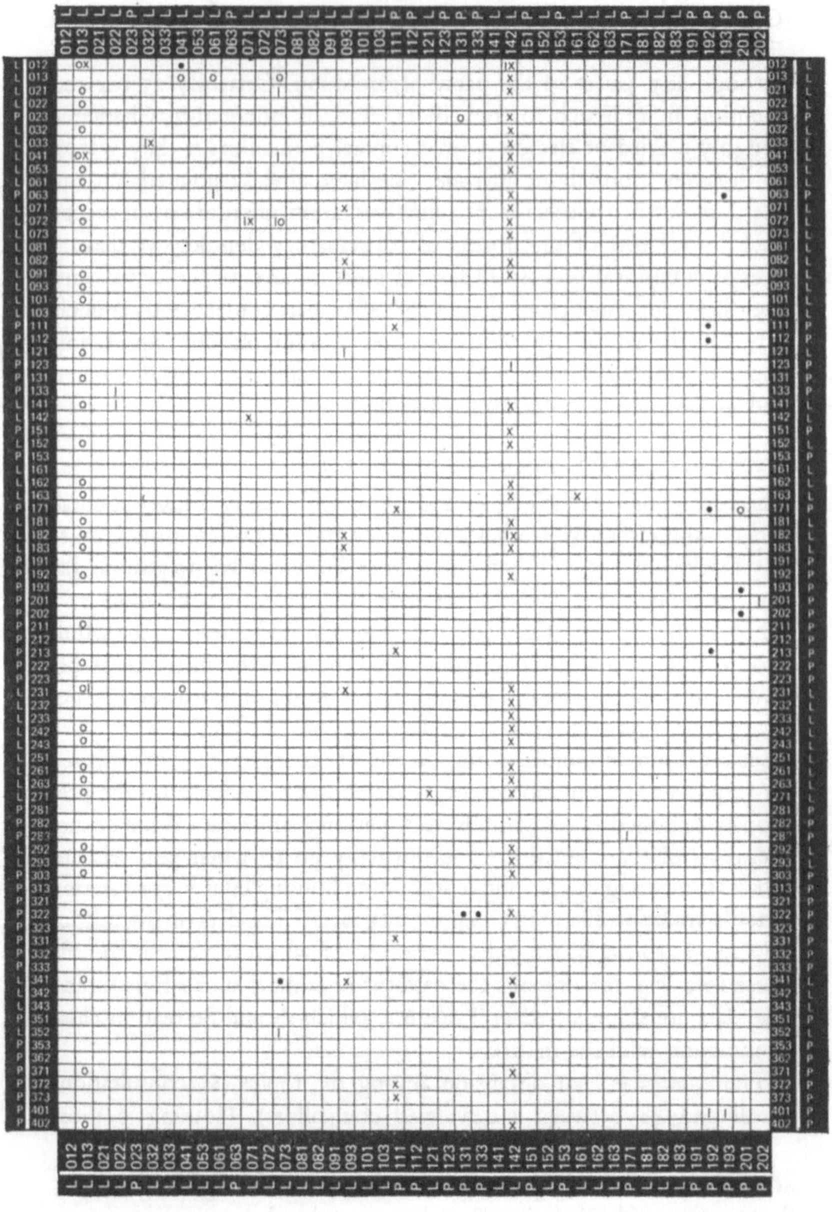

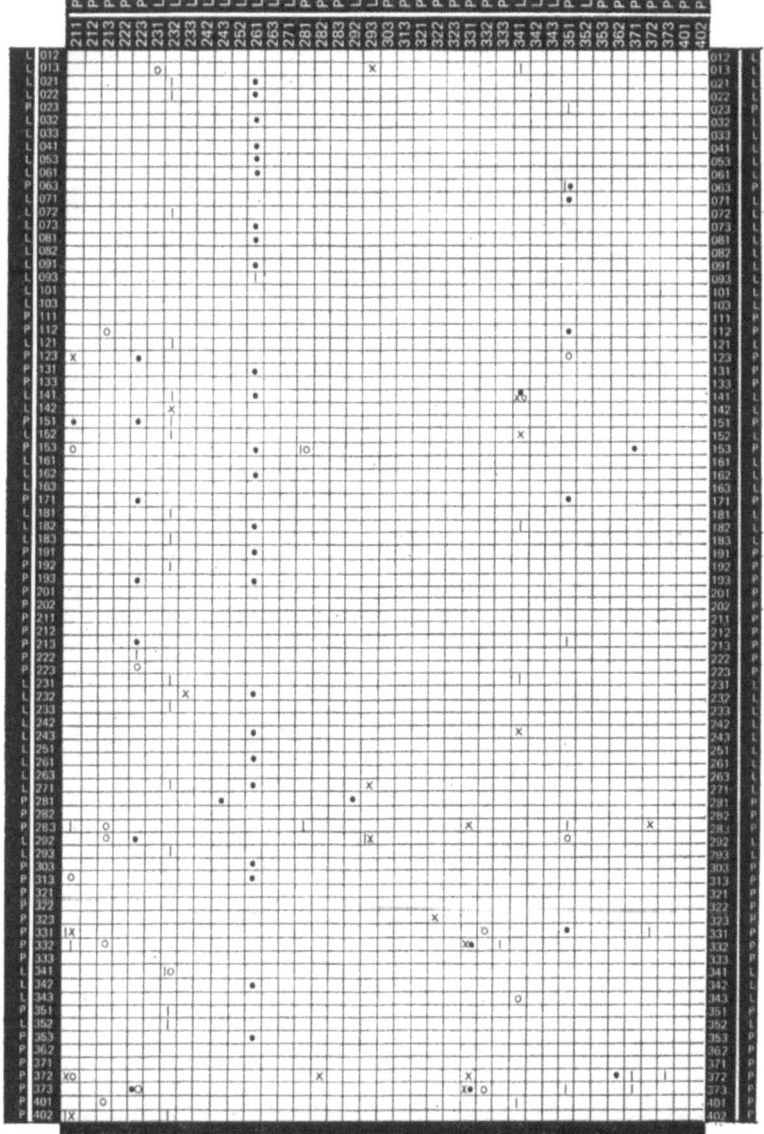

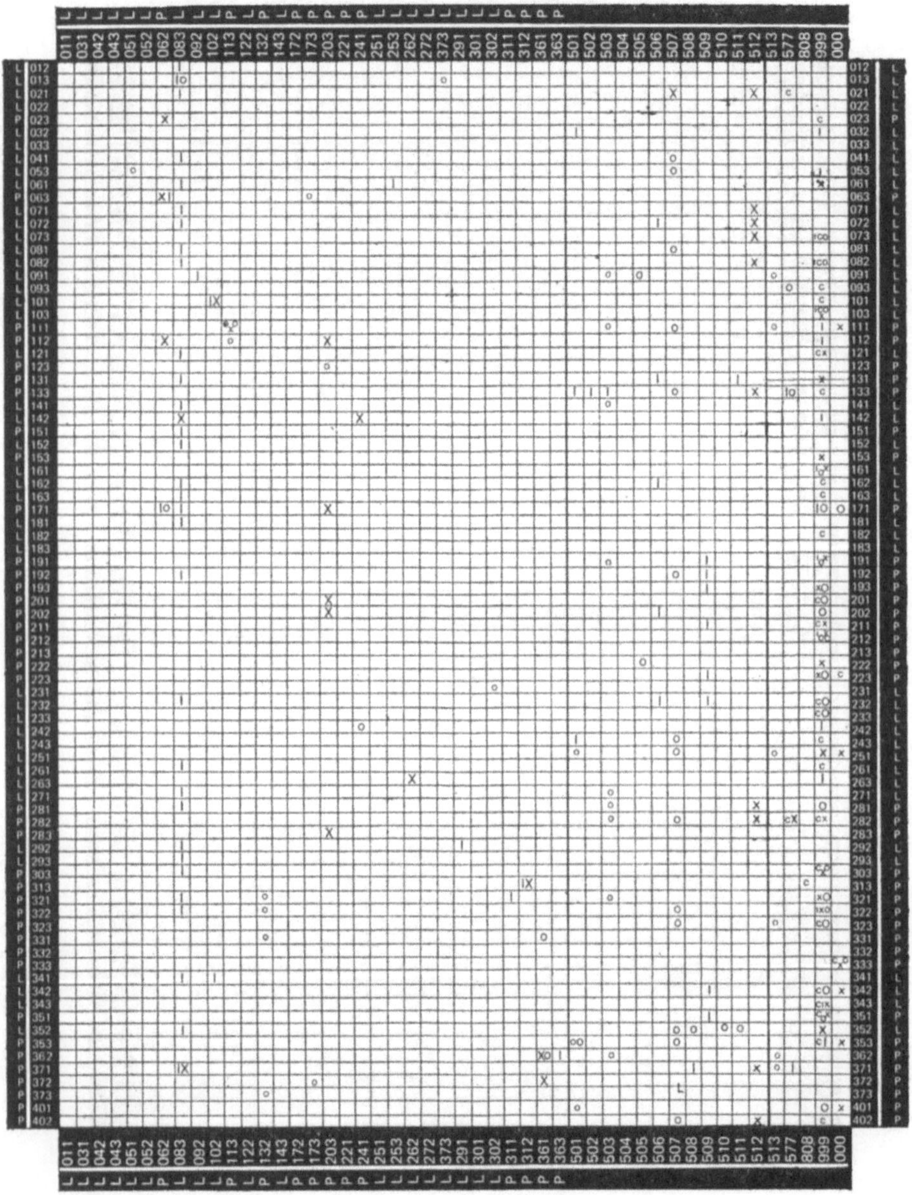

The numbers on all sides of Fig. 6.1 refer to individual councillors, who are designated as P (Progressive) or L (Labour) according to party affiliation. The first two digits in each councillor's number relate to the ward they represent (01–37). Within each ward councillors are arranged alphabetically and designated by a third digit (1, 2 or 3). Thus 011 is the first councillor (alphabetically) representing the first ward, 373 is the third councillor (alphabetically) representing the thirty-seventh ward. Numbers 513, 577, 888, 999, 000 are missing data-categories (representing replies such as 'don't know', 'other' or 'persons not on the corporation'). Designations of these numbers are ignored in the textual discussion and Table 6.1. When the 'large rectangle' is mentioned in the text, therefore, it relates to all designations except missing data-categories. Numbers 501–512 refer to various permanent corporation officials. When these designations are also excluded we have the 'smaller rectangle' mentioned in the text, which groups all councillors.

Designations are made in four general policy areas which are distinguished by the symbols used in the matrix: corporation housing is signified by 1; corporation schools by x; traffic by •; city finance by 0.

H

TABLE 6.1

Councillors' designations of other members of Glasgow corporation with whom they normally discuss corporation housing and schools, traffic problems and rates (numbers of designations)

	1 CO — All designations of named persons on corporation (within large rectangle Fig. 6.1)	2 I — All designations of named persons interviewed by us (within square only Fig. 6.1)	3 — Designation by party of all named councillors — Within party L by L	Within party P by P	Between parties P by L	Between parties L by P	4 — Designation by party of named councillors interviewed by us — Within party L by L	Within party P by P	Between parties P by L	Between parties L by P	5 C — All designations of ward colleagues (within smaller rectangle Fig. 6.1)	6 I — Designation of ward colleagues interviewed by us (within square only Fig. 6.1)	7 O — All designations of corporation officials — By Labour councillors	By Progressive councillors	8 C — All designations of convenors concerned with given topic — By Labour councillors	By Progressive councillors
Corporation housing (Pubs)	126	62	59	29	1	15	33	22	1	6	25	17	7	15	40	13
Corporation schools (Fees)	105	76	56	29	1	7	53	17	0	6	18	10	6	6	32	6
Traffic problems (Parking)	81	48	28	30	0	3	25	20	0	3	7	3	12	8	21	3
Rates (Rates)	101	73	43	27	1	8	42	23	0	8	9	6	10	12	30	8
Totals over all four topics	413	259	186	115	3	33	153	82	1	23	59	36	35	41	123	30

NOTES ON TABLE 6.1

Table 6.1 is to be read in conjunction with Fig. 6.1, some features of which the table summarises. The column headed CO relates to all designations noted in Fig. 6.1. Columns headed I relate only to designations of other persons interviewed by us on the corporation which are shown within the square on Fig. 6.1. Columns headed C relate to designations of councillors (whether interviewed by us or not) which appear within the smaller rectangle on Fig. 6.1. The column headed O relates to designations of appointed officials of the corporation which appear in the space formed when the smaller rectangle in Fig. 6.1 is subtracted from the large rectangle. Since numbers thus relate to three different bases they are not percentaged in the table. The figures in columns 3 and 7 total to the figure in column 1. Columns 5 and 8 relate to subsets of column 3. The figures in column 4 add to to the figure in column 2. Column 6 relates to a subset of column 2.

The figures are of double interest in some cases, both from the point of view of who made the designation and who is named by it. Thus the symbols in the third and fourth columns of the table relate to: designations of Labour councillors by Labour councillors (L by L); designations of Progressive councillors by Progressive councillors (P by P); designations of Progressive councillors by Labour councillors (P by L); designations of Labour councillors by Progressive councillors (L by P). In the row headings, current issues especially relevant to each topic are bracketed after each. Thus the question of introducing pubs into corporation housing estates is a specific question in the general field of housing and the side entry appears as: Corporation housing (pubs).

The only persons in Fig. 6.1 for whom all data is complete – in the sense that they can make reciprocal choices of each other for consultation – are our eighty-two interviewees. This is the reason for reporting their internal pattern of designations separately in the table. The gap between all designations and those within the square of interviewees only in Fig. 6.1 is especially great on corporation housing because the convenor of the housing committee was not interviewed: the convenors of the planning and property management committees were interviewed, however. Only one convenor is concerned with each of the other three topics: the convenor of the education committee with corporation schools, the convenor of highways with traffic problems and the City Treasurer (who is also convenor of the finance committee) with rates. These three convenors were interviewed by us.

discussed (126 total consultations, 62 between our interviewees). Schools and rates are discussed to much the same extent and fall midway between traffic and housing in the number of consultations they spark off. Schools and rates give rise to the issues on which councillors strongly divide and the similar frequencies of consultation may be significant.

The giving and taking of advice on the four topics appears to be relatively specialised.[148] Only two persons pick another for consultation on three topics and no one is chosen on four. The most extensive consultation takes place with the convenors of committees concerned with the subject. To a lesser degree the appropriate officials are similarly chosen for consultation: the City Factor on housing, Director of Education on schools and so on. Overall, officials are not consulted as

[148] On the tendency for politicians to specialise on certain issue-areas see R. A. Dahl, *Who Governs?*, p. 175; D. Matthews, *U.S. Senators and their World*, pp. 95–7; Eulau *et al.*, *Legislative System*, chap. 9.

much as one might expect but the number of references is still substantial: 76 out of a total of 413 or 18 per cent of all designations.

Perhaps the most surprising feature of the matrix is the failure to designate 54 individuals out of the total 126 and 39 out of the 82 interviewees for any consultation at all. Although the unconsulted individuals whom we interviewed themselves designated others this finding hints at the existence of extensive discontinuities in the interactions of councillors even before the matter is examined on a systematic basis. One explanation for the phenomenon of the unconsulted lies in the fact that convenors are designated in their own areas to an overwhelmingly greater extent than they designate others. Since convenors have information, contacts and influences in their own policy area it is natural that the rank and file should seek their advice and try the effects of persuasion upon them. Conversely (again in their own areas) convenors have less to gain by consulting the rank and file. It is probably true that these discontinuities and trends to hierarchy are found in almost any human association. Even highly integrated groups are likely to generate a nexus of respect and influence which will influence communication patterns. But discontinuities are probably emphasised in the case of the council by the tradition of conducting most affairs through committees and their convenors, and by the extreme departmentalisation of corporation business.

Another systematic discontinuity leaps from the matrix however – the relative absence of consultation between Labour councillors and Progressives. Only 36 out of 337 consultations of councillors take place between the parties, i.e. 11 per cent. And only 25 out of the 259 consultations of interviewees take place between the parties (10 per cent). A peculiarity of the inter-party consultations is that all but three consist of Progressive designations of Labour councillors. The explanation lies in the Labour councillor being almost invariably a convenor in the appropriate issue-area.[149] Thirty out of 33 consultations of Labour councillors by Progressives are with convenors. It seems that Progressive like Labour councillors are heavily dependent on convenors' access to information and their unique ability to hinder or expedite particular decisions. Thus inter-party communication is almost entirely enforced by institutional constraints.

Progressive designation of Labour convenors is lowest on traffic and

[149] All convenors in the council belong to the majority party. The procedures of the council which form an essential background to these communication patterns are discussed in detail in *Class, Religion*, chap. 4.

highest on corporation housing. The same is true of Labour designation of Labour convenors. The variation in these Labour designations is only relative however for their lowest total on traffic is greater than the highest Progressive total on housing (21 compared to 13). The Progressive–Labour contrast in designations of convenors helps to explain one peculiarity of these communication patterns – the greater tendency for Labour councillors to consult at all. Over all four issues Labour councillors made 189 designations of other councillors, Progressives 148, even allowing for their greater recourse to the other party.[150] Within their own party Labour councillors made 186 designations compared to Progressives' 115. On the individual topics it is only on traffic that the numbers of designations made by each side approach equality. Thus not only are Progressive consultations held less firmly within their party: less of them take place. This contrast is somewhat modified if we divide the absolute numbers of designations by the numbers of councillors interviewed in each party; the average designations by Progressive councillors are then 3·9, compared to 4·2 for Labour. The remaining contrast might be held to reflect the traditional independence and individuality of Progressive councillors as compared to the collective traditions and sterner discipline of Labour. In fact the more numerous Labour consultations by Labour are almost all directed to convenors. Membership of the same party seems to facilitate necessary consultation of these central figures. Membership of a different party cuts it to the essential minimum. So heavy is Labour reliance on convenors that their consultations (overall and on each topic) with persons other than the interested convenor are much fewer in number than Progressive consultations with those persons (overall Progressive designations come to 118 to Labours' 66).

Thus the greater volume of Labour consultation as well as the relative fragmentation of Progressive consultation spring from the same cause: Labour, being the party in power, has the convenorships. Because consultation with convenors is necessary, given the constitution of the council, the patterns we perceive here will probably have been reversed when control passed from Labour to Progressive in 1968.[151]

[150] The members of designations of officials made by Labour and Progressive councillors is almost the same: 35–41.

[151] Patterns of consultation with backbenchers on each topic were probably also reversed. Labour councillors consult convenors in part because they are experienced and expert party members: if in opposition they would still to some extent

Present consultation within the Labour party tends to the hierarchical through the previously noted tendency for many councillors to consult convenors without being consulted by them. Inside both parties the chairman and vice-chairman attract more than the average number of designations, although on these four topics the number is insignificant compared with the totals attracted by the interested convenors. It is probable that regular group meetings provide the main opportunity to get the views and information of the principal party figures.

There is also more communication between ward colleagues than can be explained on a purely random basis. It is only really noticeable on corporation housing (where 24 per cent of all designations of councillors are of ward colleagues) and on corporation schools (where 19 per cent of all designations of councillors are of ward colleagues). Both these topics involve decisions of considerable import for constituents in all wards. On traffic problems and rates, which do not have the same localised bearings, ward consultations are 11 per cent of total designations of councillors.

The discontinuities in communication associated with the special position of convenors and with ward ties do not seriously affect our expectations about the behaviour of councillors as an interacting whole. Some tendencies to hierarchy and some kinds of clustering are to be found inside any integrated social group. Much more adverse to any view of councillors as constituting an interacting group is the low level of inter-party communication. On previous evidence the total amount of interaction is greater among councillors than among partyworkers and electors. But councillors cannot be said to be more integrated than these other groups if interaction takes place largely inside each party and not between them. In that case the Labour and Progressive groups are the really cohesive bodies we should be discussing and the collectivity of councillors a conception without political reality.

We must qualify this conclusion however by considering first that the level of inter-party consultation, low though it be, is probably higher than that between partyworkers and electors. It may – we are forced to speculate – be the minimum necessary to produce the

---

consult them as well as the interested Progressive convenors. But on the other side these would now be as well as convenors the most experienced and expert Progressive Party members and would attract the disproportionate designations from Progressives which we now see the interested Labour convenors getting from Labour.

generally higher agreement of councillors. Moreover the nature of the consultations we asked about may limit the conclusions to be drawn from the reported patterns. In face-to-face, deliberate, individual consultation councillors may be primarily drawn to their party colleagues. But other opportunities for communication and support exist in the council chamber and on committees, in semi-public meetings rather than strictly individual contacts. If it were not so how could we explain the relative lack of consultation with party leaders, when we know that both parties function as solid and cohesive voting blocks on party issues? Semi-public interaction might suffice on its own to bring opinions together. A further qualification to the view of councillors as irrevocably split between their parties lies in the 18 per cent of all designations made of officials – in relatively equal numbers by Labour and Progressive interviewees. Officials (and other high-level activists such as the newspaper correspondents and pressure-group representatives) may act as go-betweens informing councillors of the other side's views, suggesting compromises, and thus bringing opinions closer together. If we add the 9 per cent of consultations between the parties[152] to the 18 per cent of consultations with officials we are approaching a significant level of genuinely integrative behaviour in the council as a whole.

These qualifications made, the evidence (however imperfect) that we actually have cast some doubt on the link between integrative behaviour, agreement and councillors' consequent freedom of action. It behoves us now to examine the connection between integrative behaviour and agreement more directly.

DIRECT EFFECTS OF INTEGRATIVE BEHAVIOUR AMONG COUNCILLORS UPON THEIR AGREEMENT

1. The questions upon which the foregoing discussion has been based can be used in conjunction with the knowledge we possess about each councillor's preferences on the issues of pubs, fees, parking and rates to provide a limited test of the assertion that integrative behaviour promotes preferential agreement. If the assertion is valid we expect that councillors who normally discuss the broad topics of corporation housing and schools, traffic problems and rates will agree more on the narrower issues which lies in that policy-area than councillors who do not normally discuss the topic. Acting on this idea we can assess the

[152] Nine per cent out of all consultations: 11 per cent of consultations *with councillors only*, as noted above.

average level of agreement among all the pairs of councillors we inter-viewed,[153] on each issue, and contrast this average level with the agree-ment of pairs among our interviewees who would consult on each corresponding broader topic.

It will be remembered that agreement on pubs, fees, parking and rates was measured along a continuum from 'agree very strongly' through 'don't know, neutral', to 'disagree very strongly' (Fig. 5.1). For pur-poses of this analysis agreement has to be expressed as a numerical value, since an average is to be taken. This numerical value can be obtained through alternative methods which make different assumptions. We can in the first place regard the various positions on the continuum as constituting a nine-point scale of distance from strong agreement: e.g. 'agree fairly strongly' is assumed to be one unit from strongest agreement, 'agree not strongly' two units, 'neutral' or 'inevitable' four units, 'disagree very strongly' eight units.[154] The assignation of interval level status to these issue-preferences implies that the distance between each position on the continuum is the same. And this impli-cation is disputable. On the other hand the assumption enables us to apply more powerful techniques to our data. To preserve this advant-age while at the same time guarding against misinterpretation we have performed a parallel analysis which disregards possibly variable feelings on the issue and proceeds on the humbler but less controversial assumption that agreement, neutrality and disagreement constitute a mutually exclusive and exhaustive trichotomy. A score of nothing can be assigned to agreement, one to neutrality, two to disagreement, and average agreements calculated on that basis[155] for all pairs of inter-viewed councillors and all pairs which consult. Results from these two types of analysis can be compared to see whether they support the same conclusions. Both can be repeated under a control for party.

In fact both the full opinion-scale and the trichotomy produce the same substantive results. On pubs and parking, communicating pairs

[153] A limitation on this analysis is of course that we can assess the agreement only of councillors we interviewed. Hence we lose all information about consultation outside the square in Fig. 6.1.

[154] We again warmly acknowledge M. J. Taylor's initial suggestion of this method of estimating agreement and his subsequent programming for the whole analysis undertaken in this section.

[155] For a similar procedure applied to voting see H. Alker Jr., 'Dimensions of Conflict in the General Assembly', *APSR* LVIII (Sep 1964) 642–6; B. M. Russett, 'Discovering Voting Groups in the United Nations', *APSR* LX (June 1966) 327–30.

show less agreement than the average for all pairs: on fees and rates, communicating pairs show more agreement than the average.[156] On both trichotomy and full opinion-scale these results are upheld for the parties on all issues except pubs, where communicating pairs inside the Labour party show more agreement than the average for all councillors and the Progressives substantially less.[157]

Substantively these findings are interesting for the fact that the issues where normal consultation increases agreement are those on which councillors as a whole are most disagreed. A case might be made for consultation on the disagreed areas being directed successfully towards mutual influence while on the more agreed areas it becomes pure information-gathering. But there is nothing to indicate that corporation schools as such are a more disputed area than housing, in spite of the fact that the specific outcrops (in the shape of the pubs and fees questions) which we are considering do contrast in this way. Moreover agreement on fees and rates between communicating pairs inside each party parallels the general increase and the parties are internally agreed on these issues. This correspondence between findings for the parties and findings for the body of councillors also rules out a possibility that the extensive designation of convenors affects results. For there are no Progressive convenors, yet the pattern of results among Progressives is identical with that discovered for councillors as a whole.

In the absence of data on a larger number of issues it is difficult to interpret these findings. What does emerge clearly is the limited effect of integrative behaviour on agreement. On the evidence of this analysis communication does increase agreement on some issues (whose character remains obscure). But its influence is not so general as we originally anticipated. The vital question for our model is whether the issues on which integrative behaviour increases agreement are in

[156] Average agreement compared with communicants' agreement on the full opinion-scale is: pubs, 2·7739 to 3·6935; fees, 4·0715 to 2·5811; parking, 2·9934 to 4·4878; rates, 3·8688 to 2·1667. The higher the figure the lower the agreement. Councillors' agreement in terms of this measure is greatest overall on pubs, next greatest on parking, next on rates and least on fees. This ordering accords with that established through the comparison of proportions on Fig. 5.1 except that the positions of rates and fees are reversed. We have here an alternative measure of agreement on these issues which was not employed in Chap. 5 because the comparison of proportions is generalisable to the single and multiple choices of alternatives which were discussed in the remainder of that chapter, whereas the assignation of numerical values is not. The trichotomised measure orders issues on councillors' agreement as follows: parking, pubs, rates, fees.

[157] Labour, 1·3939; Progressives, 7·4545.

the majority or the minority. The former finding would offer at least qualified support to our argument for councillors' integrative behaviour promoting the agreements which then buttress their collective freedom of action. Since we here find consultation associated with increased agreement on two issues and with decreased agreement on another two, the need for supplementary investigation is evident.

2. Other indicators of integrative behaviour on the four issues are in fact available. In their interviews we asked the six municipal correspondents of the Glasgow press, who are probably the best placed observers of council affairs, to rank the issues in regard to the bitterness they engendered among councillors, and the tendencies to compromise and the party solidarity they aroused. These judgements were designed to get at aspects of the collective behaviour of councillors which escape the previous examination at the level of pairs. The expression of bitterness and willingness to compromise are obvious features of non-integrative and integrative behaviour respectively. Party solidarity is included because the data from Fig. 6.1 seem to reveal it as an impediment to full interaction among councillors. Hence, weaker party solidarity will provide more opportunities for interaction between councillors of the different parties. If the connection between integrative behaviour and agreement is strong and general then the ordering of the issues on councillors' agreement should be identical with their ordering on tendencies to compromise and the reverse of their ordering on bitterness and party solidarity.

A preliminary question is the extent to which the indicators of integrative behaviour themselves coincide. As it turns out they show a perfect correspondence, allowing for ties. Bitterness and party solidarity fall into the reverse order to compromise. And with the ranking on agreement (measured through the percentage differences discussed in relation to Fig. 5.1) the ordering on all indicators shows a one-to-one relationship, positive or negative, as is appropriate for the prediction.

Taken with the previous evidence that individual consultation promoted agreement on two issues, this finding offers support to the view that integrative behaviour does count as a factor making for relative consensus and consequent autonomy among politicians.

PUBLIC AND PRIVATE SETTLEMENT OF POLITICAL ISSUES

Perhaps more immediately than in the case of integrative behaviour the politicians' autonomy has been regarded as resting on their ability to emphasise and de-emphasise political issues. Councillors are expected

TABLE 6.2

Degree of integrative behaviour shown by Glasgow councillors on four current issues, related to the extent of their preferential agreement on these four issues (rank-orderings of issues on indicators of integrative behaviour and extent of agreement)

	Rank-order of issues on indicators of integrative behaviour			Rank-order of issue on
	Bitterness	Compromise	Party solidarity	agreement on preferences
Pubs	2	1	4	1
Parking	2	2	3	2
Fees	2	2	2	3
Rates	1	3	1	4

'Pubs' refers to the proposals to have pubs in corporation housing estates; 'Parking' refers to the proposals to extend parking-meters all over the city centre; 'Fees' refers to the proposals for abolition of fee-paying in corporation schools; 'Rates' refers to the proposals for an increase in rates. Entries in the table are numerals signifying the rank-order of these four issues on three indicators of integrative behaviour and on preferential agreement on issues. The indicators of integrative behaviour are the judgements of the six municipal correspondents of the Glasgow press in reply to the following questions: 'Considering these four issues, pubs in council housing estates, abolition of fee-paying, parking-meters and rates, which would you say is the one on which councillors have shown most bitterness?' 'Which is the one of the remaining three on which councillors have shown most bitterness?' 'Which is the one where there has been least bitterness shown by councillors?' 'Considering these four issues, pubs in council housing estates, abolition of fee-paying, parking-meters and rates, which would you say is the one on which councillors have shown the most tendency to compromise?' 'On which one of the remaining three have councillors shown the most tendency to compromise?' 'On which one have councillors shown least tendency to compromise?' 'Considering these four issues, pubs in council housing estates, abolition of fee-paying, parking-meters and rates, which would you say is the one on which councillors have shown most solidarity with their party group?' 'On which one of the remaining three have councillors shown most solidarity with their party group?' 'On which one of the remaining two have councillors shown the least solidarity with their party group?' Issues are assigned a definite rank on the three indicators of integrative behaviour where at least five out of six correspondents agreed on the assignment. Where the correspondents did not agree to this extent the issues are tied – notably on the relative bitterness shown on the different issues. The measures of agreement on issue-preferences are the percentage differences between the proportions of councillors agreeing and disagreeing very strongly, between the proportions agreeing and disagreeing very strongly and fairly strongly, and between the proportions agreeing and disagreeing *in toto* without reference to strength of feeling. These have previously been presented in Table 5.1, with which the ordering of issues in terms of councillors' agreement can be checked. For the correspondence between this method and other methods of ranking these issues on the extent of councillors' agreement see note 156.

to focus the attention of electors upon some issues through their influence upon the mass media, and to play up a more limited number by flinging them into the party arena. They are expected to deflect attention from other issues by keeping them from the mass media and directing party competition away from them. These assertions, if true, would eliminate the threat to politicians' freedom of action which is posed by the restraints of party competition.

It is difficult to measure the promotion and deflection of issues directly. However an indirect test of councillors' abilities in this field – hence of many of our assertions relating to their autonomy – can be provided through their own estimates of how far they can draw attention to issues or keep attention from them. Seventy-four per cent of councillors actually thought they exercised influence in bringing issues to general attention compared to 66 per cent of partyworkers. On the reverse question of playing down issues only 23 per cent of partyworkers could even think of a problem which would be worsened by general attention. Fifty-five per cent of councillors could think of such a problem.[158] When asked directly if they could exercise influence in keeping issues from general attention councillors split almost evenly: 46 per cent thought they could, 48 per cent thought not.

On this evidence councillors do, as anticipated, show a strong desire for autonomy – stronger than partyworkers': more also attributed to themselves an influence over the promotion of issues, as is only natural. And half regard themselves as capable of the much more difficult task of muffling public debate on certain problems, although half discount their influence in that direction. This last finding is more ambiguous than the others. Should more weight attach to the half who thought they could muffle issues or to the half who denied that they could? Before we can resolve this question we must discover the effect of party on their replies and also examine the grounds which councillors advance for making these estimates of their influence.

Eighty-seven per cent of Progressive councillors feel they can bring issues to general attention compared with 65 per cent of Labour councillors. Seventy-two per cent of Labour partyworkers feel they can get attention compared to 60 per cent of Progressive partyworkers. Party thus makes Progressive councillors more confident of gaining

---

[158] When asked further what specific problems might be worsened 12 per cent of all councillors mentioned some aspect of housing, 18 per cent crime of various types, 6 per cent welfare and amenity questions. No other problem was mentioned by more than 2 per cent of all councillors.

publicity than Labour but Progressive partyworkers less confident than Labour! The difference at councillor level could be attributed to the restrictions imposed upon Labour backbenchers by their membership of the majority party: being privy to decisions largely made by convenors and forbidden to speak out of turn. As the Opposition, Progressives might be better able to skirmish in open foraging order. However officeholders in the Labour party turn out to show no more confidence than backbenchers: only 68 per cent feel they can gain publicity. It may be that the restrictions of power bind all Labour councillors equally.

TABLE 6.3

Appraisals of means of, and obstacles to, bringing issues to general attention (percentages of councillors and partyworkers saying issues can or cannot be brought to general attention, respectively)

Councillors

Issues can be brought to general attention:	First mention	Second mention	Issues cannot be brought to general attention because gained only:	First mention	Second mention
Through being a councillor	16	7	Through holding other position than R holds	16	—
Through corporation departments/officials	2	—	Through corporation departments/officials	16	—
Through central government	2	3	Through central government	16	—
Through the parties	4	—	Through the parties which carry no weight	—	5
Through non-political local organisations	2	2	Through non-political local organisations	—	—
Through public meetings	23	23	Through public meetings which are ineffective	53	42
Through the mass media	51	28	Through mass media not open to R	5	—
Through direct approaches to public	—	3	Through public who are apathetic	—	—
			Through gaining electoral victory	—	—

Partyworkers

Issues can be brought to general attention:	First mention	Second mention	Issues cannot be brought to general attention because gained only:	First mention	Second mention
Through councillors	19	15	Through councillors	14	—
Through corporation departments/officials	1	3	Through corporation departments/officials	—	—
Through central government	3	3	Through central government	3	—
Through the parties	49	15	Through the parties which carry no weight	32	5
Through non-political local organisations	1	1	Through non-political local organisations	—	—
Through public meetings	13	6	Through public meetings which are ineffective	5	—
Through the mass media	—	1	Through mass media not open to R	5	3
Through direct approaches to public	14	1	Through public who are apathetic	27	3
			Through gaining electoral victory	8	—

Base numbers for percentages in the table are: 61 for councillors who feel that issues can be brought to general attention; 19 for councillors who feel that issues cannot be brought to general attention; 78 for partyworkers who feel that issues can be brought to general attention; 37 for partyworkers who feel that issues cannot be brought to general attention. Responses were elicited by the questions: 'Do you feel that you and your colleagues on council have much influence in bringing issues to general attention?' 'Why is that?' (councillors). 'Do you feel that you and your colleagues active in ward politics have much influence in bringing issues to general attention?' 'Why is that?' (partyworkers). Responses of councillors and partyworkers who felt they had influence were coded into sixty-three detailed categories which are combined for our purposes into the eight in the table. Responses of councillors and partyworkers who felt they had no influence were coded into fifty detailed categories which are combined for our purposes into the nine in the table. The combination of the original detailed categories into those in the table can be studied through the codebooks for the Glasgow Studies held by the Social Science Research Council Data Archive at the University of Essex. The category 'through the central government' refers to all agents and representatives of central government, including M.P.s. The full reply of each respondent was noted and subsequently coded into the detailed categories. Since many people gave two replies to the questions (in terms of our detailed categories) both the first and second mentioned are noted in the table. Few persons give more than two however, so third-mentioned replies are not given. Percentages for first and second replies cannot be combined since such combination would give rise to double-counting as discussed in the text of Chapter 5. Each set of percentages (in this and following tables) relates to a base of 100 per cent but they do not always add precisely to 100 per cent because of rounding and because percentages from whom nothing was ascertained have been omitted.

The principal means to publicity – for those councillors confident that they can attain it – are the mass media (mainly newspapers). A lesser emphasis is placed on public meetings and on the platform provided by council membership. Those councillors who feel unlikely

TABLE 6.4

Progressive appraisals of means of, and obstacles to, bringing issues to general attention (percentages of Progressive councillors and partyworkers saying issues can or cannot be brought to general attention, respectively)

Progressive Councillors

Issues can be brought to general attention:	First mention	Second mention	Issues cannot be brought to general attention because gained only:	First mention	Second mention
Through being a councillor	21	3	Through holding other position than R holds	(60)	—
Through corporation departments/officials	3	—	Through corporation departments/officials	—	—
Through central government	—	3	Through central government	—	—
Through the parties	3	—	Through the parties which carry no weight	—	(20)
Through non-political local organisations	3	—	Through non-political local organisations	—	—
Through public meetings	27	36	Through public meetings which are ineffective	—	(40)
Through the mass media	42	27	Through mass media not open to R	(40)	—
Through direct approaches to public	—	—	Through public who are apathetic	—	—
			Through gaining electoral victory	—	—

to get attention predominantly stress the unrepresentativeness of public meetings. All partyworkers place a natural emphasis on getting attention through the parties. Substantial numbers also mention approaches to councillors and the public – those who feel unlikely to get attention stress the public's apathy. The great contrast between

Progressive Partyworkers

Issues can be brought to general attention:	First mention	Second mention	Issues cannot be brought to general attention because gained only:	First mention	Second mention
Through councillors	25	22	Through councillors	15	—
Through corporation departments/officials	3	3	Through corporation departments/officials	—	—
Through central government	6	—	Through central government	—	—
Through the parties	25	9	Through the parties which carry no weight	25	5
Through non-political local organisations	3	—	Through non-political local organisations	—	—
Through public meetings	19	3	Through public meetings which are ineffective	5	—
Through the mass media	—	—	Through mass media not open to R	—	5
Through direct approaches to public	19	3	Through public who are apathetic	30	—
			Through gaining electoral victory	15	—

Base numbers for percentages in table are: 33 for Progressive councillors who feel that issues can be brought to general attention; 5 for Progressive councillors who feel that issues cannot be brought to general attention (percentages based on this tiny figure are bracketed); 32 for Progressive partyworkers who feel that issues can be brought to general attention; 20 for Progressive partyworkers who feel that issues cannot be brought to general attention.

Progressive and Labour partyworkers emerges again in the reliance they place upon parties as channels of publicity. The fact that Labour predominates in Glasgow means for partyworkers that the party is better equipped to attract attention. Progressives on this level stress the ineffectiveness of their party and council group as a consequence of losing the elections. The only alternative for Progressives not confident of getting attention lies in approaching the public, which is apathetic.

A notable contrast emerges between partyworkers and councillors in their attitudes to the mass media, which are hardly mentioned by the former. But the largest numbers of both Progressive and Labour councillors emphasise their use. No other channel compares in importance for Labour councillors, although Progressives would also employ their platform in the council and at public meetings. This contrast between partyworkers and councillors presumably stems from differences in their contact with reporters and in the relative ease of access to the media with which they credit themselves.

Fifty-eight per cent of Progressive councillors consider that they can keep issues from public attention, if necessary, compared to 37 per cent of Labour councillors and 38 per cent of Labour office-holders.

TABLE 6.5

Labour appraisals of means of, and obstacles to, bringing issues to general attention (percentages of Labour councillors and partyworkers saying issues can or cannot be brought to general attention, respectively)

Labour Councillors

Issues can be brought to general attention:	First mention	Second mention	Issues cannot be brought to general attention because gained only:	First mention	Second mention
Through being a councillor	11	10	Through holding other position than R holds	—	—
Through corporation departments/officials	—	—	Through corporation departments/officials	21	—
Through central government	4	4	Through central government	14	—
Through the parties	4	—	Through the parties which carry no weight	—	—
Through non-political local organisations	—	4	Through non-political local organisations	—	—
Through public meetings	18	7	Through public meetings which are ineffective	64	42
Through the mass media	61	28	Through mass media not open to R	—	—
Through direct approaches to public	—	7	Through public who are apathetic	—	—
			Through gaining electoral victory	—	—

Labour Partyworkers

Issues can be brought to general attention:	First mention	Second mention	Issues cannot be brought to general attention because gained only:	First mention	Second mention
Through councillors	15	11	Through councillors	12	—
Through corporation departments/officials	—	2	Through corporation departments/officials	—	—
Through central government	—	4	Through central government	6	—
Through the parties	65	20	Through the parties which carry no weight	41	6
Through non-political local organisations	—	2			
Through public meetings	9	9	Through non-political local organisations	6	—
Through the mass media	—	2	Through public meetings which are ineffective	12	6
Through direct approaches to public	11	—	Through mass media not open to R	24	—
			Through public who are apathetic	—	—
			Through gaining electoral victory	—	—

Base numbers for percentages in table are: 28 for Labour councillors who feel that issues can be brought to general attention; 14 for Labour councillors who feel that issues cannot be brought to general attention; 46 for Labour partyworkers who feel that issues can be brought to general attention; 17 for Labour partyworkers who feel that issues cannot be brought to general attention.

Thus the piquant contrast persists of the Opposition feeling more confident of its ability to regulate publicity than the ruling party. Such confidence may well follow from a real contrast between the parties: the Opposition may in fact enjoy greater initiative than the dominant party in deciding which issues to publicise and which to play down. It is likely that the Labour convenors and their party colleagues more often wish to keep things quiet than the Progressives. The latter therefore must more often be in a position to decide whether they will co-operate or whether they will reveal all. This interpretation finds some support when we examine the grounds on which councillors say they can or cannot keep issues from attention. Progressives who say they can, place more emphasis on co-operation between councillors and parties in directing attention from issues. Labour councillors trust more to co-operation or management of the press. Labour councillors who feel unable to muffle issues emphasise the tendency of some councillors to talk, more than the corresponding Progressives. It is also true that Labour councillors feel rather more strongly than Progressives that issues *should* not be kept from the public, an emotion which probably derives from the party's populist traditions.

From the replies of councillors as a whole it is apparent that both those who think issues can be muffled, and those who think not, chiefly emphasise the way issues are handled by councillors and by reporters. Over the first and second responses to the question almost half those who are sceptical of the likelihood of issues being muffled (as opposed to those who think they should not be muffled) stress the role of reporters in publicising them. This emphasis is in line with the previous

TABLE 6.6

Appraisals of means of, and obstacles to, keeping issues from general attention (percentages of all councillors, Labour councillors and Progressive councillors saying issues can or cannot be kept from general attention, respectively)

All Councillors

Issues can be kept from general attention because:	First mention	Second mention	Issues cannot be kept from general attention because:	First mention	Second mention
Councillors/officials can agree/manoeuvre to keep issues quiet	53	11	Repetition: Issues cannot be kept quiet	2	5
Parties can agree/manoeuvre to keep issues quiet	14	5	Issues should not be kept quiet	25	7
			Councillors/officials will always talk	30	16
Reporters can agree to keep an issue quiet/need not be informed	31	11	Party competition always brings issues into the open	4	5
			Reporters will always find out about an issue	32	16
Public are ill-informed and their attention soon wanders	3	3	Important issues cannot be kept quiet	5	5

Progressive Councillors

Issues can be kept from general attention because:	First mention	Second mention	Issues cannot be kept from general attention because:	First mention	Second mention
Councillors/officials can agree/manoeuvre to keep issues quiet	50	9	Repetition: Issues cannot be kept quiet	6	6
Parties can agree/manoeuvre to keep issues quiet	23	5	Issues should not be kept quiet	19	—
			Councillors/officials will always talk	19	19
Reporters can agree to keep an issue quiet/need not be informed	23	14	Party competition always brings issues into the open	6	12
Public are ill-informed and their attention soon wanders	5	—	Reporters will always find out about an issue	44	19
			Important issues cannot be kept quiet	6	—

Labour Councillors

Issues can be kept from general attention because:	First mention	Second mention	Issues cannot be kept from general attention because:	First mention	Second mention
Councillors/officials can agree/manoeuvre to keep issues quiet	57	14	Repetition: Issues cannot be kept quiet	—	4
Parties can agree/manoeuvre to keep issues quiet	—	7	Issues should not be kept quiet	29	11
			Councillors/officials will always talk	36	14
Reporters can agree to keep an issue quiet/need not be informed	43	21	Party competition always brings issues into the open	7	—
Public are ill-informed and their attention soon wanders	—	14	Reporters will always find out about an issue	25	14
			Important issues cannot be kept quiet	4	7

Base numbers for percentages in the table are: 36 for all councillors who say that issues can be kept from general attention; 44 for all councillors who say that issues cannot be kept from general attention; 22 for Progressive councillors who say that issues can be kept from general attention; 16 for Progressive councillors who say that issues cannot be kept from general attention; 14 for Labour councillors who say that issues can be kept from general attention; 28 for Labour councillors who say that issues cannot be kept from general attention. There are slight discrepancies between these numbers and the numbers who replied 'yes' and 'no' to the original question whether issues could be kept from general attention, which arise because some who replied 'don't know' to the original question subsequently mentioned obstacles to keeping issues quiet. Responses were elicited by the question: 'If you and your colleagues on the council felt that a problem would be worsened by general attention being paid to it, do you think you could keep it from general attention?' 'In what way?' (*if yes*); 'Why is that' (*if no*). Responses to both follow-up questions were coded into thirty-three detailed categories which are combined for our purposes into the ten in the table. The amalgamation of detailed into general categories can again be checked on the basis of the Glasgow codebooks held by the S.S.R.C. Data Archive. The full reply of each respondent was noted and subsequently coded into the detailed categories. Since many people gave two replies (in terms of our detailed categories), both first and second are noted in the table separately in order to avoid the risk of double-counting.

stress on the role of the media in bringing issues to general attention. Thus it is important in deciding the question of how far councillors can regulate publicity to discover whether (as the sceptical fear) their attitude is to probe, publish and be damned. Fortunately, we have on this point the independent testimony of the municipal correspondents themselves.

Correspondents agree five to one that it is impossible for councillors to keep issues quiet. Four maintain that some councillors will always leak a matter to them and one stresses the willingness of one party to provide information about the other. On the other hand it is obvious from their replies that what the correspondents are really emphasising is the inability of councillors to keep things quiet without their co-operation. For all agree that they would delay revealing any item of corporation news if they were specially requested to do so by a convenor or councillors. Four out of five who were asked this question had actually been requested to delay news in the past and had done so.

It seems therefore that the fifth of all councillors who believe that issues cannot be kept quiet because of reporters are suffering from somewhat exaggerated fears: that by co-operation and agreement if not by other methods issues can be played down by councillors acting in conjunction with correspondents.[159]

[159] Correspondents agree more with partyworkers in that four out of five cannot think of any problem that would be worsened by general attention. Since their work lies in publicity this finding is not perhaps surprising. However it seems more important that they will withhold news if asked. Moreover not all news can be

Correspondents are also unanimous and in agreement with council-lors in stressing the media as the main channel through which issues can be brought to general attention. But in doing so they emphasise their dependence on news emanating from the council. Asked how they obtained information about local politics, four cited convenors and officials, one said he got it from councillors generally and one by lobby-ing corporation committees. Both councillors and correspondents therefore recognise their interdependence: an appraisal which makes for co-operation. The general trend of these findings is in fact to con-firm our expectation that councillors enjoy substantial freedom in emphasising some issues and playing down others. Many of them share this realisation, and it appears that even those who do not will benefit. Certainly their autonomy seems dependent on correspondents' co-operation. But since the views and interests of the two sides converge the councillors' dependence is not a serious limitation on their freedom of collective action.

THE IMPACT OF PARTY COMPETITION UPON ACTIVISTS COMPARED WITH ELECTORS

We have stressed the potentially disruptive influence which party competition might exercise upon politicians' autonomy. The threat stems from the assumption of our model that activists as a whole are disproportionately inclined to see their own party's electoral victory as leading to the immediate satisfaction of their political demands, and the opposing party's triumph as a sweeping threat to these demands. Since the model also assumes that activists are exceptionally consistent and tenacious in translating their political aspirations into action, this reasoning would lead to a prediction of utter conflict and division among activists, were it not qualified. For the model additionally postulates the perception of other paths to demand satisfaction, which can be followed in any political situation likely to exist in a mass democracy through sheer increases in political activity.

Although alternatives to all-out competition exists, however, any frustration of demands must carry a standing temptation to intensify and extend the party struggle. And this temptation must exist in con-stant tension with the opportunities for co-operative action already noted.

---

published: priorities must be established, and correspondents' criteria of news-worthiness most closely parallel councillors' appraisals of important problems (see Chapter 5).

The strength of the connection between demand-satisfaction and party is demonstrated by the data we present at this point, before going on to consider how this chaotic force may be limited by councillors' implicit action. The data consist firstly of the estimates given by each party's workers and electors of how far their own party clearly supports their own preferences on the current issues of pubs, fees, parking and rates, and on the problem facing Glasgow which they consider most important. These estimates are supplemented by the same groups' appraisals of how far the other party clearly opposes their own preferences. It is regrettable that we cannot extend this comparison to councillors of each party. Unfortunately, for reasons of time, these questions were not asked of councillors. On the whole what has been found true for partyworkers in the analyses undertaken in previous chapters has been found to apply with even greater force to councillors. In the case of these extremely party-related questions, however, it may be that councillors would show themselves somewhat more pessimistic about their own party and more optimistic about the Opposition. But in the absence of direct data from councillors we are forced to extrapolate from the trends observed among one set of activists to the other.

Among the appraisals there are only two exceptions from the general tendency for more partyworkers than electors to see their own party as clearly offering support and the other party as clearly opposing: these occur with the Progressives on parking. A wider gap opens between Labour partyworkers' and electors' favourable perceptions of their own party and unfavourable perceptions of the opposing party than is the case among Progressives. Except on rates and the most important problem fewer Progressive than Labour partyworkers see their own party clearly favouring their own position. On the unfavourable attitude of the other party percentages approach equality. Progressive electors are consistently more inclined than Labour electors to see their own party as favourable and the other as unfavourable. Party ties have in fact inconsistent effects at the two levels of activity.

Direct appraisals of the link between party and personal demands can be supplemented by the reports of each stratum about the action most likely to secure their preference on the four current issues (pubs, fees, parking and rates) previously considered. From the leading alternatives reported we can see how much activists, compared with electors, rely on party action to secure their demands. We can also specifically check our assumption that activists recognise other means

TABLE 6.7

Appraisals of support given by own party, and of opposition by other party, to own preferences on current issues (percentages of partyworkers and electors by party)

	Progressive Partyworkers (per cent)	Progressive Electors (per cent)	Labour Partyworkers (per cent)	Labour Electors (per cent)
Pubs				
Own party favours	44	38	73	35
Other party opposes	39	37	28	18
Fees				
Own party favours	67	47	80	45
Other party opposes	69	48	72	30
Parking				
Own party favours	35	44	48	47
Other party opposes	24	29	28	19
Rates				
Own party favours	83	65	48	30
Other party opposes	76	74	67	37
Most important problem facing Glasgow				
Own party favours	89	60	83	46

Entries are percentages who perceive own party as clearly favouring and other party as clearly opposing own preference. Percentages who perceive own party and other party as having no opinion or split and who perceive own party as clearly opposed and other party clearly favouring own preference are not reported. The four issues are: introduction of pubs into corporation housing estates (pubs); abolition of fee-paying in corporation schools (fees); extension of parking-meters all over the city centre (parking); increase in rates (rates). The survey questions from which responses reported in the table on these four issues derive are: 'Do you feel the Labour Party favours or opposes or has no opinion on the proposal to – ?' 'Do you feel the Progressive Party favours or opposes or has no opinion on the proposal to – ?' Responses on the most important problem derive from a question asked of all partyworkers and electors when they had named and discussed the most important problem which they considered to face Glasgow: 'Which party do you think would be most likely to do what you want on this, the Progressive Party, the Labour Party or wouldn't there be any difference?'

to demand-satisfaction than party-related action, and furthermore discover how affiliation with the majority and minority parties affects chosen strategies.

THE POLITICIANS 241

Not shown in Table 6.8 are the replies (considered above) of 26 per cent of electors, 5 per cent of partyworkers and 4 per cent of councillors that they would do nothing to get their way on the four issues. We present the most popular appraisals in the form used in Chapter 5 to estimate agreement, so that as well as considering substantive implications we can note the agreement of each grouping on the strategies they would adopt.

Looking first at the total strata it is obvious that very little agreement does exist on the strategies to be adopted. Each stratum divides fairly

TABLE 6.8

Agreement on appraisals of strategic action on current issues (percentages of councillors, partyworkers and electors naming the appraisals most popular among each group on first mention and differences between these percentages: proportions of those in each group out of those naming either of the two most popular appraisals on first mention who name the other most popular appraisal on their second and third mentions, i.e. degrees of overlap)

Group	Order of popularity	Substantive appraisal: Work through:	First-mention per cent endorsement	Percentage difference	Second-mention degree of overlap	Third-mention degree of overlap
All councillors	1	Party groups in council	34			
	2	Council/councillors as a body	30	4	0·13	0·02
All partyworkers	1	Party organisation outside council	32			
	2	Informal group action	25	7	0·04	0·06
All electors	1	Informal group action	23			
	2	Council/councillors as a whole	20	3	0·10	0·01
Prog. councillors	1	Council/councillors as a body	50			
	2	Party groups in council	11	39	0·13	0·09
Prog. partyworkers	1	Informal group action	28			
	2	Council/councillors as a body	24	4	0·02	0·00
Prog. electors	1	Council/councillors as a body	23			
	2	Informal group action	18	5	0·12	0·02
Lab. councillors	1	Party groups in council	56			
	2	Council/councillors as a body	14	42	0·17	0·00
Lab. partyworkers	1	Party organisation outside council	52			
	2	Informal group action	19	33	0·05	0·10
Lab. electors	1	Informal group action	25			
	2	Council/councillors as a whole	20	5	0·10	0·02

The question which elicited the responses summarised in Table 6.8 is: 'If you felt strongly about any of these problems, pubs in housing estates, eliminating fee-paying schools, extending parking-meters, raising rates, what do you think you could do?' Its intent was to get at the type of action which would be taken on any current issue. Responses were coded into fifty-nine detailed categories which were, however, so grouped as to facilitate easy combination into the nine broader groupings on which general agreement was judged for the purposes of this table. Most courses of action mentioned in the table are self-explanatory. 'Informal group action' covers action with family, friends and neigh-bours directed to petitioning, canvassing and use of public meetings. 'Non-party pressure-groups' include churches, unions, co-ops, professional groups, parents' associations, tenants', occupiers', ratepayers' associations, etc. Some electors replied that they would do nothing but this is not counted here as a substantive appraisal for purposes of estimating agreement. Bases for percentages are the total samples and party groups, except for degrees of overlap.

evenly between two leading strategies: councillors between using the party groups on council, or the council as a whole: partyworkers between the general party organisation or informal group action: electors between informal group action and working through the council or councillors as a body. The fact that non-party strategies are only slightly less popular than party strategies among activists provides support for our assumption that they recognise other means to demand-satisfaction, in the form of lobbying activities, which certainly involves (in the case of partyworkers) an increase in political activity. However, the partisan nature of the leading strategy among both councillors and partyworkers confirms previous evidence about the closer connection made by them between personal demands and party success.

The level of agreement remains low for Labour and Progressive electors and for Progressive partyworkers. It increases remarkaby however for Labour partyworkers round an alternative hardly men-tioned by Progressives – action through the general party organisation. Progressives of course lack any tight party organisation of their own, but in view of their pessimism about who runs Glasgow (Chapter 2) the concentration of Labour on the party machinery in preference to council channels is remarkable. It accords with the marked tendency of Labour partyworkers to seek information through party channels which we noted in Chapter 4. It is the councillors who most fully reveal a party split however. Progressives and Labour neatly reverse each others' leading strategies, Labour relying heavily on action through the party group on council and Progressives on council agencies as a whole. Since Labour was, at the time of interviewing, the majority party, and action passed in the Labour group, through the voting discipline of members, had a high probability of becoming council policy, it is hardly surprising that they should show this reliance: nor that Progressives should seek influence through the means of persuasion provided by detailed debate in full council and committee. But the finding is of great interest in showing the kind of constraints imposed by election results upon the day-to-day activities of councillors. It emphasises the pervasive and continuous importance of the electoral competition for the two party groupings of councillors. Even in the case of Labour councillors and partyworkers however only a bare majority of the whole group chooses party-related action: the 35 per cent of Labour councillors and 39 per cent of Labour partyworkers who do not choose party strategies or say they would do nothing, opt for strategies (only partially mentioned in the table) such as informal group action or action through council and committee debate, which are non-partisan. And in the case of Progressives we can fairly confidently assume that greater electoral success in 1966 would have increased their tendency to rely on the party group in council.

The evidence does therefore support the general prediction that activists will see their political demands as bound up more closely with their own party's success than will electors. This stronger temptation to conflict can only be offset by the stronger impulses to co-operation already noted, and which appear in the tendency to choose non-partisan as well as partisan modes of demand-satisfaction.

PARTY COMPETITION AND KNOWLEDGE OF ISSUES

One way in which we expect party conflict to be channelled is through an implicit tendency of politicians to compete only on issues that are generally known. Competition on unknown issues would not attract votes and it is a simplifying assumption of our model that competition is solely directed to that end. Politicians' ability to direct publicity to or from an issue derives much of its importance from this argument, for it then implies their ability to regulate the scope of party competitions. If the temptation to compete varies with publicity then the deflection of publicity implies removal of the temptation to compete. On the other hand the extension of competition to issues not generally known implies that politicians are only partially in control of their own destiny, for the party competition would then (in the absence of other constraints) range more or less arbitrarily over the whole range of issues and constantly threaten to interest non-activists in the resolution of the question.

The actual prediction that parties compete only on issues which are generally known can be tested in relation to the four current issues already extensively discussed – pubs, fees, parking and rates. The degree of general knowledge of an issue can be assessed directly through the replies of electors in our sample. We can also consider the coverage given to each issue in the Glasgow press. For not only have most electors been shown to regard the press as their most important source of local political information[160] but the parties will compete not so much on objectively known issues as on the issues which their leaders think are known. Since most councillors appear to regard the press as the main channel of general publicity (Tables 6.3 and 6.6) they are most likely to form their estimates of which issues are known and which are unknown from the press coverage given them.[161]

In terms of the percentages of electors who had heard of them the ordering of issues is: rates (94 per cent), pubs (85 per cent), parking (73 per cent), fees (41 per cent). The ordering in terms of press coverage is: rates (241 sq. ins), parking (43 sq. ins), pubs (12 sq. ins), fees (0 sq. ins). The two orderings agree in placing rates as best known and fees as least known, although the ranks of pubs and parking are reversed.

We have also two measures of the degree of party competition on the issues. The judgements of municipal correspondents (described in the notes to Table 6.2) as to the extent of councillors' party solidarity are available. We can also look directly in Tables 5.2 and 5.3 at the tendency for councillors' preferences to divide by party on each of these issues. Both these indicators agree in estimating party competition as most evident on rates, next on fees, then on parking and pubs.

The comparison of rankings on knowledge and degree of competition completely refutes the idea that competition varies with publicity. Rates, the most widely known and most extensively covered issue, is indeed the question most contested by the parties. But fees, the next most contested, is least known – less generally known on either measure of knowledge than the strongly agreed proposals about pubs. It is true that in the period since we finished interviewing the fees question has received extensive press coverage and it is likely that many more electors have now heard of it than was true before. There is an opening

---

[160] Table 4.4.

[161] Press coverage of the four issues has been estimated by randomly selecting twenty dates during our interviewing period for each of the five main daily newspapers in Glasgow and measuring the amount of space devoted to each of the four issues over the twenty copies in square inches, then averaging over newspapers.

therefore for maintaining that politicians may compete not only on the issues which they feel to be most generally known but also on those which they feel to have the potential for becoming known. On present evidence we have no way of testing this modified assertion, but certainly the original must be abandoned.

The fact that councillors divide most strongly on rates also invalidates another expectation, namely that politicians would be wary of entering into party competition on any issues but those on which the population was already evenly split. In the case of splits it was anticipated that the politicians likely to be electorally disadvantaged by finding themselves on the minority side would in effect refuse to compete by associating themselves with the majority viewpoint. But on rates, where popular preferences and the Progressive councillors are overwhelmingly opposed to an increase, Labour councillors strongly support it. So unanimous is popular hostility to an increase that councillors can hardly fail to perceive it, and indeed from remarks made during interviews they appeared fully aware of popular feeling. Of course being in power Labour may have to support an increase since it appears the only way to avert administrative cutbacks which would carry adverse electoral consequences anyway. But there seems no tendency on the part of Labour councillors to equivocate about their unpopular support for an increase, which would be anticipated on the basis of our theoretical arguments.[162]

Our expectation that party competition would focus only on issues which councillors (with correspondents) had had a hand in singling out seems therefore to be false. Certainly the ability to play issues up or to play them down may still contribute to councillors' freedom from external interference. But so far as we can see from our data it does not regulate the party competition.

[162] Labour councillors may also have calculated that over all the policies Labour has to offer, the extension of housing and other services would outweigh the consequent rates increase with its own voters. It is true that the electoral appeals of the party have emphasised the services provided by the rates rather than the rates themselves. But since the rates question has high visibility (it is of all our issues best known to electors) Labour is probably unable to disguise its position effectively.

7. Conclusion

In spite of the reversal of expectations in regard to party competition, our stratification model has functioned reasonably well as an explanation of the trends uncovered in the Glasgow data. Even when unsuccessful its failure has raised interesting questions, and its utility as a guide and focus for analysis has been demonstrated in the analysis of agreement, representation, communication and politicians' autonomy.

As it turns out, however, the fit of hypotheses to some data is loose. Certainly many predictions have held, but many also have been rejected. Thus while the model as it stands can explain certain aspects of political life in Glasgow it is not as comprehensive an explanation as we originally set out to provide. Nevertheless, by modifying its original postulates in the directions indicated by the data so that they do fit the Glasgow situation, we can provide a connected and plausible explanation of many of our findings. Its standing will be *a posteriori* rather than *a priori*. But it will be open to testing against further empirical evidence from Glasgow and other cities. Moreover it can provide a coherent interim interpretation of our Glasgow findings, within the context of current political research.

To derive a new model which retains the effective parts of the old and modifies the rest, the best procedure is to list systematically each area covered by initial assumptions and to consider their success or failure in that area. (Exact estimates of the success or failure of the very detailed data-predictions derived from our initial assumptions are given in Appendix B. Just as in Chapter 1 we provided a gloss on the very detailed statement of assumptions provided there, so our review here gives a summary guide to the detailed assessment of their performance.)

Having reviewed the performance of detailed predictions we can then ask whether failures stemmed from major underlying defects of the initial model or simply from localised faults in the statement of some postulates, or from both. On the basis of these reappraisals a new explanation can be proposed and justified. Finally the new postulates will be conveniently summarised, to facilitate the generation of further predictions for testing in other investigations.

SUPPORT FOR ESTABLISHED PROCEDURES

It will be remembered that our initial model postulated a strong correlation between activism (in the absence of important irreconcilable disagreement) and demand-satisfaction. Although party exerted an unanticipated effect this was only one third of the total influence exerted.

Demand-satisfaction assumed importance in our original formulation only because a further connection was postulated with support of the procedures under which demand-satisfaction was secured. This connection was shown by our data to be entirely non-existent, so far as Glasgow is concerned. Although the finding disproves our original postulate it is of great importance in casting doubt on a widely-held assumption that support for existent procedures is prompted largely by self-interest. It seems that self-interest does not prompt such support, either because it is a less potent influence on political attitudes than has been thought or because it is not so enlightened as to generate understanding of the underlying procedures under which it has been gratified.

Although the explanation for greater activist support of procedures was in terms of self-interest, it nevertheless transpired from the analysis that in Glasgow activism did promote some pro-democratic preferences and appraisals. Its influence was greater on appraisals than on preferences. On the latter in fact its effects were outweighed by those of party. On the question of majority over minority decision on pubs neither party nor activism exerted much effect: on parking, party produced a parameter of 0·15 compared to 0·20 for activism; on rates, 0·30 to 0·16; on fees, 0·45 to nothing. Correlations between personal preferences on these issues and support for the corresponding majority or minority endorsement were generally highest for electors and less consistent among activists (partyworkers and councillors equally) (Table 2.3). Attitudes to pro- or anti-representative changes in Glasgow government – the best indicator of overall procedural support – were judged to be strongly influenced by party and to be relatively unaffected by activism as such.

Another notable point which emerged from all these comparisons was that partyworkers generally show more support for democratic procedures than councillors, although councillors show more support than electors. The relationship between activism and pro-democratic feeling thus appears curvilinear rather than simply linear, that is to say that increasing activism promotes greater support up to a point, but after that point is associated with decreasing support.

On appraisals, activism seems to exert no effect and party a considerable effect over questions of the Provost's impartiality and on the question of who runs Glasgow. The reverse is the case with appraisals of non-elected groups exerting influence and the question of who gets jobs. On the question of whether changes resulting from the disappearance of parties would be beneficial or not, activism and party exert strong and equal effects. Party distinguishes between definite likes of parties and their absence, more strongly than activism, and activism between dislikes and their absence more strongly than party. But both exert reasonably strong and consistent effects over all four party appraisals. Over all pro-democratic appraisals considered in Chapter 2 activism affects four more strongly than party, party four more strongly than activism, and one is affected equally.

Conclusions about the shape of the relationship between activism and positive appraisals of Glasgow government must be limited, for only three involve councillors. But there is no indication from these that partyworkers incline more to pro-democratic appraisals. On two the expected ranking of councillors–partyworkers–electors occurs, but on appraisals of the Provost neither type of activism exerts any effect, owing to the overwhelming influence of party.

It is certainly in this area of support for procedures that initial hypotheses have proved least successful, and it is fortunate that it forms a relatively self-contained claim of reasoning so that alterations can be introduced without predetermining the shape of the other two chains. The problems deriving from unanticipated findings are threefold: the connection between activism and pro-democratic feeling must be explained without recourse to demand-satisfaction; the stronger pro-democratic preferences of partyworkers compared to councillors must be contrasted with the prevalence of the anticipated order on appraisals; and the generally stronger effects of party than of activism accounted for.

Fortunately it is easy to put forward reasons for a link between activism and pro-democratic feeling, other than self-interest through demand-satisfaction. For one thing activists have been found to have a more complex appreciation of political processes, including their location on a wider time-span. Thus they are more likely to realise that the flow and ebb of party competition and political conflict is necessarily bounded to some extent by procedural constraints – otherwise the parties themselves could not exist in the same shape, let alone the present representative character of government. In a society where certain abstract procedural beliefs (such as majority rule and minority rights) are overwhelmingly shared, activists are better able as a result of their greater political exposure to perceive and support their embodiment in governmental procedures in a city where we have shown them to be actually put into practice.[163] Moreover one of our original assumptions (Assumption X) points to greater activist consistency in carrying attitudes over into behaviour, and activists' identification with a party (which in a democracy defined operationally by Neubauer's index has a fair chance of taking over the government at some stage) must help generate some support for the forms through which it will exercise power. Thus their wider and more vicarious identifications and greater consistency are capable of promoting activist support for existent procedures even when they do not see their own political self-interest as being involved.

By itself this explanation of stronger activist support for procedures does not account for the curvilinear relationship with democratic preferences and the linear relationship with democratic appraisals. If activism increases support for democracy, why does it not do so in the same way over both preferences and appraisals? However, further characteristics can be regarded as differentiating councillors from partyworkers: these are in the first place their greater knowledge of the detailed workings of government and more accurate information. Knowledge and accuracy should secure greater agreement on correct appraisals of the necessary role of parties and on the representative nature of Glasgow government (its placing on Neubauer's scale and the analysis of Chapter 3 shows that it is representative in actual fact). On the other hand a second differentiating factor can be conceived as rendering councillors less agreed than partyworkers in preferences and strongly evaluative appraisals. This factor consists in councillors' exposure to a much wider range of conflicting demands and pressures than partyworkers. We have already noted councillors' greater stress on their own mixed role (Table 3.2). Councillors are forced to be at the same time party strategists and public representatives, upholders of majority rule while forced to seek the co-operation of pressure groups for governmental and party ends. They are also in the position of having to seek efficient running of the government through strategies such as giving more power to officials, even if these run counter in some respects to

---

[163] Chapter 1 above. Evidence on the overwhelming adherence of British activists and electors to abstract democratic procedures is presented in Budge, *Agreement*, chap. 8. For the greater support of activists for specific procedural applications and their more widespread perception of government as democratic see Budge, chaps 8 and 9.

I

their own ideals of participatory democracy. Partyworkers on the other hand can follow participatory ideals free from governmental, pressure group, and substantially from constituency, constraints. On this interpretation we should expect partyworkers to endorse purely democratic preferences with less qualification than councillors, as in fact they seem in Glasgow to do.

Both partyworkers and councillors must however be seen as subject to one overriding constraint on their procedural views – their party. Even if most activists are prompted to initial involvement by primary groups or general political interest, both still operate through attachments to a party, and a plurality of councillors owe their position on the council directly to party agencies.[164] Glasgow activists' whole political career is pursued within the context of a party, and their outlook is liable to be shaped by this concrete experience and by interaction with fellow partisans more powerfully than by general ideals, however potent these may otherwise be.

Historical analysis shows that differences between the parties were not simply produced by the struggle for power but also by the ideologies they were formed to promote.[165] Our findings show that these ideological emphases persist at the present day, and extend to views about the functioning of government. Historically the Progressives arose as an anti-party coalition: members still distrust party and emphasise the role of the corporation as an administrative and governing body. Labour adherents continue to sympathise with the concept of party as a link between rulers and ruled, and as the best method of ensuring responsible government. While the history and beliefs of Progressive and City Labour parties are peculiar to Glasgow, similar broad differences can be traced between the parties of most contemporary mass democracies. Thus it is likely that a parallel ideological division will affect the procedural attitudes of activists in most of these polities.

A further procedural effect of the party division in Glasgow can be discerned in the difference between the party in power and the party out of power. Pure partisan loyalty is liable to make adherents of the government party support established procedures and to make opposition adherents more critical, and again the institutional difference will be general and not limited to Glasgow.

It is noticeable from our findings that partisan differences among Glasgow activists rarely produce diametrically opposed preferences or

[164] *Class, Religion*, chap. 5.
[165] Ibid., chap. 4; *The Political Development of Modern Glasgow*, chap. 4.

appraisals: the only cases of outright division are in fact support for the majority on fee-paying and appraisals of changes resulting from the disappearance of parties. Rather, party differences tend to moderate or enhance enthusiasm for the same procedures. What activists of one party might push in the procedural field, the others would neglect, rather than oppose outright.

Partisan differences affect electors only slightly: they are as a whole liable to translate their personal preferences into support for majority or minority (Tables 2.2–2.4) on current issues, and possibly following through their own interests as they see them, support the representative principle in any governmental changes. On almost all matters however they include larger numbers who are apathetic or lack an opinion about the point under discussion and their appraisals and preferences tend to be less focused.

Within the overall context of parties which differ rather than conflict outright on procedural matters, activists' relatively stronger democratic feeling can still be seen as a moderating influence on their confrontations and so as contributing to a reduction in the potential for disagreement. This was a feature of the original assumptions. But any new formulation must take explicit account of the precondition that outright partisan conflict is absent, and also of the different shapes taken by the relationship of activism to pro-democratic appraisals on the one hand, and to democratic preferences and evaluations on the other.

Since the reasoning relating to procedures has always been rather independent of the other elements in the model, it is possible to suggest a tentative form for procedural relationships at this stage. This may require further amendment after the reviews of other areas if they reveal a general defect in the original model. But at this state the actual procedural findings are fresh in mind, so it may be as well to link them immediately with the new formulation. We start, as in Fig. 1.1, with the absence of important irreconcilable disagreement, which we have in fact found to be absent in Glasgow as predicted. We regard such an all-pervasive salient disagreement as likely to alienate the defeated side from the procedural rules and political system under which its defeat was secured. When such disagreement is absent we now regard one of its main effects as being to dampen down controversy between the parties over procedural matters, prompting the differences of emphasis which we discovered in Glasgow, but not outright opposition. Such differences of emphasis still have the potential to spark outright opposition quite quickly however, under a sufficient stimulus – which in our

Fig 7.1

A new formulation of the relationship between activism, party, democratic preferences and democratic appraisals

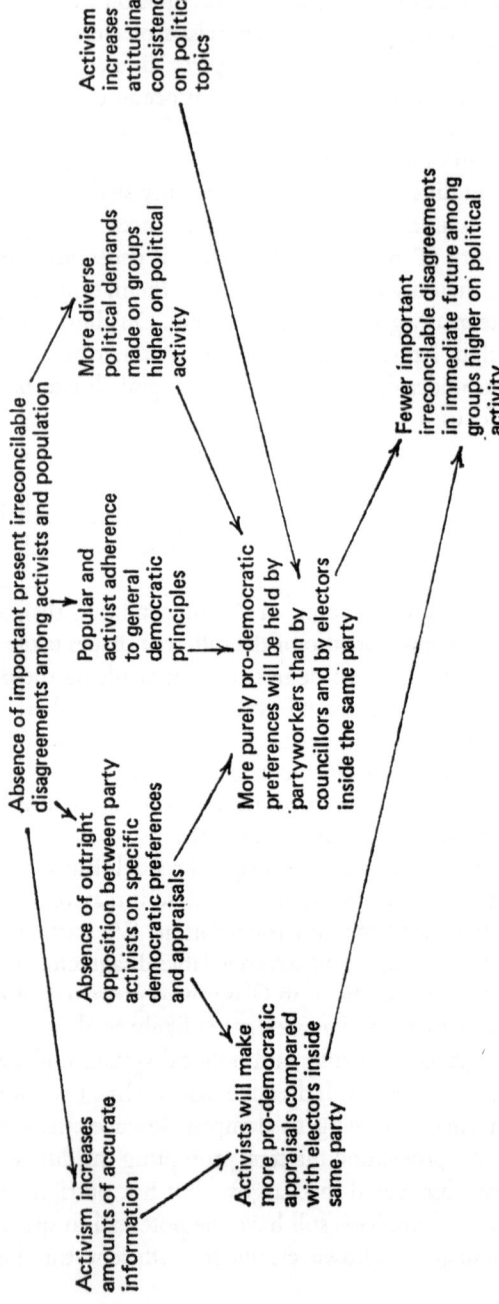

interpretation is the generation of a salient and irreconcilable disagreement. The arrow linking this factor to the absence of outright party opposition on procedures is dotted, since it is possible that intervening issue agreements to be discussed below may help to dampen down procedural opposition so that this is not a final formulation. The absence of fundamental disagreement also implies that the general and rather vague attachments to democracy which population and activists share are not put under any strain. Further, the more involved activists – the councillors – find themselves exposed to the diverse and conflicting pressures mentioned earlier, since no one overmastering political concern imposes consistency by deflecting other pressures altogether. On the side of preferences a general characteristic of activists – their ability to think through political consequences more logically and clearly – would seem to work against the disorder introduced by conflicting pressures, by better enabling activists to link the abstract beliefs in democracy which they share with the rest of the population with their specific applications in Glasgow government. In the case of middle-level activists – the partyworkers – less exposed to conflicting pressures, this ability promotes strong unqualified pro-democratic preferences. In the case of high-level activists – the councillors – this ability is smothered to some extent by the qualifications entailed by the actual exercise of power. It wins through to the extent that it still prompts councillors to stronger pro-democratic preferences than electors.

On the side of appraisals we borrow the assumption about greater accuracy produced by activism (again dependent on the absence of fundamental disagreement, which might debar some activists from access to official sources) to explain the relationship between increasing activism and the pro-democratic nature of purely factual appraisals – within the bounds set by party.

Fig. 7.1 presents a more complicated scheme than the left-hand chain of Fig. 1.1. The greater number of postulates are however required to fit the relatively complex nature of our findings. Where our original expectations have not been so rudely overturned more of the original simplicity can be preserved.

REPRESENTATION

Perhaps the central finding from the investigation of representative-constituent relationships was the better fit to the overall pattern of issue-preferences of the party-microcosm models compared with the stratification model. On the other hand it can be argued that special-purpose representation models might be expected to provide a better overall fit anyway: that when the minority of party-related issues are excluded (as envisaged by our original argument) the stratification model fits current issue-preferences almost as well as other models and had the advantage, which they have not, of being generalisable to wider areas of politics than representation. In any case it remains true that the preferences of councillors and partyworkers coincide more with each other than either does with electors, but only within the parties. Even on non-partisan issues cross-strata correlations within the parties are very slightly higher than cross-party correlations within the strata – not the other way round as our original hypotheses predicted.

The stratification model can however be used to provide a plausible explanation for the greater coincidence of preference between party-workers and electors in high-turnout wards compared with low-turn-out wards when no greater coincidence appears for councillors and electors. Partyworkers can be regarded as standing at less of a political distance from electors than councillors and thus as more likely to interact and thus agree with electors when they are on average more active.

On role perceptions more councillors than partyworkers and more partyworkers than electors are found to have ward, city and party orientations, and this holds both for the total groups and within parties. On appraisals too initial expectations are upheld: councillors' and party-workers' general issue appraisals are more accurate than those made by electors, and more accurate for both partyworkers and electors in high- than in low-turnout wards. General accuracy is accompanied (as expected) by extreme inaccuracy in activist perceptions of constituents' issue preferences, but activists are better able to assess constituents' preferences in high-turnout compared to low-turnout wards.

COMMUNICATION

The general inaccuracy of each stratum's appraisals of the others' opinions tends to confirm original expectations about gaps and dis-continuities in the flow of communication between one stratum and the other. Certainly reports of reading habits, sources of local inform-ation and ways of hearing about issues confirm that members of each stratum rely more on each other than on members of other strata for their information and are all heavily dependent on the mass media. As also anticipated the main gap opens between activists and electors: partyworkers rely on councillors to a great extent for their information.

Reported methods of seeking additional information – whether about issues or constituents' opinions – revealed a potential for considerably more cross-stratum interaction than is apparent in normal periods. Partyworkers also reported themselves as actually having more contacts with electors and councillors than had been anticipated. One finding which links closely with the representation analysis was the report of somewhat greater contact between electors and partyworkers in high-turnout wards. This helps explain the higher coincidence of issue-preferences between partyworkers and electors in such wards, within the same party.

Communication patterns seem to be affected only marginally by party influence. Labour partyworkers rely for information more heavily than Progressives on their more efficient party machine. Progressive electors resemble partyworkers more closely than Labour electors, but this is probably due to their occupational and class status and level of education rather than to more directly partisan influences.

A classification of current issues

	Simple	*Complex*
Partisan	Abolition of fees	Rates
Non-partisan	Pubs in Estates Parking-meters School-integration	Housing problem Traffic problem Finance problem Education problem

Fig. 7.2

Overall, the communication data do not force very extensive modifications in the original postulates. If we concentrate on periods when no intense political feelings are roused (as the absence of important irreconcilable disagreements implies) we need make additional allowance only for the contacts of partyworkers with councillors and with some electors. The change from our original communication model to our new formulation is illustrated in Fig. 7.2. Now we show partyworkers as linked with both councillors and electors, but since in both cases it seems to be a case of partyworkers approaching the other strata we show the councillor and elector arrows pointing in different directions from partyworkers to the other stratum. And since party-workers' contact seems to be with a rather restricted group of electors rather than with a representative selection we show that arrow as dotted rather than solid.

NON-DIRECTED AGREEMENT

Stratification assumptions lead to a ranking of political strata according to the extent to which opinions coincide internally within each activist and party grouping as well as across them. As we have seen, predictions about the cross-coincidence of issue-preferences (covered in the representation analysis) were not strongly upheld. The original stratification model is much more successful in its prediction that internal coincidences of opinion increase with activism, for both total and party groups. However it once more has greater success with appraisals than with preferences. The predicted ordering is substantially encountered on six current issues and substantially absent on four. Both potential issues generate preferences which conform to the prediction. Over the variety of appraisals examined in Chapter 5 the anticipated ordering of non-directed agreement is found on all but appraisals of Glasgow government and of voting, which are affected by the partisan influences already discussed.

While party operates consistently to increase preferential agreement on fees (and to increase Labour agreement and decrease Progressive on traffic and education) its effects on other issues are mixed and no systematic pattern can be discerned.

POLITICIANS' AUTONOMY AND PARTY COMPETITION

The analysis of autonomy and competition focused many concerns of the previous discussion. Expectations derived from the stratification theory added up to an integrated picture of the politicians' ability to deflect popular and party pressures into certain narrow areas. In many respects our findings support these ideas. Councillors' issue preferences correspond roughly but by no means exactly to those of electors, so the former do not simply reflect the latter. And we know from the analysis of representation that activists do not shape preferences to fit their perceptions of constituents' attitudes, for the two hardly correspond. Moreover the more complex considerations which activists bring to the formulation of their preferences provide good reason why they should wish to cushion simplistic popular demands. Their ability as well as desire to do this is reflected in the confidence of the majority of councillors about bringing issues to general attention, and of half about keeping issues if necessary from public attention. The correspondents' testimony shows that in fact issues can be played down if councillors so wish.

As far as we can judge another theoretical connection, between integrative behaviour and agreement on issues, is also upheld by our evidence. The fact that councillors have emerged from the communication analysis as the most interactive group would then link with findings on non-directed agreement to indicate that councillors have the basis for mutual co-operation among themselves, which would seem necessary for autonomous action.

However the patterns of interaction which we traced among councillors were heavily concentrated inside the parties, tempered somewhat by institutional constraints which forced opposition consultation of convenors, and some recourse to permanent officials on the part of both parties.

This finding can be taken as indicating again that the common experiences of activists are substantially limited by partisan loyalties. We had expected that partisan feelings would be stronger among activists as in fact is found to be the case (Table 6.7). Against our expectations however we found no evidence that activists constrained their stronger partisan feelings by limiting party competition either to the issues they had helped publicise or to issues on which the populace divided evenly. The fact that party competition is not limited in the expected ways forces some reconsideration of the earlier responses on bringing issues to attention and keeping issues from attention. It is obvious that party differences do affect councillors' replies here (Tables 6.4–6.6). The Opposition Progressives were much more confident of their ability to manage news than the majority Labour party: it is possible that news management is involved in party competition and used by each party to focus attention on issues where they feel themselves to have an advantage over the other side.

EVALUATION OF ORIGINAL POSTULATES IN LIGHT OF FINDINGS AS A WHOLE

One basic assumption behind the initial formulation has not been shaken by findings from the data: this is that activism and party are the two main influences shaping political behaviour and attitudes in Glasgow. It is true that these are the only factors whose influence has been systematically evaluated throughout the discussion (although influences such as class, religion, education and area have also been considered at various points). Nevertheless party and activism have shown reasonably high correlations with most of the attitudes considered. There is strong reason for thinking that where they show weak relationships, the hidden variable dampening the overt connection is one we could not control: namely the common Glasgow environment. Only in a comparative analysis however could one explicitly evaluate the strength of community influences relative to party and activism. Within the framework of our theory we should expect the main community differences to be related to the degree of democracy and the presence or absence of important irreconcilable disagreements.

The initial postulates in Fig. 1.1 linked the prior absence of adverse economic conditions, increasing socioeconomic disparities and strong political disagreements to the absence of present disagreements of that sort, and these in turn to the increase of integrative behaviour with political activism. We have not had sufficiently extensive evidence to put the anticipated relationships to a particularly searching test but what evidence we have does not refute them.

The actual link between more integrative behaviour and greater activism has been upheld, and the assumed connection between integrative behaviour and greater agreement on factual appraisals also receives substantial support from the data, if we distinguish purely factual appraisals from the more evaluative appraisals directly related to party competition in elections and legislature. An anomaly occurs in the finding that integrative behaviour is heavily concentrated among activists of the same party. For purely factual agreements among activists spread across party lines. These concurrent findings would seem to indicate that agreements on appraisals may have some source other than interactive behaviour among activists. Such a source might be sought in the overwhelmingly upheld Assumption XI of Fig. 1.1 – already used to explain activist concurrence on pro-democratic appraisals – that activism increases the accuracy of factual appraisals. Increasing accuracy would then satisfactorily account for increasing agreement on the correct appraisal. Thus although the postulated connection between integrative behaviour and factual agreement passes the direct tests to which it has been subjected, it may be strategic to revise it so as to fit better with the overall pattern of findings, and to relate factual agreement rather to activists' greater accuracy.

In Glasgow the greater agreement of activists on purely factual appraisals is accompanied by their greater agreement on potential issue-preferences. So there seems no need to modify the connection assumed between these types of agreement by the original theory. Moreover both initial assumptions (IX and X in Figs. 1.1 and 1.2) about communication between strata has been well upheld. No important form of communication between strata has been discovered other than individual contacts, meetings and mass media (IX). The inaccuracy of each stratum's appraisals of other strata's preferences is so extreme that it does indeed seem that the mass media, the main source of local political information, do not purvey knowledge of the preferences of electoral sub-groups nor of individual elected representatives (X). So inaccurate are such appraisals – extending to activists' views of the apathy of electors in even the most important political problem – that we might well in any reformulation strengthen the assumption to state that the mass media do not provide information on the preferences on most issues of electors or representatives or activists. This also implies (in accordance with findings) that we exclude from expectations about the accuracy of activist appraisals those appraisals relating to political reactions of other strata.

As far as the assumptions on party competition (Fig. 1.2) are concerned, we have had no disconfirmation of the general postulate linking activism to a greater carryover of appraisals into behaviour. The general impression that activist attitudes show greater internal consistency, which has emerged from the analysis, in fact supports this postulate so far as it goes. We have also discovered that a majority of activists do continue in politics in order to promote causes which they have at heart, and that most of those active at the time of our survey had been politically active in the previous time-period. These are both derivations from the assumption that activists see some political demands as being gained by increasing or maintaining their political activity rate. (Assumption XIII (a), Fig. 1.2). The further finding – that activists are more prone to see their party as supporting and the other party as opposing their own issue-stands (Table 6.7) – upholds the supplementary assumption that activists see other political demands as being gained by party vote-maximisation (Assumption XIII(b)). And widespread activist recognition of the role of councillors in governing the city supports the assumption that activists see a minimal requirement for vote-maximisation as efficient running of government and the services it provides (Assumption XV, Fig. 1.2). On the other hand the fact that party competition was not confined to publicised issues knocks out this offshoot from that chain of reasoning (Assumption XIV).

In evaluating the success of postulates in the original model we have so far kept clear of the more complicated question of how preferential agreement on current issues relates to integrative behaviour and greater activist agreement on potential issues, which has also been discovered (Assumptions IV; VI and VII, Fig. 1.1).

These connections are complicated for several reasons. Even if we take the mixed set of findings on preferential agreement as supporting our original model, we still have to face the difficulty raised previously with factual appraisals. Since integrative behaviour is confined largely within the parties at activist level, it is difficult to avoid the conclusion on our initial assumptions that preferential agreement must also be higher among activists of one partisan group than among activists as a whole. But secondly the findings on higher activist agreement *vis-à-vis* electors were by no means as clear-cut for preferences as they were for appraisals. For dichotomised reactions on five current issues a party model of representation was discovered to fit marginally better than the stratification model (even with allowance made for party competition). When consideration was given to the intensity of preferences on these five issues the stratification model held, and agreement was increased by party only on the fees issue. Nevertheless on three out of four problems mentioned as important partyworkers agreed less than electors, both across and within the parties.

Since the stratification model was confirmed on preferential agreement on the majority of current issues involved in each comparison it is possible to stick to the original simple formulation. The varied character of the findings suggests however that a reformulation would help prediction, and thus understanding of the patterns which preferential agreement on current issues can take.

What findings do we want to explain? First, that activists agree less than electors on some current issues and on some agree more. In part this finding can be met, as the original formulation anticipated, by dividing current issues between partisan and non-partisan. But we should make this classification explicit in the new formulation by introducing party directly into the main chain of reasoning, so that the validated assumptions of Fig. 1.2 are conflated with the validated assumptions of Fig. 1.1. Making explicit mention of party then allows us to modify the postulate of integrative behaviour in line with the patterns of advice-seeking actually discovered among councillors.

As with procedural preferences however we have to take account of certain curvilinear patterns of preference (notably among Progressives on rates) and issues where the order of agreement was quite reversed, notably on the housing, finance and traffic problems. Party is not the sole extraneous influence here for the reversal continued within parties. The most promising approach to this problem of the negative or curvilinear relationship between activism and issue agreement is probably to draw a distinction between simple and complex issues. Simple issues would then be issues in which no very long-term or indirect considerations were involved beyond the immediate and widely known problem on hand. Of our issues the introduction of pubs to housing estates and extension of parking-meters are simple in this sense. The abolition of fee-paying and integration of the school-systems are somewhat more complicated in terms of religious repercussions, but certainly are not highly technical nor likely to produce very unexpected results. Rates, finance, housing, traffic and probably education are on the other hand problems with multifarious bearings upon other policy decisions and unexpected and unresolved twists. These are complex issues. It is to be expected that top activists' exposure to conflicting pressures – already mentioned in the discussion of procedures – and their longer-term, more theoretically oriented viewpoint might lead them here to lesser agreement than groups which viewed the issue simplistically. These might possibly be partyworkers but certainly electors.

A modified formulation of normal communication flows between political strata

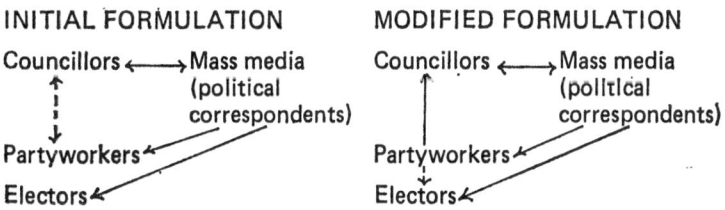

Fig. 7.3

By combining the partisan–non-partisan distinction with the simple-complex we have a fourfold classification to which the Glasgow issues are assigned in Fig. 7.3.

CHARACTERISTICS OF ACTIVISM

Before going on to summarise the suggestions for a revised model, in a figure comparable to Figs. 1.1 and 1.2, it is as well to reconsider the nature of what, with party, remains the central concept in the scheme. In the course of analysis and discussion we have drafted into our interpretation as explanations and assumptions many of the characteristics we take to be associated with greater political activity. Before our final statement of the effects we expect it to exert, we are as well to consider the correlates of activism more carefully and systematically than has been done hitherto. It will help if in the first place we list the major activist characteristics which have been considered in isolation at previous points in the discussion. These are their:

Long-term, theoretically-oriented view of political processes.
Logical consistency between attitudes, and between attitudes and behaviour.
Accuracy and amount of political information.
Strong partisan commitment and feeling.
Responsibility for carrying on government and administration.
Subjection to increasingly varied political demands.
Higher rate of integrative behaviour.

The general accuracy of activists' factual appraisals (to which we can add the sheer amount of political information they possess), the consistency between their attitudes and behaviour, their higher interaction and stronger partisan feelings are validated assumptions of the initial model (XI, XII, IV, and XIII(b), Figs. 1.1 and 1.2). The internal consistency of their attitudes, the wider temporal and theoretical context within which they locate political problems, and their subjection to varied demands (expressed in their greater endorsement of mixed roles) are findings of the analysis.

It is noteworthy that the influence of the various activist characteristics cannot all work in the same direction. The tendency to internal consistency in activists' attitudes and their ready translation into overt behaviour must be countered by the varied political demands to which they are subject, as a result of which they often betray greater inconsistency. The institutional restraints of government must equally often prevent a ready transition from appraisals and preferences into action. While the accuracy of their information, their consistency and higher rates of interaction must work to promote agreement, their stronger partisan commitments and differing governmental responsibilities must constantly spread disagreement. Since one party or set of parties normally assumes governmental responsibilities, leaving the others with only truncated or potential responsibilities, implication or non-implication in government may become linked to party differences. This seems, for example, to have happened with support for procedures. While on the one hand activists' wider views of politics may promote greater agreement if there is a validated theory or accepted expert to whom they have access (as in public health matters), in other fields the competing theories may produce more disagreement than would exist in a simpler frame of reference. The end-result may be greater activist cynicism about the efficacy of any policy which might totally overwhelm their natural impulse to translate ideas into action. This argument ties into the distinction between simple and complex issues made above.

The effect of taking a hard look at different activist characteristics and their conflicting effects is to modify our previous assumptions about greater preferential agreement being constantly associated with activism. We must now recognise that different patterns of relative agreement will emerge, depending on the type of issue and the activist characteristics which predominate in the particular situation.

A NEW MODEL OF PREFERENTIAL AGREEMENT ON CURRENT ISSUES

Figure 7.4 incorporates many of the suggestions made earlier about the reformulations of initial theory (including those summarised in Figs. 7.1–7.3). For the moment we will concentrate on its treatment of preferential agreement on current issues, before commenting on other changes.

In regard to simple non-partisan issues the original assumptions still hold: that is, we anticipate that the more integrative behaviour of activists will promote greater preferential agreement, and that because these issues are non-partisan the greater concentration of integrative behaviour within the party groupings will not affect activists' generally greater agreement.

With regard to simple partisan issues our original reasoning can be modified to conform to the Glasgow findings. Since integrative behaviour tends to appear more among the party groupings of activists than among activists as a whole, then agreement on partisan issues ought to be more pronounced inside these party groupings. Within each party activists will still agree more, but given their stronger

Fig. 7.4

A Reformulated Model Relating to Intra-strata Cohesion and Party Competition with accompanying Communication Restraints in a Mass Democracy

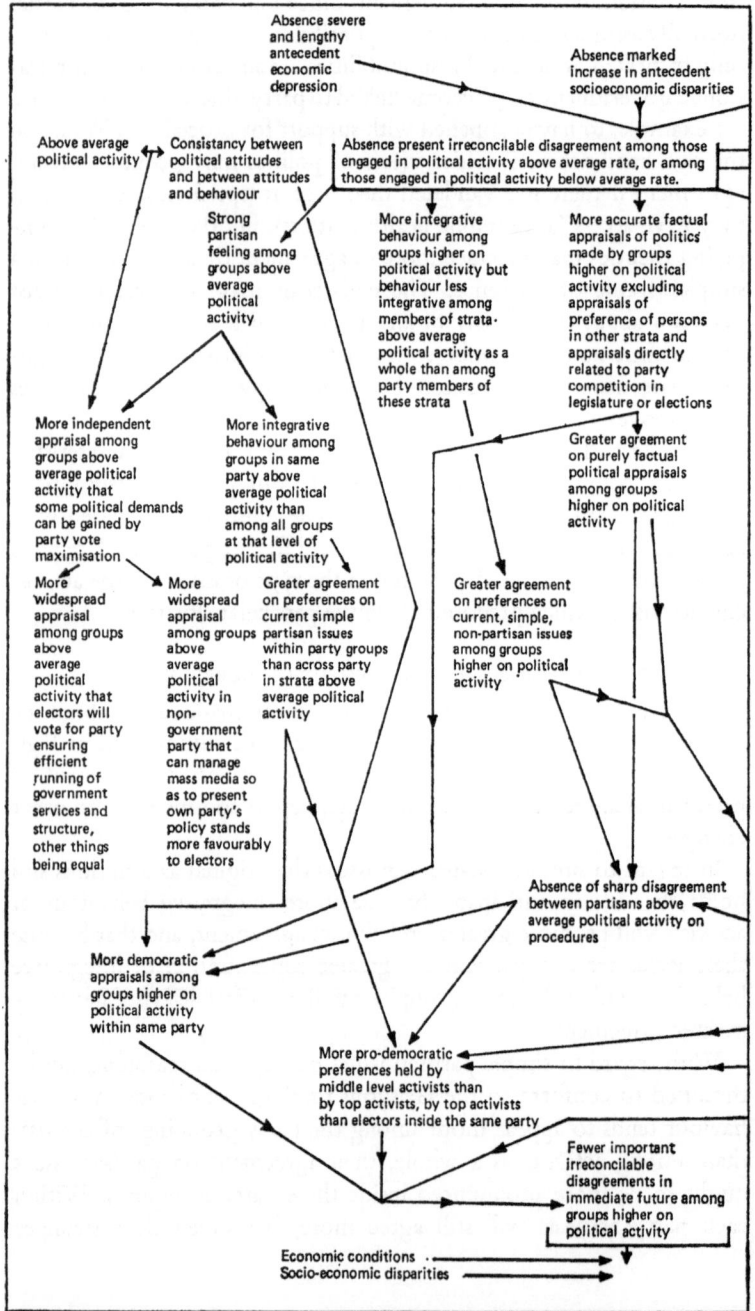

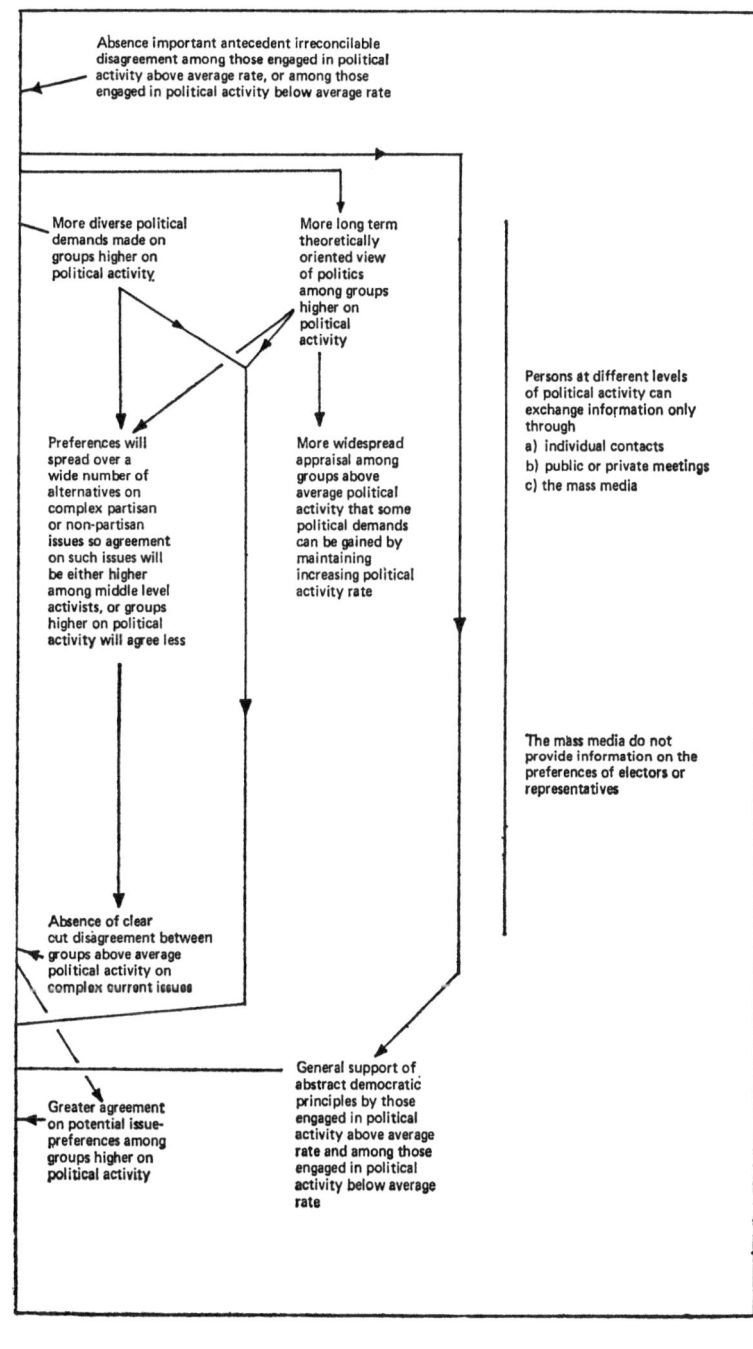

Absence important antecedent irreconcilable disagreement among those engaged in political activity above average rate, or among those engaged in political activity below average rate

More diverse political demands made on groups higher on political activity

More long term theoretically oriented view of politics among groups higher on political activity

Preferences will spread over a wide number of alternatives on complex partisan or non-partisan issues so agreement on such issues will be either higher among middle level activists, or groups higher on political activity will agree less

More widespread appraisal among groups above average political activity that some political demands can be gained by maintaining increasing political activity rate

Persons at different levels of political activity can exchange information only through
a) individual contacts
b) public or private meetings
c) the mass media

The mass media do not provide information on the preferences of electors or representatives

Absence of clear cut disagreement between groups above average political activity on complex current issues

General support of abstract democratic principles by those engaged in political activity above average rate and among those engaged in political activity below average rate

Greater agreement on potential issue-preferences among groups higher on political activity

partisan feelings they will agree less across party on partisan issues than the general population.

In the case of complex issues – whether partisan or non-partisan – other factors come into play. These are the diverse pressures felt by activists and secondly their broader frame of reference. Both influences seem likely to make the preferences of activists – certainly of top activists – on these issues more diffuse and less clear-cut than those of persons less cross-pressured and more simplistic in their approach. On certain complex issues the persons with most clear-cut and agreed preferences may be middle-level activists but they are most likely to be electors. The fact that top activists may agree less or least does not imply sharp disagreement. Instead what we envisage as the typical situation here is a wide spread of endorsements over numerous preferences, in response to the variety of different pressures experienced on the issue and numerous divergent diagnoses of the problem.

Thus three different states of agreement can be envisaged as emerging on current issues. The greater agreement of activists as such on simple non-partisan issues operates as in Fig. 1.1 to increase their agreement on potential issue-preferences. The sharp disagreement among activist party groups on simple partisan issues does not affect agreement on potential issue-preferences because by definition the parties have not taken a stand on these: if they did take a stand they would become current issues. Relatively diffuse activist disagreement (whether within or cross party) on complex issues can be conceived as reducing the strains on procedures set up by sharp focused partisan clashes on simple partisan issues. The impact of these two types of current issue is to produce the differences of emphasis on activists' procedural preferences and appraisals which were noted earlier, but to banish sharp disagreement from that area. Generally, both sets of activist partisans will support democratic procedures but adherents of the governing party will show more enthusiasm for them than adherents of the opposition. From this connexion one can proceed to the whole chain of reasoning summarised in Fig. 7.1.

THE GENERAL REFORMULATION OF THE STRATIFICATION MODEL

Apart from new assumptions about current issue-preferences, Fig. 7.4 contains a considerable number of validated assumptions taken over from Figs 1.1 and 1.2. One of the reasons why the reformulated model is more complicated to summarise than the original is the fact that the effects of political stratification and of party competition are conflated instead of being presented separately. The assumptions relating to communication constraints are the same: so are those on the conditions leading to an absence of present important irreconcilable disagreements. Again this factor is a central component of the theoretical scheme. As before it is presumed to promote integrative behaviour – indirectly among partisan groups of activists and directly among activists as a whole. Integrative behaviour then leads to the different states of preferential agreement on simple current issues already discussed.

Closely related to the discussion of preferential issue-agreements is the question of agreement on purely factual appraisals, including issue-appraisals. Because of the concentration of integrative behaviour among party groups of activists, accompanied by a spread of factual agreements over all activists, we now regard such agreements as being promoted by the connection of accuracy with activism, rather than by integrative behaviour. We assume that activism is associated with accuracy only in the absence of fundamental disagreement however, for in the crisis atmosphere which that would promote, rumour and hearsay would flourish, while many activists might be debarred from access to the official agencies on which they normally rely for their information. Again greater agreement on factual appraisals is regarded as directly promoting agreement on potential issue-preferences, and thus contributing indirectly to activist avoidance of fundamental disagreement in the next time-period. We also postulate some influence of activists' factual agreement on their preferential agreement on simple non-partisan current issues. Shared appraisals should facilitate shared preferences where party is not involved and complex technical considerations absent.

The absence of important irreconcilable disagreement is in a separate but related chain of reasoning assumed to promote the existence of stronger partisan feeling among activists, on the grounds that the presence of such a disagreement cross-cutting party lines would tend to promote new political alignments among activists which would reduce attachments to the established parties. Linked with the postulates of stronger partisan feeling and greater consistency between activist attitudes and behaviour are assumptions from Fig. 1.2 about the importance attached by activists to party vote-maximisation, and their perception that this in part depends on meeting a minimal popular demand for efficient government.

In view of our reappraisal of party differences in attitudes towards management of news, we now regard activists' ability to emphasise some issues and de-emphasise others as directed towards the advantage of their own party rather than towards buttressing activists' autonomy as such. Where an activist sees a point that will benefit his own party and rebound adversely on its competitors he will seek publicity, and where the situation is reversed he will try to play the issue down. We have thus in the reformulated model abandoned the attempt to predict exactly what issues will be subjects of party competition; we simply accept that some will be partisan and others not.

The stronger partisan feeling of activists is expected to produce more integrative behaviour inside each party group at the same level of activity, in the manner detailed above. This tendency for activists to split quite sharply on party lines on many issues is then expected to contribute to the differing degrees of support offered by different parties to procedures (in terms both of preferences and appraisals about the functioning of government).

The link between the more strongly cross-pressured situation of activists and the absence of fundamental disagreement has been raised in the review of support for procedures: such disagreement would crowd out other concerns (by definition lesser) so that activists would then not be cross-pressured. When they are cross-pressured top activists would tend to be less wholehearted in their preferences for pure democracy than middle-level activists, and their varied concerns and loyalties would contribute to the diffuse disagreement we expect on complex current issues. To this diffuse disagreement the more sophisticated view of political processes taken by activists may also contribute. Again the absence of fundamental disagreement seems likely to promote the long-term theoretical view: where activist feelings boil over into resentment and rage, immediate concrete action is likely to ensue without reflection on consequences.

One appraisal which a more complex view of politics is likely to foster is the knowledge that lobbying and increased personal pressure group activity is in many cases more likely to gain one's ends than campaigning for the party. This is the old Assumption XIII(a) from Fig. 1.2 which proved useful in providing some orientation towards recruitment findings. It is here linked to the general model in a new and perhaps more plausible way, and still receives considerable support from its validated predictions.

A final connection is made in our reformulation between the absence of important irreconcilable disagreement and the general support for abstract democratic principles shown by both activists and population.

A considerable body of evidence now exists for both Britain and the United States that support for democratic procedures at a very general and abstract level is practically universal.[166] The presence of such support can be explained by simple socialisation into the prevailing societal norms. But obviously a fundamental and pervasive disagreement, where the overwhelming necessity seemed to carry one's own policies, would reduce any commitment to majority rule and minority rights, even in the abstract. Where general support exists, however, it is by no means certain that it necessarily will be carried over into specific pro-democratic preferences and appraisals: in fact evidence already reviewed in Chapter 2 shows that the ability to do this presupposes certain reserves of reasoning ability and knowledge which are available mainly to such groups as the better-educated and particularly the politically active. In Fig. 7.4 we link our assumptions about the more complex views taken by activists of political processes, the consistency of their attitudes and behaviour, and their greater factual accuracy, to their ability to make the transition between the general democratic beliefs held by all to favourable and specific preferences and appraisals about Glasgow government. As noted previously we do also allow for the fact that party disagreements will affect the emphasis of the support given by activist partisans of different colours.

FINAL CONSIDERATION OF THE REFORMULATED MODEL

In the discussion of our data we have run the gamut between detailed assessments of Glasgow history to relatively abstract general formulations. There is no hiatus between these concerns, for the Glasgow experience has throughout been the touchstone by which we assessed the model, and the model has formed the best interpretation we could apply to the Glasgow experience. The fact that this interpretation generates expectations about politics in other cities adds to its general interest but does not detract from its explanation of specifically Glasgow patterns. The general form of the model and its ability to generate predictions for other polities does on the other hand render it an interim rather than a final explanation of the Glasgow patterns. For if it fails to accomodate findings from other cities it must again undergo modification to fit the new data as well as those we have derived on Glasgow.

We have stated the new model in some detail but have not subjected it to the full formalisation and systematisation applied to our initial

[166] The evidence for the United States is summarised in Budge, *Agreement*, chap. 1, and for Britain is presented in chaps 8 and 9.

model in Appendix B. The statement of assumptions summarised in Fig. 7.4 is, we hope, sufficiently full to allow other investigators to formalise them overall or in sections, in accordance with their requirements. Obviously – since it has been stated so as to fit all our data – all the validated derivations and associated data-predictions stated in Appendix B can be deduced from this model. Interesting extensions can also be made which can be tested on data generated for areas we have not explored here, whether for Glasgow or other polities.

Other investigators may not be willing to invest so many resources in formalisation of models as we have done, but may nevertheless seek to interpret some of their more general findings as confirmation or rejection of the model presented in Fig. 7.4. For their benefit we can at this point set out some general guidelines, which are implied in our detailed reasoning. These guidelines concentrate on the relationships, under various conditions, of activism and party, the central determinants of our scheme.

Where important irreconcilable disagreements are absent we should expect the effects of activism to relate to those of party just as they have done with our Glasgow data. Generally speaking, activism should have stronger effects than party over purely factual appraisals. On evaluations of voting party should be stronger, and on procedural appraisals party and activism should exert varying effects which overall approximate equality. On issue-preferences the different patterns of relative agreement described above should emerge from simple partisan, simple non-partisan, and complex issues. These relative effects of activism and party can probably be most easily assessed through Coleman's Effect Parameters, but any of the statistics we have employed will give exact values which can be compared with those we have derived for Glasgow.

Suppose an important irreconcilable disagreement is present, what will be its influence on the relative effects exerted by party and activism on political behaviour and attitudes? Two possible lines of effect can be envisaged, depending on whether the disagreement coincides with party lines or cross-cuts them.

If such a fundamental and pervasive disagreement exists between parties the general effect will be to increase the importance of party divisions relative to activism. Party feeling will be evident among general population as well as among activists. All issues will tend to be partisan and to generate party-based cleavages. All cross-strata correlations of preferences between partisans will thus increase and all cross-party correlations for any stratum will decrease. The accuracy of activist appraisals will generally decrease, although the accuracy of cross-strata appraisals of partisan preferences will increase, since party will form a clearer reference-point. There will be outright opposition between the parties on procedural practices and appraisals.

If on the other hand a fundamental disagreement cross-cuts party lines, both activist and party influences should decrease. What has been said about the influence of party in the previous paragraph will now apply not to party but to the two groupings differentiated on the central disagreement. The influence of activism will diminish, if and until conditions change to restore the lines of party division and political stratification which we found in Glasgow in 1966.

Appendix A: Study Design

SURVEY PROCEDURES

As mentioned in the introduction, the data for this study derive from survey interviews with 563 electors, 82 municipal councillors, 118 partyworkers and 6 municipal correspondents, conducted in Glasgow during the year 1966. This appendix presents the study design – how the respondents were selected, the interviews conducted, the data processed and analysed.

Work began in September 1965. A pilot questionnaire for electors was drawn up by the authors and administered to a small quota sample of electors. On the basis of these results and of comments from friends and colleagues three draft interview schedules were put together – one each for electors, partyworkers and councillors. In December 1965 the draft schedules were administered to a random sample of 150 electors in three Glasgow wards, 20 partyworkers nominated by the Glasgow Progressive and Labour parties, and a small quota sample of councillors in Greenock. In addition, one Glasgow councillor from each party was asked to comment on the draft councillor schedule. Following necessary revisions indicated by the field tests, the final schedules for electors, partyworkers and councillors were fielded in February 1966.

Students in a first-year politics course conducted most of the electors' interviews as part of their training in methods of survey research. For most, the field test of the draft schedule provided them with their first interviewing experience in the field. Second- and third-year politics students interviewed the partyworkers on a paid basis, the draft schedule again serving as their field training. These same students followed up the more difficult elector interviews. All interviews with councillors were conducted by the authors.

The final elector sample was a systematic selection of 749 citizens from the register of electors (1966) of the city of Glasgow.[167] Of these 563 were successfully interviewed. Out of the 186 not interviewed, ten had died since the register was made up, 17 were too ill to reply to questions, 49 had moved from their listed address, 33 could not be contacted, 61 refused to be interviewed and 16 could not be interviewed for various other reasons.

The deceased electors cannot be counted as part of the initial sample, so the effective sample was 739, yielding a response rate of 76 per cent, a figure which

[167] Given a population of size N and a desired sample of size n, then the sampling interval $k — N/n$. A systematic sample is obtained by a random start between 1 and k and then taking every kth individual on the list. See Hubert Blalock, *Social Statistics*, p. 397.

compares favourably with recent British and American political surveys.[168] Furthermore, this figure is the strictest possible response rate one could reasonably apply. Several of the ill and infirm respondents were individuals who were senile or else mental incompetents who, as a result of their permanent incapacitation, are not effectively part of the Glasgow electorate. In addition, a number of the non-contacts had occupations, such as serving as seamen, which effectively removed them from the Glasgow electorate for long periods of time. Nor is the register an infallible document. Although a citizen cannot exercise his right to vote in Glasgow unless his name is on the register, it does not follow that the register, compiled annually by the office of the Electoral Registration Officer of the city of Glasgow, is accurate and up to date. One of the electors chosen in the sample, for instance, had died three years previously; three of the non-contacts were with respondents at addresses which no longer existed, the dwelling having been demolished to make way for the expanding corporation redevelopment programme; a number of the removals had left years, not months, previous to their selection. In the latter two instances we can confidently expect that at the time of their selection a number of these electors were already on another register of electors in their new home areas.[169] Were these factors taken into account in calculating the response rate, it would stand significantly above 76 per cent.

The sample of partyworkers was obtained in a more complicated manner. After consultation with members of the municipal Labour Party organisation, it was decided to interview all Labour Party ward secretaries and chairman. The Progressive Party has no ward secretaries or chairman in most wards, and so, after consultation with party members, it was decided to interview two partyworkers per ward whom the city Progressive party office would name.

Party organisations, however, are not the models of efficiency they are in theory supposed to be. The Labour Party itself could furnish only the names of the ward secretaries. The chairmen's names had to be obtained from the secretaries themselves. To make matters worse, the interviewers soon discovered that in some wards those named were actually former secretaries, and in these

[168] Cf. Frank Bealey, Jean Blondel and W. P. McCann, *Constituency Politics* (London 1965) Appendix 2; Budge and Urwin, *Scottish Political Behaviour*, chap. 3; R. S. Milne and H. C. McKenzie, *Straight Fight* (London, 1954) and *Marginal Seat* (London, 1958) Appendices; L. J. Sharpe, *A Metropolis Votes* (London, 1963) pp. 56–8; Joseph Trenamen and Denis McQuail, *Television and the Political Image* (London, 1961) pp. 257–8. For a summary of American work with higher response rates see Leslie Kish, *Survey Sampling* (New York, 1965) pp. 539 ff. But see also Aage Clausen, 'Response Validity, Vote Report' (unpublished) *passim* which gives a report on the 1964 University of Michigan sample of the national electorate and also indicates that national surveys in the U.S. usually do not include those in hotels, large rooming houses, old people's homes, convents, etc., which are included on the register of electors.

[169] Two of the removals had in fact emigrated.

wards the interviewer asked the respondent to name the present party secretary rather than the chairman. The Progressive Party was even less well run. Not only was the list of workers out of date, but in some cases it was inaccurate. For example, one of the workers nominated was a fourteen-year-old girl who had helped distribute literature in an election; another was a charwoman who had at one time cleaned a hall rented by the party; several others had only once contributed to the party and disclaimed any political involvement. For both parties a number of individuals listed as active were no longer living at the addresses furnished by the party. None the less, despite the above problems, interviews were obtained with 118 out of 148 individuals named as active in the Labour and Progressive parties. Although the population from which the sample is drawn is not well-defined, the response rate is once again respectably high.

For the councillor survey we attempted to interview all 113 municipal councillors, i.e. 111 ward councillors, the Deacon Convenor, and the Dean of Guild. Successful interviews were obtained with 82. While there were but a handful of direct refusals, many of the councillors remained simply too elusive to pin down for an interview time.

Interviewing of the electors and partyworkers was completed in May 1966. Interviewing of the councillors was completed in September 1966. The roots of the theoretical model were developed in May 1966, and it was at this time, therefore, that the role of the mass media in linking the political strata became especially evident, and consequently it was decided to interview the municipal correspondents. The authors developed the interview schedule during the summer of 1966 and administered the interviews to the municipal correspondents in September and October 1966. These six correspondents, representing the *Daily Record, Daily Express, Evening Citizen, Evening Times, Glasgow Herald* and *The Scotsman* comprise the entire set of regular municipal correspondents for the Glasgow and Scottish newspapers. In addition, the correspondents of the *Herald* and the *Times* double as the municipal correspondents for BBC and STV respectively, so that our data cover all those who are regularly engaged in gathering information about the politics of the Glasgow Municipal Corporation for dissemination to the general public.

Using standard procedures, the authors developed and tested codes for the three major surveys. During June 1966 the elector and partyworker interview schedules were coded by students, all of whom had participated in the interviewing. In September and October the authors themselves coded the councillor schedules. In order to assess the reliability of the codes, 10 per cent of the schedules were coded independently by two coders. The results indicated that all single-column codes had nearly 100 per cent reliability and that double- and treble-column codes employed for open-ended questions had an acceptably high level of reliability in almost all cases – only three out of 34 multiple-column codes had a correspondence of less than 80 per cent of independent coding decisions. A list of codes and their reliabilities is reprinted with our codebooks and data in the British Social Science Data Archive, at the University of Essex.

Once transferred to machine-readable media, the data were submitted to a second check for logical consistency and wild coding. Unfortunately, at the time we began the data analysis, no general-purpose-consistency check programme was available to us in Britain, so the data had to be sent to the Inter-university Consortium for Political Research at the University of Michigan for this purpose. Since to await the full results of the consistency check would have entailed a delay of over one year, the work for this book was carried out on the 'uncleaned' version of the data. Results of the consistency check, however, have indicated no frequently occurring patterns of error, so we are confident that the 'uncleaned' data in fact more than meet ordinary standards of good-quality survey data. Since some errors were discovered, however, subsequent analyses of the 'cleaned' data may show slight discrepancies in their findings when compared with the findings published in this volume. The cleaned data, together with codebooks, are obtainable from the British Social Science Data Archive at the University of Essex.

REPRESENTATIVENESS OF THE SAMPLES

The accuracy of a random sample depends basically upon the size of the sample, not the size of the population. For a random sample of 739, the effective size of our sample of Glasgow electors, the sampling error in estimating any population parameter should be no greater than a maximum of 3·6 per cent in 19 of 20 cases. Moreover, the accuracy of the sample estimate increases as the parameter being estimated deviates from 50 per cent: e.g. we can be 95 per cent confident that an estimate of 50 per cent will be within 3·6 per cent of the 'true' proportion, but we can be equally confident that an estimate of 10 per cent will be within 2·4 per cent of the true proportion.[170]

Unfortunately, in practice, numerous biases are introduced into social-science samples, such as ours. To begin with, there is the problem of non-response. Some 8 per cent of those in the electors sample refused to be interviewed and another 16 per cent would not be interviewed for other reasons. These non-responses may be from individuals who have some social or political characteristics in common which distinguish them from the more co-operative and available citizens who were successfully interviewed. And even if those interviewed do not form a biased sample, the measurements taken may be inaccurate, or the respondents may give answers which they feel the investigators wish to hear or which they believe emphasise the positive aspects of their own characters, regardless of the veracity of the answers. Finally, the sampling lists from which the samples are drawn may be incomplete, biased, or otherwise

[170] Cf. Kish, pp. 50–3; Trenamen and McQuail, pp. 257–8.

inadequate, so that no sample drawn from them will be representative of the population.

For the elector survey the third type of problem is irrelevant. By law, only those citizens on the register of electors can vote, so our listing, therefore, is complete. Table A.1, which contains comparisons of the sample data with census and election data for Glasgow, indicates, however, that there may be some biases in the sample data resulting from non-response and from prevarication.

While the sample distribution closely resembles the population with regard to sex of respondents, it appears that some biases have crept into the data with regard to marital status, age, education and home ownership. Single people are for the most part younger and less settled than married couples. Not having children, they need spend less time at home, especially in the evenings. Also, if they do not live with their parents, single people tend to move house more frequently than older married people. All these factors make single individuals more difficult to locate for interviews and consequently increase the likelihood that they will be under-represented in a sample survey. And there is one additional factor that must be taken into consideration. Although all possible voters are on the register of electors, it does not follow that the register is a complete enumeration of all adult citizens. Some people are bound to be missed, and these are likely to be people who move house often or who are otherwise difficult to find at home, i.e. those missed are likely to include a disproportionately large percentage of single people. And since these same people tend to take less interest in politics than citizens with family responsibilities, they are less likely to check that the provisional register contains their names, and more likely, therefore, to be excluded.

Virtually the same considerations apply when we attempt to explain the seeming under-representation of 21-9-year-olds in the sample. They include a large proportion of single individuals, and like single people, they tend to be more difficult to locate and less active and interested in politics than the average citizen. It should also be noted that the census figure includes 20-year-olds, thus slightly inflating the percentage which is compared with the young voters in the sample.

Although the bias in the education distribution, an apparent under-representation of the lower educated, looks greater than those of single individuals and young electors, we do not think that it signifies a serious distortion in the sample. The sample figures include all electors over 21 in 1966; the census figures represent the education levels of those over 25 in 1961. This means that all the 21-9-year-olds in our sample are excluded from the census figures. Yet these citizens, who recently came of voting age, entered the electoral rolls with a minimum school-leaving age of 15, and in a period of great expansion in the British education system. In light of this, the apparent under-representation of the lower educated looks more natural. It would indeed be suspicious if the sample and census education distributions were practically the same. A combination of factors may explain the under-representation of private and the over-representation of public rentals in the sample. Glasgow's public housing and urban redevelopment programmes have continued on a massive scale since 1961, and as a result there was undoubtedly a greater ratio of public to private rentals at the time of the survey than in 1961. And who lives in the public housing units? The waiting list is long, and for the most part those in the units are long-time Glasgow residents, most often families and old-age pensioners. While many families and old people rent privately, privately rented accommodation is also sought by those excluded from the public housing lists – young men and women, single people, and those who have recently moved to Glasgow. These are the very people who are most likely to be left off the electoral register and when they are on the register, are most likely to be missed by interviewers.[171]

The most serious biases discovered in the sample centre about the report of actual vote. Here it seems that a substantial number of electors found it too tempting to appear as good citizens and to report that they voted when in fact they had not. For the 1964 General Election, the prevarication does not produce any serious errors. There is an 8 per cent over-report of turnout, but this is to be expected in a sample survey. It is reasonable to surmise that those who are repeatedly away from home whenever an interviewer calls, are as likely to be away from home whenever an election takes place. Also, the official turnout figure is based upon the entire electoral register, 5 to 10 per cent of which, as we have seen, consists of electors who have died or moved away. The former type of elector is excluded from survey samples while the latter type is unlikely to be interviewed. Both these factors lead to the expectation of a higher reported turnout for the sample than for the population. The over-report of a Labour vote in the sample, however, suggests that a number of electors, especially Labour supporters, were prevaricating when they told interviewers they had voted.

When it comes to the 1965 municipal election vote, a prevarication is likely to have been the modal response received from Labour supporters. Progressive supporters, however, also over-reported their votes. While a portion of the 27 per cent over-report of the vote is due to inadequacies in the electoral register, and the relative absence from the sample of those groups who do not often vote, most of the bias is undoubtedly due to intentional or perhaps un-witting misrepresentation on the part of the electors, especially Labour supporters. And this misrepresentation occurred, despite efforts to curb it by prefacing the question on municipal elections with the statement, 'many people

[171] It must also be emphasised that the comparison of sample and census data is dependent upon the tenuous assumption that the average number of persons per private and public housing units is about equal.

TABLE A.I

Sample statistics and population parameters for Glasgow electors

Criterion	Sample (per cent)	Glasgow (per cent)
Sex		
Men	47	46
Women	53	54
Marital status		
Single	14	21
Married	73	68
Widowed	12	11
Divorced	1	1
Age		
21–29	15	21
30–39	18	19
40–49	22	19
50–59	19	19
60–69	13	13
70 and over	9	9
Refused and NA	2	—
Education – Terminal age		
Under 15	59	73
15	25	16
16	7	4
Over 16	8	5
Home ownership		
Owner-occupier	19	18
Rent privately	29	44
Rent public housing	50	38
NA	2	—
1964 General Election		
Labour	48	43
Conservative	28	28
Non-voter	19	27
Other	4	2
1965 Municipal Election		
Labour	33	15
Progressive	24	17
Non-voter	38	65
Other	5	3

Sources: Sex, marital status, age, education, home ownership – Census 1961; class – General Election vote – *The Times Guide to the House of Commons*, 1966; Municipal election vote – Private files, E. W. S. Craig and *Glasgow Herald*.

All census figures refer to percentage of adult population, 20 and over, 1961, with the following exceptions; terminal education is calculated on these 26 and over, and home ownership refers to percentages of dwelling units rather than individuals.

don't find time to vote in local elections'. This obvious out made no difference to the electors; a good proportion of them were more willing to polish their self-image as good citizens than to exercise the good citizen's fundamental right to vote.

In sum, however, the data in Table A.1 suggest that subject to the caution of an over-report of political activity, there is little reason to suggest that the elector sample is an unrepresentative sample of the Glasgow electorate.

The 'representativeness' of the partyworker and councillor samples can be dealt with summarily. The sample of partyworkers is not a probability sample drawn from a well-defined population, so its representativeness cannot be evaluated directly. It suffices to note that interviews were obtained from party-workers in each ward, and there is no reason to believe that the information is faulty. With the councillors the intention was not to sample but to interview everyone. Of the 82 we successfully interviewed, 54 per cent were Labour as compared to 57 per cent of the council, and 13 per cent were convenors of standing committees as opposed to the actual figure of 15 per cent of the councillors. With regard to party and office, therefore, it looks as if the 82 councillors interviewed are not a biased sample of the whole.

STATISTICAL TESTS

To some readers it may seem odd that we have not applied standard tests of significance to our data when the book is concerned with the comparison of results from the data analysis with the predictions of the model. Instead, the reader finds that we have concentrated on differences of percentages and on strengths of relationships.

There are basically two reasons for this procedure. First, all standard tests of significance assume that the samples dealt with are random samples of the populations they represent. Our samples do not meet this criterion. As we have seen, the elector sample under-represents ill people, people with mobile jobs, people who are rarely at home, and people who are distrustful of interviewers. The partyworker sample is drawn from a population which is not well-defined, but it is, in any case, not a random sample. For the councillors, in spite of the 'representativeness' of the sample, there are no grounds to argue that the sample is random. In fact, the sample represents these councillors who were willing to give interviews – that is, it is clearly not random.

Second, statistical tests tell only whether or not some relationship is 'signifi-cant' at some predetermined level of certainty. This significance, however, depends mostly on the N of the samples. A difference of 2 or 3 per cent may be statistically significant but have little meaning at all with regard to our model. On the other hand, a large percentage difference may be insignificant statistically, but because of its direction it may carry considerable theoretical importance for our model.[172]

For readers who feel uncomfortable unless they see some level of significance presented at the bottom of each table we have tried to provide sufficient data to allow calculation of any test statistics that may be desired. Our own preference has been to proceed with the analysis by looking at the type, direction and strength of the relationships rather than their statistical significance.

[172] Cf. Hanan Sevin, 'A Critique of Tests of Significance in Survey Research', *American Sociological Review*, XXII (1957) 519–27; John Tukey, 'The Future of Data Analysis', *Annals of Mathematical Statistics*, 33 (1962) 1–67.

Appendix B: Detailed Statement of the Predictive Model discussed in Chapter 1

PART ONE – MODE OF PRESENTATION
Our model is presented here through five different types of statement:

(a) *Definitions* which characterise all variables in the model at the conceptual level;
(b) *Assumptions* which we make about the generalised relationships between the defined variables;
(c) *Operational assumptions* about the values assumed by the independent variables in Glasgow in the first half of 1966 – the specific situation in which the model is tested;
(d) *Derivations* which state consequences implied by definitions and assumptions, but have the property lacking in these parent statements of ready translation into certain specific predictions about our data (i.e. *data-predictions*).
(e) *Data-predictions* which are specifications of findings we expect to get from our survey data on the basis of the equivalence we judge to exist between them and the various derivations of the model. Thus the data-predictions are the only statements in this Appendix not logically but only judgementally related to the others. They constitute operationalisations for our data of the derivations from the generalised model. Since other persons' judgements of what might constitute adequate operationalisations may differ from ours we group data-predictions under the derivation to which they refer, so that the reader himself may judge the equivalence and thus ultimately the adequacy of the test of the model which has been made against our Glasgow data.

Definitions and assumptions are the only statements to be encountered in Part Two (The Generalised Model). Operational assumptions occur only at the very outset of Part Three (Operationalisation of the Model): thereafter in Part Three only derivations and attendant data-predictions appear. The different statements are numbered differently and distinguished as far as possible by the type used.

PART TWO – ASSUMPTIONS AND DEFINITIONS
ASSUMPTION I. **There will be no irreconcilable disagreement among those engaging in an average rate of political activity in a mass territorial democracy on current political issues they regard as most important**

K

nor among those in the same mass territorial democracy engaging in a higher rate of political activity than average on the current political issues they regard as most important, provided that:

(a) no antecedent lengthy and severe economic depression has occurred;
(b) there has been no marked antecedent increase in objective or subjective socioeconomic stratification;
(c) antecedent political issues formerly regarded as most important by those engaging in an average rate of political activity have not been characterised by irreconcilable disagreements among those so engaging;
(d) antecedent political issues formerly regarded as most important by those formerly engaging in a higher rate of political activity than average have not been characterised by irreconcilable disagreements among those so engaging.

DEFINITION I.1. A *mass territorial democracy* is any political system:

(i) which is composed only of the population of a given territorial area;
(ii) where the population is too large to allow decision-makers to be known personally by the majority of electors;
(iii) which is distinguished by high observance of fundamental present political procedures.

DEFINITION I.2. *Fundamental present political procedures* are:
At elections

(i) Every elector can vote for any of the candidates put forward in his constituency.
(ii) In assessing the result of the election in a constituency the weights assigned to each vote are identical.
(iii) The candidate(s) having the greater number of votes in each constituency is (are) elected.

During the pre-voting period

(iv) Any elector may nominate a candidate or set of candidates for election.
(v) All electors can possess identical information about the candidates standing for election.

During the post-voting period

(vi) That party (or group of parties) having the greatest number of winning candidates over all constituencies (calculated on the basis of the last election or last series of elections) controls decision-making in the chief decision-making offices and bodies.

(vii) Decisions taken by these offices and bodies are obeyed.

During the inter-election stage

(viii) Winning candidates give help to electors from their constituency who ask for help.

(ix) The chief decision-making offices and bodies will not habitually take actions which are clearly opposed to the preferences of the majority of electors.

DEFINITION I.3. An *irreconcilable disagreement* exists where:

(*a*) Restrictions have not been imposed upon choice of alternatives by the question which prompts the responses.

(*b*) Relatively equal proportions in any group endorse different alternatives or different sets of related alternatives.

(*c*) These different alternatives are judged by a trained observer to be incapable of simultaneous adoption as Government policy.

DEFINITION I.4. A *current issue* is any topic on which a course of action is presently being urged by or upon the Government through representative bodies, pressure-groups or the mass media.

DEFINITION I.5. Those engaging in a *higher rate of political activity than average* in Glasgow are municipal correspondents of the Glasgow press, local councillors and partyworkers. All others engage in an *average rate of political activity*.

DEFINITION I.6. A political system is said to be *stratified in objective socio-economic terms* to the extent that members of its population:

(*a*) consume goods and services at unequal rates;

(*b*) enjoy unequal social prestige.

DEFINITION I.7. A political system is said to be *stratified in subjective socio-economic terms* to the extent that members of its population identify with different objective socioeconomic strata.

ASSUMPTION II. **In a mass territorial democracy if the irreconcilable disagreements specified in Assumption I are absent and if a group (A) engages in a higher rate of political activity than any other group (B) then group (A) will agree more than group (B) that some of its members' political demands are conceded.**

DEFINITION II.1. Councillors and municipal correspondents engage in a *higher rate of political activity* than partyworkers, partyworkers than electors who attend public meetings, electors who attend public meetings than electors who vote in local elections, electors who vote in local elections than electors who do not vote in local elections.

DEFINITION II.2. A *group** is any set of people selected from the population of a political system either randomly or in accordance with specified criteria.

DEFINITION II.3. A group (A) *agrees more* than another group (B) when:

(i) the alternative or set of related alternatives most often mentioned by members of group (A) is endorsed by a higher proportion of the members of group (A) than the proportion in group (B) which endorses the alternative or set of related alternatives most often mentioned by members of group (B) and

(ii) the proportion of members of group (A) endorsing the most often mentioned alternative or set of related alternatives is substantially higher than the proportion of members of group (A) sharing the next most often mentioned alternative or set of related alternatives.

ASSUMPTION III. **In a mass territorial democracy if a group (A) agrees more than any other group (B) that some of its members' political demands are conceded then group (A) will display positive behaviour towards fundamental present political procedures to a greater extent than group (B).**

DEFINITION III.1. A group (A) is said to exhibit *positive behaviour* towards any object, group, person or concept to a greater extent than group (B) when the behaviour of a higher proportion of the members of group (A) than of the members of group (B) towards that object, group, person or concept is classed by a trained observer as showing identification, acceptance or support.†

ASSUMPTION IV. **In a mass territorial democracy if the irreconcilable disagreements specified in Assumption I are absent and if a group (A)**

* The definition of *group* employed in this Appendix is unusual in that it does not imply an element of conscious adherance and interaction among the group's members. It is however convenient for us to employ the term more widely and this wide sense is employed consistently through the model.

† What is taken as identification, acceptance or support will vary with the observational scheme being employed and the data available. In the commonly used Bales Interaction Process Analysis Categories this would be any reaction falling into 'positive reactions (agreement)' [R. F. Bales, *Interaction Process Analysis: A Method for the Study of Small Groups* (Cambridge, Mass., 1950) p. 9]. In Chapter 6 we make use of the judgements of municipal newspaper correspondents as to whether councillors displayed more or less bitterness, tendencies to compromise and party solidarity on issues in order to decide which issues were the focus of more positive behaviour among councillors.

engages in a higher rate of political activity than any other group (B) then group (A) will display integrative behaviour over more current issues than group (B).

DEFINITION IV.1. A group (A) is said to exhibit *integrative behaviour* to a greater extent than group (B) when the behaviour of a higher proportion of the members of group (A) than of the members of group (B) towards other members of the same group is classed by a trained observer:

either as positive behaviour
or as spontaneously seeking or giving information, opinions or suggestions.*
and when the behaviour of a majority of the members of group (A) towards non-members of group (A) is not classed by the trained observer either as positive behaviour or as spontaneously seeking or giving information, opinions or suggestions.*

ASSUMPTION V. **In a mass territorial democracy if a group (A) displays integrative behaviour to a greater extent than any other group (B) on any current issue then group (A) will agree more on preferences on that current issue than group (B).**

DEFINITION V.1. A *preference* is a choice of one course of action or a set of related courses of action, out of a greater number available for choice.

ASSUMPTION VI. **In a mass territorial democracy if a group (A) displays integrative behaviour over more current issues than any other group (B) then group (A) will agree to a greater extent than group (B) over all factual appraisals of politics.**

DEFINITION VI.1. A *factual appraisal* is a non-preferential judgement of an object, group, person or concept.

ASSUMPTION VII. **In a mass territorial democracy if a group (A) agrees to a greater extent than any other group (B) on its preferences on current issues and if group (A) agrees to a greater extent than group (B) over all factual appraisals of politics then group (A) will agree to a greater extent than group (B) on its preferences on potential issues.**

DEFINITION VII.1. A *potential issue* is any topic on which preferences may be expressed which is not a current issue.

---

* Again the definition can be operationalised in terms of Bales Interaction Process Analysis Categories (any reaction falling into 'positive reactions' (agreement), attempted answers and questions). The data we have limits us on the whole to reported or intended discussion with others as indicators of integrative behaviour.

ASSUMPTION VIII. In a mass territorial democracy if a group (A) displays positive behaviour towards fundamental present political procedures to a greater extent than any other group (B) and if group (A) agrees to a greater extent than group (B) on its preferences on potential issues then there will be fewer irreconcilable disagreements among group (A) on issues considered important by group (A) in the future than among group (B) on issues considered important by group (B) in the future.

ASSUMPTION IX. In a mass territorial democracy the only ways in which persons engaged in a higher rate of political activity can initiate or receive communication on any political issue or topic with groups of people engaged in a lower rate of political activity is through:

(a) face-to-face discussion with individuals;
(b) through various types of public or committee meetings (spontaneously summoned or routine);
(c) through the mass media.

ASSUMPTION X. In a mass territorial democracy the mass media do not provide accurate appraisals of the preferences of electors in each constituency or of most individual elected representatives.

> DEFINITION X.1. An *accurate political appraisal* is an appraisal which conforms to established research findings of political science.

ASSUMPTION XI. In a mass territorial democracy if and only if a group engages in a higher rate of political activity than average, then most factual appraisals of politics made by the group (other than those relating to the opinions of individuals or small sub-groups engaging in an average rate of political activity) will be accurate.

ASSUMPTION XII. In a mass territorial democracy if and only if a group (A) is higher on political activity than the average rate for the population then group (A) will behave politically to a greater extent than any other group in accordance with its members' perceptions of how to gain some of their demands on current issues.

ASSUMPTION XIII. In a mass territorial democracy if a group (A) is higher on political activity than average then group (A) will perceive to a greater extent than any other group that some of their demands on current issues can be gained by:

(a) maintaining/increasing their present rate of political activity:
(b) maximising the vote attracted by their party at the next election.

ASSUMPTION XIV. In a mass territorial democracy if a group (A) perceives to a greater extent than any other group (B) that some demands on current issues can be gained by maximising the votes attracted by their party at the next election then group (A) will perceive to a greater extent than group (B) that party vote-maximisation varies with the extent to which the party is generally known to satisfy to a greater extent than other parties the demands made by:

(i) enough electors to constitute a numerical majority of those voting in relevant elections;
(ii) most party-supporters engaging in a higher rate of political activity than average.

ASSUMPTION XV. In a mass territorial democracy if a group (A) perceives to a greater extent than any other group (B) that party vote-maximisation varies with the extent to which the party is generally known to satisfy to a greater extent than other parties the demands made by enough electors to constitute a numerical majority of those voting in relevant elections then group (A) will perceive to a greater extent than group (B) that a demand is made by almost all electors for the governmental structure and services of the democracy to be run efficiently.

PART THREE – OPERATIONALISATION OF MODEL

OPERATIONAL ASSUMPTION A. Glasgow is a mass democracy.

OPERATIONAL ASSUMPTION B. During the period antecedent to February–July 1966 no lengthy or severe economic depression occurred in Glasgow.

OPERATIONAL ASSUMPTION C. During the period antecedent to February–July 1966 neither objective nor subjective socioeconomic stratification increased in Glasgow.

OPERATIONAL ASSUMPTION D. During the period antecedent to February–July 1966 there were no irreconcilable disagreements among those then engaging in average rates of political activity in Glasgow on current issues then regarded as most important by those so engaging.

OPERATIONAL ASSUMPTION E. During the period antecedent to February–July 1966 there were no irreconcilable disagreements among those in Glasgow then engaging in a higher rate of political activity than average on the current issues then regarded as most important by those so engaging.

DERIVATION 1. **There will be no irreconcilable disagreement on preferences among those in Glasgow engaging in a higher rate of political activity than average on the current issue they regard as most important.**
(From Ass. I; Op. Ass. A, B, C, D, E)

> DATA PREDICTION 1.1. The combined group of Glasgow councillors and partyworkers, when asked what the corporation should do about the problem facing Glasgow which they consider most important, will not endorse in relatively equal numbers courses of action judged incapable of simultaneous adoption as corporation policy.
> (Tested Chap. 5: supported)

DERIVATION 2. **There will be no irreconcilable disagreement on preferences among those engaging in an average rate of political activity in Glasgow on the current issue they regard as most important.**
(From Ass. I; Op. Ass. A, B, C, D, E)

> DATA PREDICTION 2.1. The systematic sample of Glasgow electors, when asked what the corporation should do about the problem facing Glasgow which they consider most important, will not endorse in relatively equal numbers courses of action judged incapable of simultaneous adoption as corporation policy.
> (Tested Chap. 5; supported)

DERIVATION 3. **Within any subdivision of Glasgow respondents a group (A) which has a higher rate of political activity than group (B) will exhibit as compared to group (B) greater agreement that some of its members' political demands are conceded.**
(From Ass. I, II; Op. Ass. A, B, C, E)

> DATA PREDICTION 3.1. When asked how likely they are to succeed if they do anything about the proposals to have pubs in corporation housing estates, abolish fee-paying in corporation schools, extend parking-meters all over the city centre and increase rates, proportionately more Glasgow councillors and correspondents than partyworkers, more partyworkers than local voters, more local voters than local non-voters will say that they are very likely or quite likely to succeed on all or some of these proposals. This will apply to the comparison of strata as a whole and within any party.
> (Tested Chap. 2: supported)

DERIVATION 4.A. **Within any subdivision of Glasgow respondents, a group (A) which agrees more than group (B) that some of its political demands are conceded will exhibit as compared to group (B) more positive behaviour towards fundamental present political procedures.**
(From Ass. III; Op. Ass. A)

DERIVATION 4.B. **Within any subdivision of Glasgow respondents identi-fied by any criterion except agreement that some political demands are conceded, a group (A) which has a higher rate of political activity than group (B) will exhibit as compared to group (B) more positive behavi-our towards fundamental present political procedures.**
(From Ass. I, II, III; Op. Ass. A, B, C, D, E)

DATA PREDICTION 4.1. Proportionately more of the group who feel likely to succeed as specified under D.P. 3.1 than Glasgow councillors and corre-spondents, more councillors and correspondents than partyworkers, more partyworkers than local voters, more voters than non-voters will say that the majority of people in Glasgow rather than the directly affected minority should decide on the proposals to have pubs in corporation housing estates, abolish fee-paying in corporation schools, extend parking-meters all over the city centre and increase rates. This will apply to the comparison of strata as a whole and within any party.
(Tested Chap. 2: not supported)

DATA PREDICTION 4.2. There will be a proportionately larger gap between those endorsing preferences for change in Glasgow government which strengthen representative principles and those endorsing preferences for change in Glasgow government which weaken representative principles among those who feel likely to succeed as specified under D.P. 3.1 than Glasgow councillors and correspondents, among councillors and corre-spondents than among partyworkers, among partyworkers than among local voters, and among voters than among non-voters. This will apply to the comparison of strata as a whole and within any party.
(Tested Chap. 2: not supported)

DATA PREDICTION 4.3. Proportionately more of the group who feel likely to succeed as specified under D.P. 3.1 than Glasgow councillors and corre-spondents, more councillors and correspondents than partyworkers, more partyworkers than local voters, more voters than non-voters will say that the Lord Provost stands for the whole of Glasgow rather than just his own party group. This will apply to the comparison of strata as a whole and within any party.
(Tested Chap. 2: not supported)

DATA PREDICTION 4.4. Excluding Glasgow councillors and correspondents, proportionately more partyworkers than local voters and more voters than non-voters will say that no special groups are given preference over other people when applying for corporation jobs. This will apply to the com-parison of strata as a whole and within any party.
(Tested Chap. 2: supported)

DATA PREDICTION 4.5. Proportionately more of the group who feel likely to succeed as specified under D.P. 3.1 than Glasgow councillors and correspondents, more councillors and correspondents than partyworkers, more partyworkers than local voters, more voters than non-voters will say that parties are necessary or inevitable when asked what difference in the way the corporation is run would follow if there were no parties on Glasgow corporation. This will apply to the comparison of strata as a whole and within any party.

(Tested Chap. 2: not supported)

DATA PREDICTION 4.6. Excluding councillors and correspondents, proportionately more of the group who feel likely to succeed as specified under D.P. 3.1 than partyworkers, more partyworkers than local voters, more voters than non-voters will mention definite likes about the party other than their own, and definite dislikes about their own party. This will apply to the comparison of strata as a whole and within any party.

(Tested Chap. 2: not supported)

DATA PREDICTION 4.7. Proportionately more Glasgow councillors and correspondents than partyworkers and more partyworkers than local voters, will say that a councillor's responsibilities include representation of his ward. This will apply to the strata as a whole and within any party.

(Tested Chap. 3: supported)

DATA PREDICTION 4.8. In higher-turnout wards proportionately more electors than in lower-turnout wards will say that a councillors' responsibilities include representation of his ward. This prediction excludes lower-turnout wards where more electors feel likely to succeed as specified under D.P. 3.1. This will apply to the whole group of electors and within any party.

(Tested Chap. 3: not supported)

DATA PREDICTION 4.9. Proportionately more of the group who feel likely to succeed as specified under D.P. 3.1 than Glasgow councillors and correspondents, more councillors and correspondents than partyworkers, more partyworkers than local voters, more voters than non-voters will deny that any people or groups not successfully competing in elections have so much influence on corporation affairs that the interests of the majority are ignored. This will apply to the comparison of strata as a whole within any party.

(Tested Chap. 2: not supported)

DATA PREDICTION 4.10. Excluding councillors and correspondents proportionately more of the group who feel likely to succeed as specified under

D.P. 3.1 than partyworkers, more partyworkers than local voters, more voters than non-voters will say that councillors or the Labour Party runs Glasgow. This will apply to the comparison of strata as a whole and within any party.
(Tested Chap. 2: not supported)

DERIVATION 5. **Within any subdivision of Glasgow respondents a group (A) which has a higher rate of political activity than group (B) will exhibit integrative behaviour to a greater extent over more current issues than group (B).**
(From Ass. I, IV; Op. Ass. A, B, C, D, E)

DATA PREDICTION 5.1. Glasgow partyworkers will name personal contacts with other partyworkers as their best source of local political information to a greater extent than electors will name personal contacts with other electors. This will apply to the comparison of strata as a whole and within any party.
(Tested Chap. 4: supported)

DATA PREDICTION 5.2. Most Glasgow partyworkers will not name personal contacts with electors as their main source of local political information. This will apply to the whole group of partyworkers and within any party.
(Tested Chap. 4: supported)

DATA PREDICTION 5.3. Glasgow councillors and correspondents will hear of the proposals to have pubs in corporation housing estates, abolish fee-paying in corporation schools, extend parking-meters all over the city centre and increase rates from other councillors to a greater extent than partyworkers will hear of the same proposals from other partyworkers, and partyworkers will hear of these proposals from other partyworkers to a greater extent than electors will hear of the same proposals from other electors. This will apply to the comparison of strata as a whole and within any party.
(Tested Chap. 4: supported)

DATA PREDICTION 5.4. Most Glasgow councillors and correspondents will not hear of the proposals to have pubs in corporation housing estates, abolish fee-paying in corporation schools, extend parking-meters all over the city centre and increase rates from partyworkers or electors. This will apply to the whole group of councillors and within any party.
(Tested Chap. 4: supported)

DATA PREDICTION 5.5. Most Glasgow partyworkers will not hear of at least three out of the proposals to have pubs in corporation housing estates, abolish fee-paying in corporation schools, extend parking-meters all over the city centre and increase rates, from electors. This will apply to the whole group of partyworkers and within any party.
(Tested Chap. 4: supported)

DATA PREDICTION 5.6. Most Glasgow partyworkers will not regard one of their tasks as contacting councillors or higher party officials nor contacting people in the ward. This will apply to the whole group of partyworkers and within any party.
(Tested Chap. 4: supported)

DATA PREDICTION 5.7. When asked directly, most Glasgow partyworkers will not say that the advice or help they give to people in the ward includes political discussion. This will apply to the whole group of partyworkers and within any party.
(Tested Chap. 4: supported)

DATA PREDICTION 5.8. When asked directly, most Glasgow partyworkers will say *either* that they are in contact with the City Labour Party or Progressive Association occasionally or never, *or* will not mention policy matters as the subject of contact. This will apply to the whole group of partyworkers and within any party.
(Tested Chap. 4: supported)

DATA PREDICTION 5.9. When asked directly most Glasgow partyworkers will say *either* that they are in contact with councillors occasionally or never, *or* will not mention political problems as the subject of contact. This will apply to the whole group of partyworkers and within any party.
(Tested Chap. 4: supported)

DATA PREDICTION 5.10. Most Glasgow partyworkers will not discuss at least three of the proposals to have pubs in corporation housing estates, abolish fee-paying in corporation schools, extend parking-meters all over the city centre and increase rates with electors. This will apply to the whole group of partyworkers and within any party.
(Tested Chap. 4: supported)

DATA PREDICTION 5.11. Most Glasgow councillors will not say they talk to electors directly affected by issues, approach constituents directly or through non-political organisations, spontaneously summon public meetings or see partyworkers in order to discover what their constituents are thinking on at least three of the proposals to have pubs in corporation housing estates,

abolish fee-paying in corporation schools, extend parking-meters all over the city centre and increase rates. This will apply to the whole group of councillors and within any party.
(Tested Chap. 4: not supported)

DATA PREDICTION 5.12. Most Glasgow partyworkers will not say they talk to electors directly affected by issues, approach constituents directly or through non-political organisations, spontaneously summon public meetings or see councillors in order to discover what their constituents are thinking on at least three of the proposals to have pubs in corporation housing estates, abolish fee-paying in corporation schools, extend parking-meters all over the city centre and increase rates. This will apply to the whole group of partyworkers and within any party.
(Tested Chap. 4: not supported)

DATA PREDICTION 5.13. When asked directly, proportionately more Glasgow partyworkers in higher-turnout wards than partyworkers in lower-turnout wards will say that the advice or help they give to people in the ward includes political discussion. This will apply to the whole group of partyworkers and within any party.
(Tested Chap. 4: not supported)

DATA PREDICTION 5.14. Proportionately more Glasgow partyworkers in higher-turnout wards than partyworkers in lower-turnout wards will discuss with electors at least three of the proposals to have pubs in corporation housing estates, abolish fee-paying in corporation schools, extend parking-meters all over the city centre and increase rates. This will apply to the whole group of partyworkers and within any party.
(Tested Chap. 4: supported)

DATA PREDICTION 5.15. Proportionately more Glasgow councillors and partyworkers in higher-turnout wards than councillors and partyworkers in lower-turnout wards will say they talk to electors directly affected by issues, approach constituents directly or through non-political organisations, or spontaneously summon public meetings in order to discover what constituents are thinking on at least three of the proposals – to have pubs in corporation housing estates, abolish fee-paying in corporation schools, extend parking-meters all over the city centre and increase rates. This will apply to the whole group of councillors and partyworkers and within any party.
(Tested Chap. 4: not supported)

DATA PREDICTION 5.16. Proportionately more Glasgow councillors and partyworkers in higher-turnout wards than councillors and partyworkers in lower-turnout wards will make accurate appraisals of their constituents' preferences in regard to at least three of the proposals to have pubs in corporation housing estates, abolish fee-paying in corporation schools, extend parking-meters all over the city centre and increase rates. This will apply to the whole group of councillors and partyworkers and within any party.

(Tested Chap. 3: supported)

DERIVATION 6. **Within any subdivision of Glasgow respondents, a group (A) which displays more integrative behaviour on a current issue than group (B) will agree more on its preferences on that issue than group (B).**
(From Ass. V; Op. Ass. A)

DATA PREDICTION 6.1. Glasgow councillors will show more agreement in their preferences on those issues where they are judged by municipal correspondents to show less bitterness, more tendency to compromise, less party solidarity. And conversely.

(Tested Chap. 6: supported)

DATA PREDICTION 6.2. Glasgow councillors who normally discuss with each other corporation housing, corporation schools, traffic problems and rates will show greater agreement than the average for all councillors in their preferences on at least three of the proposals to have pubs in corporation housing estates, to abolish fee-paying in corporation schools, to extend parking-meters, to increase rates, respectively. This will apply to the whole group of councillors and within any party.

(Tested Chap. 6: not supported)

DERIVATION 7. **Within any subdivision of Glasgow respondents identified by any criterion except integrative behaviour on current issues a group (A) which has a higher rate of political activity than group (B) will agree more on preferences over more current issues than group (B).**
(From Ass. I, IV, V; Op. Ass. A, B, C, D, E)

DATA PREDICTION 7.1. On the proposals to have pubs in corporation housing estates, abolish fee-paying in corporation schools, extend parking-meters all over the city centre, increase rates, and integrate Catholic and Protestant schools, Glasgow councillors and correspondents will agree on their preferences to a greater extent than partyworkers, and partyworkers will agree on their preferences on these same current issues to a greater extent than local voters, and local voters will agree on their preferences on these same current issues to a greater extent than non-voters. This will apply to the comparison of strata as a whole and within any party.

(Tested Chap. 5: supported)

DATA PREDICTION 7.2. On at least three of the proposals to have pubs in corporation housing estates, abolish fee-paying in corporation housing estates, extend parking-meters all over the city centre, increase rates and integrate Catholic and Protestant schools, Glasgow councillors will agree on their preferences among themselves across party to a greater extent than they will agree with the preferences of partyworkers and electors.
(Tested Chap. 3: not supported)

DATA PREDICTION 7.3. On at least three of the proposals to have pubs in corporation housing estates, abolish fee-paying in corporation schools, extend parking-meters all over the city centre, increase rates and integrate Catholic and Protestant schools, Glasgow partyworkers will agree on their preferences among themselves across party to a greater extent than they will agree with the preferences of councillors and electors.
(Tested Chap. 3: not supported)

DATA PREDICTION 7.4. On at least three of the proposals to have pubs in corporation housing estates, abolish fee-paying in corporation schools, extend parking-meters all over the city centre, increase rates and integrate Catholic and Protestant schools, Glasgow ward councillors and ward electors will agree on their preferences to a greater extent in higher-turnout wards than in lower-turnout wards. This will apply to the comparison of strata as a whole and within any party.
(Tested Chap. 3: not supported)

DATA PREDICTION 7.5. On at least three of the proposals to have pubs in corporation housing estates, abolish fee-paying in corporation schools, extend parking-meters all over the city centre, increase rates and integrate Catholic and Protestant schools, Glasgow ward partyworkers and ward electors will agree on their preferences to a greater extent in higher-turnout wards than in lower-turnout wards. This will apply to the comparison of strata as a whole and within any party.
(Tested Chap. 3: supported)

DATA PREDICTION 7.6. Glasgow partyworkers will agree on their preferences on at least three of the problems of housing and redevelopment, finance, education and roads to a greater extent than electors. This will apply to the comparison of strata as a whole and within any party or class.
(Tested Chap. 5: not supported)

DERIVATION 8. **Within any subdivision of Glasgow respondents identified by any criterion except integrative behaviour on current issues a group (A) which has a higher rate of political activity than group (B) will**

agree to a greater extent than group (B) on a majority of factual appraisals on politics.

(From Ass. I, IV, V, VI; Op. Ass. A. B, C, D, E)

DATA PREDICTION 8.1. Glasgow councillors and correspondents will agree on their factual appraisals of important problems in Glasgow to a greater extent than partyworkers, partyworkers will agree on their appraisals of the same problems to a greater extent than local voters, and voters will agree on their appraisals of the same problems to a greater extent than non-voters. This will apply to the comparisons of strata as a whole and within any party.

(Tested Chap. 5: supported)

DATA PREDICTION 8.2. Glasgow councillors and correspondents will agree on their factual appraisal of the preferences of most Glaswegians on the most important problem facing Glasgow, to a greater extent than partyworkers, and partyworkers will agree on appraisals of the same preferences to a greater extent than electors. This will apply to the comparisons of strata as a whole and within any party.

(Tested Chap. 5: supported)

DATA PREDICTION 8.3. Glasgow councillors and correspondents will agree on their factual appraisals of which class and religious groups support which party to a greater extent than partyworkers, and partyworkers will agree on their appraisals of these same patterns of support to a greater extent than electors. This will apply to the comparisons of strata as a whole and within any party.

(Tested Chap. 5: not supported)

DATA PREDICTION 8.4. Glasgow councillors and correspondents will agree on their factual appraisals of the most effective action to get their demands satisfied on an issue to a greater extent than partyworkers, partyworkers will agree on their appraisals of this same action to a greater extent than local voters and voters will agree on their appraisal of this same action to a greater extent than non-voters. This will apply to comparisons of strata as a whole and within any party.

(Tested Chap. 5: supported)

DATA PREDICTION 8.5. Glasgow councillors and correspondents will agree on their factual appraisals of the results of eliminating political parties from Glasgow corporation to a greater extent than partyworkers and party workers will agree on their appraisals of these same results to a greater extent than voters. This will apply to comparisons of strata as a whole and within any party.

(Tested Chap. 5: supported)

DATA PREDICTION 8.6. Glasgow councillors and correspondents will agree on their factual appraisals of what classes exist and what types of people constitute them to a greater extent than partyworkers, and partyworkers will agree on their appraisals of these same classes and types to a greater extent than electors. This will apply to comparisons of strata as a whole and within any party.

(Tested Chap. 5; supported)

DATA PREDICTION 8.7. Glasgow councillors and correspondents will agree on their appraisals of group influence on corporation affairs to a greater extent than partyworkers, and partyworkers will agree on their appraisals of this same group influence to a greater extent than electors. This will apply to comparisons of strata as a whole and within any party.

(Tested Chap. 5: not supported)

DATA PREDICTION 8.8. Glasgow councillors will agree on what current issues should not/cannot be mentioned in newspapers to a greater extent than Glasgow partyworkers. This will apply to comparisons of strata as a whole and within any party.

(Tested Chap. 6: supported)

DATA PREDICTION 8.9. On the proposals to have pubs in corporation housing estates, abolish fee-paying in corporation schools, extend parking-meters all over the city centre and increase rates, Glasgow partyworkers will agree on the stand taken by the Progressive and Labour parties to a greater extent than local electors. This will apply to comparisons of strata as a whole and within any party.

(Tested Chaps 3 and 5: supported)

DATA PREDICTION 8.10. On at least three of the proposals to have pubs in corporation housing estates, abolish fee-paying in corporation schools, extend parking-meters all over the city centre and increase rates, Glasgow partyworkers and electors will agree on the stand taken by the Progressive and Labour parties to a greater extent in higher-turnout wards than in lower-turnout wards. This will apply to comparisons of strata as a whole and within any party.

(Tested Chap. 3: supported)

DATA PREDICTION 8.11. On their appraisals of who runs Glasgow, Glasgow partyworkers will agree to a greater extent than local electors. This will apply to comparisons of strata as a whole and within any party.

(Tested Chap. 5: supported)

L

DATA PREDICTION 8.12. On their appraisals of whether any group gets preference in corporation jobs Glasgow partyworkers will agree to a greater extent than local electors. This will apply to comparisons of strata as a whole and within any party.

(Tested Chap. 5: not supported)

DERIVATION 9. **Within any subdivision of Glasgow respondents identified by any criterion except agreement on preferences on current issues and factual appraisals of politics or integrative behaviour on current issues, a group (1) which has a higher rate of political activity than group (2) will agree more on preferences on potential issues than group (2).**

(From Ass. I, IV, V, VI, VII; Op. Ass. A, B, C, D, E)

DATA PREDICTION 9.1. On their preferences for change in Glasgow government, Glasgow councillors and correspondents will agree to a greater extent than partyworkers, and partyworkers will agree to a greater extent than local electors. This will apply to comparisons of strata as a whole and within any party.

(Tested Chap. 5: supported)

DATA PREDICTION 9.12. On their preferences as to the responsibilities attributed to councillors, Glasgow councillors and correspondents will agree to a greater extent than local voters, and voters will agree to a greater extent than non-voters. This will apply to comparisons of strata as a whole and within any party.

(Tested Chap. 3 and 5: supported)

DERIVATION 10. **In Glasgow a group which has a higher rate of political activity than average will seek to discover the current issue preferences of those engaged in an average rate of political activity through the mass media or through routine committee or public meetings rather than through face-to-face discussion with individuals engaged in average rate of political activity or through spontaneously summoned committee or public meetings.**

(From Ass. I, IV, IX; Op. Ass. A, B, C, D, E)

DATA PREDICTION 10.1. Most Glasgow councillors will say that they would try to discover what their constituents were thinking on the proposals to have pubs in corporation housing estates, abolish fee-paying in corporation schools, extend parking-meters all over the city centre, and increase rates, through newspapers or television or through ward committee meetings or party meetings rather than through talking to electors directly affected by issues, approaching constituents directly or through non-political organisations, or spontaneously summoning public meetings. This will apply to the whole group of councillors and within any party.

(Tested Chap. 4: not supported)

DATA PREDICTION 10.2. Most Glasgow partyworkers will say that they would try to discover what their constituents were thinking on the proposals to have pubs in corporation housing estates, abolish fee-paying in corporation schools, extend parking-meters all over the city centre, and increase rates, through newspapers or television or through ward committee meetings or party meetings rather than through talking to electors directly affected by issues, approaching constituents directly or through non-political organisations, or spontaneously summoning public meetings. This will apply to the whole group of partyworkers and within any party.
(Tested Chap. 4: not supported)

DERIVATION 11.* **In Glasgow the preferences of the persons (other than those whose rate of political activity is above average) who attend routine public and committee meetings are not representative of the preferences of all those engaged in an average rate of political activity over most current issues.**
(From Ass. I, II, III, IV, V; Op. Ass. A. B, C, D, E)

DATA PREDICITION 11.1. On the proposals to have pubs in corporation housing estates, abolish fee-paying in corporation schools, extend parking-meters all over the city centre and increase rates less than 75 per cent of Glasgow electors will mention routine public or committee meetings as means of getting further information. This will apply to the whole group of electors and within any party.
(Tested Chap. 4: supported)

DERIVATION 12. **In Glasgow those engaging in an average rate of political activity will rely mainly on the mass media for their political information.**
(From Ass. I, IV, IX; Op. Ass. A, B, C, D, E)

DATA PREDICTION 12.1. Most Glasgow electors will name newspapers, radio or television as their best source of local political information. This will apply to the whole group of electors and within any party.
(Tested Chap. 4: supported)

DATA PREDICTION 12.2. On at least three of the proposals to have pubs on corporation housing estates, abolish fee-paying in corporation schools, extend parking-meters all over the city centre and increase rates, most

---

* Although Derivation 11 is vital to our argument we have no data bearing directly upon it. A very weak data-prediction can be formed if we assume that one necessary but not sufficient condition for the derivation holding true for Glasgow is that those attending meetings do not constitute an overwhelming majority of the electorate. For in that case their views would be representative in a statistical sense no matter how different they were from the remaining electors. Such a prediction forms only an incomplete test, however, which leaves the more important implications of the derivation untested.

Glasgow electors will name newspapers, radio or television as the way they heard about the proposal. This will apply to the whole group of electors and within any party.

(Tested Chap. 4: supported)

DERIVATION 13A. **Within any subdivision of Glasgow respondents those engaging in a higher rate of political activity than average will make inaccurate appraisals of the preferences on current issues of persons engaging in an average rate of political activity in their respective constituencies.**

(From Ass. I, II, III, IV, V, IX, X; Op. Ass. A, B, C, D, E)

DERIVATION 13B. **Within any subdivision of Glasgow respondents those persons engaging in an average rate of political activity will make inaccurate factual appraisals of the preferences on current issues of their respective constituency representitives.**

(From Ass. I, II, III, IV, V, IX, X; Op. Ass. A, B, C, D, E)

DATA PREDICTION 13.1. Most Glasgow councillors' appraisals of their constituents' preferences on the proposals to have pubs in corporation housing estates, abolish fee-paying in corporation schools, extend parking-meters all over the city centre and increase rates will not correspond to their constituents' preferences as ascertained through the sample survey. This will apply to the whole group of councillors and within any party.

(Tested Chap. 3: supported)

DATA PREDICTION 13.2. Most Glasgow partyworkers' appraisals of their constituents' preferences on the proposals to have pubs in corporation housing estates, abolish fee-paying in corporation schools, extend parking-meters all over the city centre, and increase rates, will not correspond to their constituents' preferences as ascertained through the sample survey. This will apply to the whole group of partyworkers and within any party.

(Tested Chap. 3: supported)

DATA PREDICTION 13.3. Most Glasgow electors' appraisals of their ward-councillors' preferences on the proposals to have pubs in corporation housing estates, abolish fee-paying in corporation schools, extend parking-meters all over the city centre, and increase rates will not correspond to their ward-councillors' preferences as ascertained through the survey. This will apply to the whole group of electors and within any party.

(Tested Chap. 3: supported)

DERIVATION 14. **Within any subdivision of Glasgow respondents a group**

(A) which engages in a higher rate of political activity than average will make more accurate factual appraisals of politics than any other group (B) which engages in an average rate of political activity. This excludes appraisals of the opinion of individuals or small sub-groups engaging in an average rate of political activity.

DATA PREDICTION 14.1. Glasgow correspondents, councillors and party-workers will make appraisals of Glaswegians' preferences on the most important problem facing Glasgow corresponding more closely to the survey findings on electors' preferences than will electors' appraisals.
(Tested Chap. 6: not supported)

DATA PREDICTION 14.2. Glasgow correspondents, councillors and party-workers will make appraisals of the support given to the political parties by religious and class groups which correspond more closely to the survey findings on class and religious group voting than will electors' appraisals. This will apply to comparisons of strata as a whole and within any party.
(Tested Chap. 5: not supported)

DATA PREDICTION 14.3. Glasgow partyworkers will make appraisals of the Progressive and Labour parties' stands on the proposals to have pubs in corporation housing estates, abolish fee-paying in corporation schools, extend parking-meters all over the city centre and increase rates, which correspond more closely to party councillors' preferences on these proposals as ascertained by the survey than will electors' appraisals. This will apply to comparisons of strata as a whole or within any party.
(Tested Chap. 3: supported)

DERIVATION 15. **Within any subdivision of Glasgow respondents most factual appraisals of politics made by a group which engages in a higher rate of political activity than average will be accurate. This excludes appraisal of the opinions of individuals or small sub-groups engaging in a different rate of political activity.**
(From Ass. XI; Op. Ass. A)

DATA PREDICTION 15.1. The majority of appraisals made by Glasgow correspondents, councillors and partyworkers of Glaswegians' preferences on the most important problem facing Glasgow will correspond to survey findings on electors' preferences.
(Tested Chap. 6: not supported)

DATA PREDICTION 15.2. The majority of appraisals made by Glasgow correspondents, councillors and partyworkers of the support given to the political parties by religious and class groups will correspond to survey findings on class and religious group voting. This will apply to the whole groups of correspondents, councillors and partyworkers and within any party.

(Tested Chap. 5: supported)

DATA PREDICTION 15.3. The majority of appraisals made by Glasgow party-workers of the Progressive and Labour parties' stands on the proposals to have pubs in corporation housing estates, abolish fee-paying in corporation schools, extend parking-meters all over the city centre and increase rates will correspond to party councillors' preferences on these proposals as ascertained by the survey. This will apply to the whole group of party-workers and within any party.

(Tested Chap. 3: supported)

DERIVATION 16. **Within any subdivision of Glasgow respondents most members of a group which engages in a higher rate of political activity than average will make the appraisal that most communication between groups distinguished by higher and lower rates of political activity is through the mass media.**

(From Ass. I, II, III, IV, V, IX, XI; Op. Ass. A, B, C, D, E)*

DATA PREDICTION 16.1. Most Glasgow correspondents will say that council-lors and partyworkers can bring issues to general attention only through newspapers, radio or television.

(Tested Chap. 6: supported)

DATA PREDICTION 16.2. Most Glasgow councillors will say that they can bring issues to general attention only through newspapers, radio or tele-vision. This will apply to the whole group of councillors and within any party.

(Tested Chap. 6: supported)

DATA PREDICTION 16.3. Most Glasgow partyworkers will say that they can bring issues to general attention only through newspapers, radio or tele-vision. This will apply to the whole group of partyworkers and within any party sub-group of partyworkers.

(Tested Chap. 6: not supported)

DATA PREDICTION 16.4. Most Glasgow correspondents will say that coun-cillors can keep issues from general attention through preventing their mention in newspapers, radio or television.

(Tested Chap. 6: supported)

* Our assumptions rank as previous research findings. Therefore the assumption that activists' appraisals are accurate means that on this point they will correspond to our assumptions and these lead to the conclusion that the only real channel of communica-tion is the mass media.

DATA PREDICTION 16.5. Most Glasgow councillors will say that they can keep issues from general attention through preventing them being mentioned in newspapers, radio or television. This will apply to the whole group of councillors and within any party or class.
(Tested Chap. 6: supported)

DERIVATION 17. **Within any subdivision of Glasgow respondents most persons presently engaged in a higher rate of political activity than average have engaged in a higher rate of political activity than average for a considerable portion of their past lives.**
(From Ass. XII, XIII; Op. Ass. A)

DATA PREDICTION 17.1. Most Glasgow councillors engaged in political work before they became councillors. This will apply to the whole group of councillors and within any party.
(Tested Chap. 1: supported)

DATA PREDICTION 17.2. Most Glasgow partyworkers have engaged in political work for at least the previous five years. This will apply to the whole group of partyworkers and within any party.
(Tested Chap. 1: supported)

DATA PREDICTION 17.3. A substantial number of Glasgow councillors and partyworkers came from an extended family one at least of whose members engaged in political candidatures or party work. This will apply to whole groups of councillors and partyworkers and within any party.
(Tested Chap. 1: supported)

DATA PREDICTION 17.4. A substantial number of Glasgow councillors and/ or partyworkers have an occupation or position which involves them in political work, i.e. are lawyers, trade-union officials, ministers, pressure-group representatives, etc. This will apply to the whole groups of councillors and partyworkers and within any party.
(Tested Chap. 1: supported)

DERIVATION 18. **Within any subdivision of Glasgow respondents persons engaged in a higher rate of political activity than average will maintain that activity in order to gain some of their demands on current issues.**
(From Ass. XII, XIII; Op. Ass. A)

DATA PREDICTION 18.1. Most Glasgow councillors will say that they continue as councillors because of their policy interests or desire to promote causes or groups' well-being. This will apply to the whole group of councillors and within any party.
(Tested Chap. 1: supported)

DATA PREDICTION 18.2. Most Glasgow partyworkers will say that they engage in political activity because of their policy interests or desire to promote causes or groups' well-being. This will apply to the whole group of partyworkers and within any party.

(Tested Chap. 1: supported)

DERIVATION 19. **Within any subdivision of Glasgow respondents a group (A) engaged in a rate of political activity higher than average will see the satisfaction of their demands on current issues as being affected by the electoral success of their party to a greater extent than any other group (B) engaged in an average rate of political activity.**

(From Ass. XII, XIII; Op. Ass. A)

DATA PREDICTION 19.1. Proportionately more Glasgow councillors and partyworkers than electors will see one of the main jobs of a councillor as being to carry out party policy or carry out election promises and remaining true to his political ideology. This will apply to comparisons of strata as a whole and within any party.

(Tested Chap. 3: supported)

DATA PREDICTION 19.2. A substantial number of Glasgow partyworkers will see one of their main functions as being electoral or organisational activity on behalf of their party. This will apply to the whole group of partyworkers and within any party.

(Tested Chap. 3: supported)

DATA PREDICTION 19.3. On at least three of the proposals to have pubs in corporation housing estates, abolish fee-paying in corporation schools, extend parking-meters all over the city centre, and increase rates, proportionately more partyworkers than electors will see their own party as favouring their own preference on the proposal. This will apply to the comparisons of strata as a whole and within any party.

(Tested Chap. 6: supported)

DATA PREDICTION 19.4. On the problem they consider most important proportionately more partyworkers than electors will see their own party as most likely to do what they want. This will apply to the comparisons of strata as a whole and within any party.

(Tested Chap. 6: supported)

DERIVATION 20. **Within any subdivision of Glasgow respondents a group (A) engaged in a higher rate of political activity than average will wish to know what are the political demands of Glaswegians to a greater extent than any other group (B) engaged in an average rate of political activity.**

(From Ass. XII, XIII, XIV; Op. Ass. A)

DATA PREDICTION 20.1. Most Glasgow councillors and partyworkers will not abstain from seeking information about their constituents' views on the proposals to have pubs in corporation housing estates, abolish fee-paying in corporation schools, extend parking-meters all over the city centre and increase rates. This will apply to the whole groups of councillors and party-workers and within any party.
(Tested Chap. 4: supported)

DERIVATION 21. **Within any subdivision of the Glasgow respondents identified by any criterion except party, those engaged in a higher rate of political activity than average will display less integrative behaviour over those current issues which receive greater coverage from the mass media than over the current issues which receive less coverage from the mass media.**
(From Ass. XII, XIII, XIV; Op. Ass. A)

DATA PREDICTION 21.1. Glasgow councillors will be judged by correspond-ents to show more bitterness on the proposals to extend parking-meters all over the city centre and increase rates, which were given most coverage by Glasgow newspapers from February to July 1966, than on the proposals to have pubs in corporation housing estates and abolish fee-paying in cor-poration schools, which were given least coverage by Glasgow newspapers from February to July 1966.
(Tested Chap. 6: not supported)

DATA PREDICTION 21.2. Glasgow councillors will be judged by correspond-ents to show less tendency to compromise on the proposals to extend parking-meters all over the city centre and increase rates, which were given most coverage by Glasgow newspapers from February to July 1966, than on the proposals to have pubs in corporation housing estates and abolish fee-paying in corporation schools, which were given least coverage by Glasgow newspapers from February to July 1966.
(Tested Chap. 6: not supported)

DATA PREDICTION 21.3. Glasgow councillors will be judged by correspond-ents to show most solidarity with their party group on the proposals to extend parking-meters all over the city centre and increase rates, which were given most coverage by Glasgow newspapers from February to July 1966, than on the proposals to have pubs in corporation housing estates and abolish fee-paying in corporation schools, which were given least coverage by Glasgow newspapers from February to July 1966.
(Tested Chap. 6: not supported)

DATA PREDICTION 21.4. On their distribution of preferences as ascertained through the survey data Glasgow councillors will show more solidarity with their party group on the proposals to extend parking-meters all over the city centre and increase rates, which were given most coverage by Glasgow newspapers from February to July 1966, than on the proposals to have pubs in corporation housing estates and abolish fee-paying in corporation schools, which were given least coverage by Glasgow newspapers from February to July 1966.

(Tested Chap. 6: not supported)

DERIVATION 22. **Within any subdivision of the Glasgow respondents identified by any criterion except party those engaged in a higher rate of political activity than average will display less solidarity on those issues which receive most coverage from the mass media than on those which receive less coverage from the mass media.**

(From Ass. V, XII, XIII, XIV; Op. Ass. A)

DATA PREDICTION 22.1. Glasgow councillors will disagree more in their preferences on the proposals to extend parking-meters all over the city centre and increase rates, which were given most coverage by Glasgow newspapers from February to July 1966, than on the proposals to have pubs in corporation housing estates and abolish fee-paying in corporation schools, which were given least coverage by Glasgow newspapers from February to July 1966.

(Tested Chap. 6; not supported)

DATA PREDICTION 22.2. Glasgow partyworkers will disagree more on their preference on the proposals to extend parking-meters all over the city centre and increase rates, which were given most coverage by Glasgow newspapers from February to July 1966, than on the proposals to have pubs in corporation housing estates and abolish fee-paying in corporation schools, which were given least coverage by Glasgow newspapers from February to July 1966.

(Tested Chap. 6: not supported)

DERIVATION 23. **Within any subdivision of Glasgow respondents, persons engaging in a higher rate of political activity than average will act to run the governmental structure and services efficiently.**

(From Ass. XII, XIII, XIV, XV; Op. Ass. A)

DATA PREDICTION 23.1. Most Glasgow councillors and most correspondents and most partyworkers will say that one of a councillor's main responsibilities is to run the city and its services efficiently. This will apply to the whole groups of councillors and partyworkers and within any party.

(Tested Chap. 3: supported)

Index

Abelson, R. P., 15 n
Activism, activists, activity
  ability to emphasise or de-emphasise
    issues, 268
  absence of fundamental disagree-
    ment, 268
  absence of irreconcilable disagree-
    ments, 192, 194
  abstract beliefs in democracy, 253
  activist, non-activist distinction, 41,
    98
  agreement on democratic funda-
    mentals, 11, 16, 30, 35, 82
  agreement on preferences, 165, 266
  agreement on purely factual apprai-
    sals, 258
  agreement with electors, 30
  appraisal of constituency opinion,
    163
  and agreement on issues, 166, 261
  and constituents' issue preferences,
    254, 260
  and demand-satisfaction, 247-8
  and democratic principles, 47, 253,
    268
  and effect parameter, 78
  and electors, 113, 117-18, 161-2, 200
  and family background, 32
  and group interests, 31
  and impact of party competition,
    12-13, 71, 79, 74, 238-43
  and integrative behaviour, 258
  and issue politics, 31
  and mass media, 124, 126, 133
  and parties, 35, 41, 74, 257, 266-8,
    270
  and political consistency, 20
  and popular opinion, 18
  and sanctions, 18
  as sources of information to council-
    lors, 223
  attachments to party, 25, 51, 79, 250
  attitudes to political procedures, 48,
    59

behaviour and political perceptions,
    20, 201, 257
carrying attitudes over into behavi-
    our, 249
characteristics of, 11, 13, 262-3
cleavages among, 10, 15. *See also*
    Cleavages
commitment to existing constitu-
    tional arrangements, 16
communication between strata, 254
comparison with electors, 11, 14-15,
    36
contrasted with apathy of anti-
    democratic, 46
demand-satisfaction, 18, 43, 50-4, 67,
    240
democratic appraisals, 249, 251
democratic feeling as moderating
    influence, 251
democratic preferences, 249, 251,
    268
discussions with partyworkers, 158-9
distribution of opinion, 94
effect on appraisals, 247, 248
effects, 9, 42
electoral success, 18
equivalence of, 8, 13
formulation of own preferences, 256
hierarchy of activity, 13, 18
homogeneity, 11
increased activism in high-turnout
    wards, 118
increases in political activity, 238
influence of, 271-2
integrative behaviour and greater
    preferential agreement, 263
integrative behaviour of, 165, 260,
    267
interaction among, 12, 15-18, 41,
    200
interaction with group members,
    41
interaction with non-activists, 18,
    29

Politicians—*cont.*
autonomy of and competition, 18, 167, 199–261
British parliamentary, 12, 73
competition on issues, 243, 245
freedom from electoral prompting, 205
freedom of action, 209
influence on social and political affairs, 48
integrative behaviour of 203, 226
link between political actions and electors' opinions, 203, 245
main concerns of, 202
political participation, 13
relationship between ward politicians and their constituents, 200
responsiveness to electors, 80
Polsby, N., Dentler, R. A., and Smith, P. A., 34n
Population, 47
and party feeling, 270
attachment to democracy, 253
Glasgow population, 192, 208
Predictive model (for complete statement *see* Appendix B), 5–6, 7, 9, 14–42, 55, 59, 63, 97, 113, 116, 123, 160, 164, 183–6, 244, 247, 253–4, 256, 260–1, 263–6. *See also* Models of representation
and Glasgow politics, 38
and information-flow, 124–5
as research strategy, 33
assumptions, 8, 14–15, 18, 20, 28, 35
data predictions, 8, 35
definitions, 15, 21, 28, 35
derivations, 35
general reformulation, 266–70
recruitment predictions, 33
success and failures, 167–9
success ratio of predictions, 33, 51, 71–2, 78–9
Pressure groups, 1, 20, 249
Progressive councillors, 31, 51, 53, 59–61, 65–6, 87–8, 245. *See also* Councillors
agreement, 95–7, 172–3
agreement among communicating pairs, 225
agreement compared with total groups on appraisals related to voting behaviour, 192

agreement compared with total groups on general political appraisals, 190
agreement compared with total groups on issues, preferences, 188–9
agreement on changes that would occur if Glasgow did not have parties, 180–1
agreement on group influence in Glasgow, 177–8
agreement with constituents, 99, 100
agreement with supporters, 100
and bringing issues to general attention, 231, 233–6, 237n
and high-turnout wards, 113, 115–16, 166
and issues, 92–3
and party effects, 77
and pro-party sentiment, 72
and their constituents, 101
and the Lord Provost, 74
appraisals of constituents' preferences, 102, 114–15, 154–5
appraisals of own preferences, 102
as minority opposition, 101
consultation with Labour councillors, 220
consultation within party, 221–2
levels of accuracy, 103
means of seeking influence, 243
meetings with principal party figures 222
party discipline, 221
promotion of issues, 228
strategic action on issues, 241–2
supporters' discernment of councillors' positions, 168
use of mass media, 233
ward and city role of councillors, 86
Progressive electors, 65, 66. *See also* Electors
agreement, 173, 242
agreement about groups' influence in Glasgow, 177–8
agreement compared with total groups on appraisals related to voting behaviour, 192
agreement compared with total groups on general political appraisals, 190
agreement compared with total groups' issue preferences, 188–9